THE M. & E. HANDBOOK SERIES

SALE OF GOODS AND HIRE-PURCHASE

THE M. & E. HANDBOOK SERIES

SALE OF GOODS AND HIRE-PURCHASE

WILLIAM T. MAJOR, M.A., LL.B.
Barrister-at-Law

SECOND EDITION

MACDONALD & EVANS LTD
8 John Street, London W.C.1
1971

First published September 1965
Reprinted November 1966
Second edition September 1971

©

MACDONALD AND EVANS LIMITED
1971

S.B.N. 7121 1924 8

Printed in Great Britain by
UNWIN BROTHERS LIMITED
WOKING AND LONDON
(HL 9934)

PREFACE TO THE SECOND EDITION

IT is hoped that these study notes will continue to be of value to students preparing for examinations with a sale of goods and hire-purchase content. The law of hire-purchase, which was treated only briefly in the first edition, is now dealt with in sufficient detail to cause the title to be changed to indicate the expansion.

This HANDBOOK assumes a knowledge of the general principles of contract law, which should be revised before beginning a study of sale of goods and hire-purchase.

Method of study. It is recommended that this HANDBOOK be used as follows:

(a) Read through the main text quickly two or three times so as to get an overall picture of the subject.

(b) Work carefully through the book chapter by chapter, making constant reference to the *Sale of Goods Act*, 1893, and the *Hire-Purchase Act*, 1965, as appropriate.

(c) Use the Progress Tests to measure your grasp of the subject.

(d) Try writing full answers to the specimen examination questions in Appendix VI.

Examination questions. I wish to thank the following examining bodies for giving their kind permission to use questions from past examination papers:

The Chartered Institute of Secretaries (C.I.S.), who gave permission to include questions from the Mercantile Law papers of the final examination.

The Association of Certified and Corporate Accountants (A.C.C.A.), who gave permission to include questions from the Mercantile Law papers of the intermediate examination.

The Institute of Chartered Accountants (C.A.), who gave permission to include questions from the English Law papers of the final examination.

August 1971   W.T.M.

CONTENTS

vii

TABLE OF CASES

(Where the facts are noted, the page number is in italics)

CHAPTER I

THE CONTRACT OF SALE OF GOODS

THE SALE OF GOODS ACT, 1893

1. Sources. The law relating to contracts of sale of goods is to be found mainly in:

(*a*) the *Sale of Goods Act*, 1893; and
(*b*) the *Hire-Purchase Act*, 1965; and
(*c*) the common law.

2. The Sale of Goods Act, 1893. The Act codifies the law relating to the sale of goods, but the rules of common law, save in so far as they are inconsistent with the express provisions of the Act, continue to apply: *s*. 61 (2).

Where an Act is designed as a codification, difficulties may arise as to the relationship between the codifying statute and the common law. In *Vagliano* v. *Bank of England* (1891), a House of Lords case, Lord Herschell said, "I think the proper course is in the first instance to examine the language of the statute, and to ask what is its natural meaning, uninfluenced by any considerations derived from the previous state of the law; and not to start with enquiring how the law previously stood, and then, assuming that it was probably intended to leave it unaltered, to see if the words of the enactment will bear an interpretation in conformity with this view."

THE CONTRACT OF SALE OF GOODS

3. Definition. A contract of sale of goods is a contract whereby the seller transfers or agrees to transfer the property in goods to the buyer for a money consideration, called the price: *s*. 1 (1).

(*a*) *A contract of sale may be in writing* (either with or without seal), or by word of mouth, or partly in writing and partly by word of mouth, or may be implied from the conduct of the parties: *s*. 3.

1

(*b*) *A contract of sale may be absolute or conditional:* s. 1 (2).

(*c*) *The essential parties* to a contract of sale are buyer and seller.

4. Terms of the contract. The express and implied terms of the contract of sale are its contents. It is the terms of the contract which define the rights and obligations of the parties.

5. Goods. "Goods" includes all chattels personal other than things in action and money: the term includes emblements, industrial growing crops, and things attached to or forming part of the land which are agreed to be severed before sale or under the contract of sale: *see* s. 62 (1). The goods which form the subject of a contract of sale may be either existing goods, owned or possessed by the seller, or goods to be manufactured or acquired by the seller after the making of the contract of sale: *see* s. 5 (1).

(*a*) *Future* goods means goods to be manufactured or acquired by the seller after the making of the contract of sale: *see* s. 5 (1) and s. 62 (1).

(*b*) *Specific* goods means goods identified and agreed upon at the time the contract of sale is made: s. 62 (1).

(*c*) *Emblements* are *annual* crops produced by agricultural labour, *e.g.* wheat, flax, potatoes.

6. Sale and agreement to sell. Where under a contract of sale the property in the goods is transferred from the seller to the buyer, the contract is called a *sale*; but where the transfer of the property in the goods is to take place at a future time or subject to some condition thereafter to be fulfilled, the contract is called an *agreement to sell*: s. 1 (3).

NOTE
- (*i*) An agreement to sell becomes a sale when the time elapses or the conditions are fulfilled subject to which the property in the goods is to be transferred: s. 1 (4).
- (*ii*) Where by a contract of sale the seller purports to effect a present sale of future goods, the contract operates as an agreement to sell goods: s. 5 (3).

7. Contracts of sale affected by hire-purchase legislation. Certain credit sale and conditional sale agreements are affected by the provisions of the *Hire-Purchase Act*, 1965.

(*a*) *Conditional sale agreements* affected by the Hire-Purchase Act are those under which:

(*i*) the purchase price or part of it is payable by instalments; and

(*ii*) the total purchase price does not exceed two thousand pounds; and

(*iii*) the property in the goods is to remain in the seller (notwithstanding that the buyer is to be in possession of the goods) until such conditions as to the payment of instalments or otherwise as may be specified in the agreement are fulfilled; and

(*iv*) the purchaser is not a body corporate.

(*b*) *Credit-sale agreements* affected by the Hire-Purchase Act are those where:

(*i*) the purchase price is payable by five or more instalments; and

(*ii*) the total purchase price exceeds thirty pounds but does not exceed two thousand pounds; and

(*iii*) the purchaser is not a body corporate; and

(*iv*) the agreement is not a conditional sale agreement as defined above.

NOTE

(*i*) The Hire-Purchase Act provides that credit sale agreements and conditional sale agreements as defined are *unenforceable by the seller* unless in writing.

(*ii*) The Hire-Purchase Act provides that, in the case of conditional sale agreements, the implied terms are as for hire-purchase agreements and that these cannot be varied or negatived by agreement. Sections 12–15 of the *Sale of Goods Act*, 1893, do not apply to conditional sale agreements.

(*iii*) In the case of conditional sale agreements, the buyer cannot pass good title to a *bona fide* purchaser of the goods; *s.* 25 (2) of the Sale of Goods Act does not apply to conditional sales as defined: *see* XI.

8. Goods which perish.   Where goods which are the subject of a contract of sale perish, the following rules apply:

(*a*) Where there is a contract for the sale of specific goods, and the goods without the knowledge of the seller have perished at the time when the contract is made, the contract is void: *s.* 6.

(*b*) Where there is an agreement to sell specific goods, and subsequently the goods, without any fault on the part of the seller or buyer, perish before the risk passes to the buyer, the agreement is thereby avoided: *s*. 7.

9. Capacity to buy and sell. Capacity to buy and sell is regulated by the general law concerning capacity to contract and to transfer and acquire property: *see s*. 2.

NOTE
- (*i*) Where necessaries are sold *and delivered* to an infant or to a person who by reason or mental incapacity or drunkenness is incompetent to contract, he must pay a reasonable price therefor: *see s*. 2.
- (*ii*) "Necessaries" means goods suitable to the condition in life of such infant or other person, and to his actual requirements at the time of the sale and delivery: *see s*. 2.
- (*iii*) A person attains full age when he reaches the age of eighteen: *Family Law Reform Act*, 1969, *s*. 1. At this age a person ceases to be an infant, or minor, and may begin to enjoy full contractual capacity.

OTHER DISPOSITIONS OF GOODS

10. Sale and other dispositions. The *Sale of Goods Act*, 1893, applies only to contracts of sale of goods as defined above. The Act does not apply to other dispositions of goods.

11. Bailment. Under a bailment, the bailor parts with possession of the goods, but he retains the ownership of them. Under a contract of sale, the seller undertakes to part with possession *and* ownership.

12. Pledge (or pawn). A pledge is a bailment of goods by a borrower as a security for a loan.

13. Hire-purchase. A hire-purchase agreement is a bailment coupled with an option to purchase the goods.

NOTE
- (*i*) The option to purchase may or may not be exercised. In any case, it is exercisable only when all agreed hiring payments have been made.
- (*ii*) The hirer under a hire-purchase agreement is not a "buyer" within the meaning of the Sale of Goods Act until such time as he exercises his option.

14. Mortgage of goods. A mortgage of goods occurs where the parties go through a form of sale as a security for a loan. The borrower transfers the property in the goods to the lender on condition that the property will be re-transferred upon the repayment of the loan.

15. Contracts for work and materials. Where the substance of the contract is an undertaking to use skill in producing a particular article, the contract may be one for work and materials, and not a contract for sale of goods. The distinction can be difficult to make in practice.

NOTE

(*i*) A contract to paint a portrait has been held to be a contract for the exercise of skill and experience of the artist, and not a contract of sale of goods: *Robinson* v. *Graves* (1935).

(*ii*) A contract to make and supply a set of false teeth has been held to be a contract of sale of goods: *Lee* v. *Griffin* (1861). Similarly, a contract to make and supply ship's propellers has been held to be a contract of sale of goods: *Cammel Laird & Co. Ltd.* v. *Manganese Bronze Co. Ltd.* (1934).

PROGRESS TEST 1

1. The *Sale of Goods Act*, 1893, is a codifying Act. How should such statutes be interpreted? (**2**)

2. Define a contract of sale of goods. (**3**)

3. Explain fully what you understand by the term "goods." (**5**)

4. Distinguish between a sale and an agreement to sell. (**6**)

5. What is (*i*) a conditional sale agreement and (*ii*) a credit sale agreement? Are these governed by any statute other than the *Sale of Goods Act*, 1893? (**7**)

6. What rules govern the capacity to buy and sell? (**9**)

7. How does a contract of sale of goods differ from (*i*) a contract of hire-purchase and (*ii*) a contract for work and materials? (**13, 15**)

8. A, a photographer, agrees with B to make a portrait of B's wife for a fee of £5. In a subsequent dispute over this agreement, it becomes necessary to advise the parties as to whether their agreement is governed by the *Sale of Goods Act*, 1893. How would you advise on this point?

9. C enters into a contract to sell a consignment of grain "now lying in D's warehouse" to E. Unknown to either party, D's warehouse was destroyed by fire at the time of the agreement and none of the grain was saved. How has the fire affected the contractual rights of C and E?

CHAPTER II

THE SELLER'S DUTIES

THE DUTY TO DELIVER THE GOODS

1. Express and implied terms. The duties owed by the seller to the buyer are defined by the terms, express and implied, of the contract. A term will be implied to give effect to the presumed but unexpressed intentions of the parties according to the general rules of contract law. Or a term may be implied to give effect to any of the provisions of *ss.* 12–15 of the Act.

The main duties of the seller are concerned with delivery of the goods, transfer of title, the description and quality of the goods and their fitness for purpose. By *ss.* 12–15, terms are implied (*i.e.* imposed on the seller) with respect to all of these duties except delivery. But by *s.* 55 the seller may contract out of these implied obligations by the simple expedient of an exemption clause. This chapter is particularly concerned with the duties of the seller as they arise out of the various implied terms as the law stands at the present time. The serious criticisms of this part of sale of goods law and the proposals for reform will be discussed later in Chapter X. The Law Commission's draft clauses in amended form are set out in Appendix II.

2. Delivery. It is the duty of the seller to deliver the goods in accordance with the terms of the contract of sale: *see s.* 27. *Delivery* means voluntary transfer of possession from one person to another: *s.* 62 (1). A transfer of ownership of the goods does not necessarily take place at the time of delivery.

3. Manner of delivery. Whether it is for the buyer to take possession of the goods or for the seller to send them to the buyer is a question depending in each case on the contract, express or implied, between the parties. Apart from any such contract, express or implied, the place of delivery is the seller's place of business, if he have one, and if not, his residence:

6

provided that, if the contract be for the sale of specific goods which, to the knowledge of the parties when the contract is made, are in some other place, then that place is the place of delivery: *s.* 29 (1).

(*a*) *Delivery may be actual, e.g.* where the seller sends the goods to the buyer, or where the buyer collects the goods from the seller.

(*b*) *Delivery may be constructive, e.g.* where the key of a warehouse is given, so that the goods lying there may be collected by the buyer.

(*c*) *Delivery may be symbolic, e.g.* by the transfer of a document of title.

(*d*) *The seller may not deliver* by instalments without the buyer's consent: *see s.* 31 (1).

(*e*) *Goods in the possession of a third party.* Where the goods at the time of sale are in the possession of a third person, there is no delivery by seller to buyer unless and until such third person acknowledges to the buyer that he holds the goods on his behalf. But this rule does not apply where delivery is made by the transfer of a document of title: *s.* 29 (3).

(*f*) *Expenses.* Unless it is otherwise agreed, the expenses of and incidental to putting the goods into a deliverable state must be borne by the seller: *s.* 29 (5). Goods are in a *deliverable state* when they are in such a state that the buyer would, under the contract, be bound to take delivery: *s.* 62 (4).

4. Time of delivery. The time for delivery is the time, if any, fixed in the contract of sale. But where, under the contract of sale, the seller is bound to send the goods to the buyer, but no time for sending them is fixed, the seller is bound to send them within a reasonable time: *see s.* 29 (2).

(*a*) *"Reasonable time."* What is a reasonable time is a question of fact: *s.* 56.

(*b*) *Time of delivery.* Demand or tender of delivery may be treated as ineffectual unless made at a reasonable hour. What is a reasonable hour is a question of fact: *s.* 29 (4).

(*c*) *Delivery and payment concurrent conditions.* Unless otherwise agreed, delivery of the goods and payment of the price are concurrent conditions, that is to say, the seller may be ready and willing to give possession of the goods to the buyer in exchange for the price: *see s.* 28.

5. Delivery, examination and acceptance. Where goods are delivered to the buyer, which he has not previously examined, he is not deemed to have accepted them unless and until he has had a reasonable opportunity of examining them for the purpose of ascertaining whether they are in conformity with the contract: *s.* 34 (1).

(*a*) *Examination.* Thus, unless otherwise agreed, when the seller tenders delivery of goods to the buyer he is bound, on request, to afford the buyer a reasonable opportunity of examining the goods for the purpose of ascertaining whether they are in conformity with the contract: *s.* 34 (2).

(*b*) *Refusal to accept.* Unless otherwise agreed, where goods are delivered to the buyer and he refuses to accept them, having the right to do so, he is not bound to return them to the seller, but it is sufficient if he intimates to the seller that he refuses to accept them: *s.* 36.

(*c*) *Acceptance.* The buyer is deemed to have accepted the goods when he intimates to the seller that he has accepted them, or when the goods have been delivered to him, and he does any act in relation to them which is inconsistent with the ownership of the seller, or when, after the lapse of a reasonable time, he retains the goods without intimating to the seller that he has rejected them: *s.* 35.

6. Delivery to a carrier. Where, in pursuance of a contract of sale, the seller is authorised to send the goods to the buyer, delivery of the goods to a carrier, whether named by the buyer or not, for the purpose of transmission to the buyer is *prima facie* deemed to be a delivery of the goods to the buyer: *s.* 32 (1).

(*a*) *Contract with carrier.* Unless otherwise authorised by the buyer, the seller must make such contract with the carrier on behalf of the buyer as may be reasonable having regard to the nature of the goods and the other circumstances of the case. If the seller omits to do so, and the goods are lost or damaged in course of transit, the buyer may decline to treat the delivery to the carrier as a delivery to himself, or may hold the seller responsible in damages: *s*. 32 (2).

(*b*) *Marine insurance.* Unless otherwise agreed, where goods are sent by the seller to the buyer by a route involving sea transit, under circumstances in which it is usual to insure, the seller must give such notice to the buyer as may enable him to insure them during their sea transit, and, if the seller fails to do so, the goods shall be deemed to be at his risk during such sea transit: *s*. 32 (3).

7. Delivery and risk. Where the seller of goods agrees to deliver them at his own risk at a place other than that where they are when sold, the buyer must, nevertheless, unless otherwise agreed, take any risk of deterioration in the goods necessarily incident to the course of transit: *s*. 33.

THE DUTY TO PASS GOOD TITLE

8. Property. Under a contract of sale, the seller transfers, or agrees to transfer, the property in goods to the buyer: *s*. 1 (1).

NOTE
  (*i*) "Property" means the general property in goods, and not merely a special property: *s*. 62 (1); *i.e.* ownership or *dominium* and not merely a limited interest.
  (*ii*) The right to property in goods is called *title* to goods.

9. Delivery and the passing of property. Property in the goods sold may pass from the seller to the buyer concurrently with delivery or otherwise. The general rule is that property passes when the parties intend that it shall pass: *see s*. 17.

10. The seller's right to sell. In a contract of sale, unless the circumstances of the contract are such as to show a different intention, there are the following implied terms:

(*a*) *Seller's right to sell.* An implied condition on the part of the seller that in the case of a sale he has a right to sell the goods, and that in the case of an agreement to sell he will have a right to sell the goods at the time when the property is to pass: *s*. 12 (1).

(b) *Quiet possession.* An implied warranty that the buyer shall have and enjoy quiet possession of the goods: *s.* 12 (2).

(c) *Freedom from encumbrance.* An implied warranty that the goods shall be free from any charge or encumbrance in favour of any third party, not declared or known to the buyer before or at the time when the contract is made: *s.* 12 (3).

NOTE

(i) Any right, duty or liability which would arise under the above implied terms may be varied or negatived by exemption clause, or by a course of dealing between the parties: *s.* 55 and X, **4–15**.

(ii) Where the seller is in breach of the implied condition in *s.* 12 (1), and the true owner of the goods recovers them from the buyer, the buyer can maintain a claim for the price he paid as money paid for a consideration that has totally failed; it matters not that *restitutio* is impossible: *Rowland* v. *Divall* (1923); *see also Butterworth* v. *Kingsway Motors Ltd.* (1954).

(iii) Section 12 does not apply to conditional sale agreements as defined in the *Hire-Purchase Act*, 1965.

CASES

Rowland v. *Divall* (1923), C.A.: R bought a motor car from D for £334. Two months after the sale, R, who was a motor dealer, sold the car to X for £400. Some two months later, the police took the car from X, as it had been stolen before it came into D's possession. R refunded the £400 to X and brought this action to recover the £334 from D. HELD: D was in breach of the condition implied in *s.* 12 (1). There was a *total* failure of consideration, and R was entitled to recover all the money he had paid. It was immaterial (i) that R had possession of the car for two months, and (ii) that *restitutio* was not possible.

Niblett Ltd. v. *Confectioners' Materials Co. Ltd.* (1921), C.A.: Sellers agreed to sell a quantity of tins of condensed milk at a price to include insurance and freight from New York to London. The buyers paid the price on receipt of the shipping documents. The tins arrived bearing labels with the brand name "Nissly." The Nestle Co. objected that the use of the word "Nissly" was an infringement of the Nestlé trade mark. The Commissioners of Customs detained the consignment, obliging the buyers to remove the labels in order to obtain possession. The tins were then sold without labels and at a loss. HELD: there was a breach of the implied condition in *s.* 12 (1) that the seller had a right to sell the goods.

DESCRIPTION, QUALITY AND FITNESS OF THE GOODS

11. Accordance with terms. It is the duty of the seller to deliver to the buyer goods which accord with the terms, express and implied, of the contract: *s.* 27. To the extent that there is no express or implied term describing the goods, the common law rule *caveat emptor* applies.

In *Wallis* v. *Russell* (1902), an Irish appeal case, FitzGibbon, L. J., said that "*caveat emptor* does not mean—in Law or Latin —that the buyer must 'take care.' It applies to the purchase of specific things, *e.g.*, a horse or a picture, upon which the buyer can, and usually does, exercise his own judgment; it applies also whenever the buyer voluntarily chooses what he buys; it applies also where, by usage or otherwise, it is a term of the contract, express or implied, that the buyer shall not rely on the skill or judgment of the seller. But it has no application to any case in which the seller has undertaken, and the buyer has left it to the seller, to supply goods to be used for a purpose known to both parties at the time of the sale."

12. Correspondence with description. Where there is a contract for the sale of goods by description, there is an implied condition that the goods shall correspond with the description: *s.* 13.

   (a) Exclusion of term. The implied term as to correspondence with description may be negatived or varied by express agreement, or by the course of dealing between the parties, or by usage, if the usage be such as to bind both parties to the contract: *s.* 55; but note *Andrews* v. *Singer* (1934).

   (b) Extent of correspondence with description. Where the implied term as to correspondence with description is not excluded, the degree to which goods must correspond with the contract description is limited only by the maxim *de minimis non curat lex* (the law does not concern itself with trifles). This places a heavy burden on the seller to deliver goods which are exactly in accordance with the contract description: *see Arcos* v. *Ronaasen* (1932); *Macpherson Train* v. *Howard Ross* (1955).

(c) *When sale by description occurs.* There is a sale of goods, *i.e.* future goods or unascertained goods. And even where the buyer sees the goods before or at the time of the sale, there may be a sale by description if the buyer or seller describes the goods, or the class to which they belong: *Beale* v. *Taylor* (1967). There may be a sale by description of a normal retail transaction in a shop: *Grant* v. *Australian Knitting Mills* (1936); *Godley* v. *Perry* (1959).

(d) *Extent of description.* The description may concern any aspect of the goods, *e.g.*

    (i) specifications as to quantity or amount;
    (ii) specifications as to measurement and size;
    (iii) specifications as to quality;
    (iv) specifications as to packing or labelling;
    (v) specifications as to shipment.

(e) *Delivery of mixed goods.* Where the seller delivers to the buyer the goods he contracted to sell mixed with goods of a different description, not included in the contract, the buyer may accept the goods which are in accordance with the contract and reject the rest, or he may reject the whole: *s.* 30 (3) and *see Re Moore & Co. Ltd.* and *Landauer & Co.* (1921), C.A.

NOTE: Section 13 does not apply to conditional sale agreements as defined in the *Hire-Purchase Act*, 1965.

CASES

Varley v. *Whipp* (1900): V contracted to sell to W a second-hand reaping machine. W had not seen the machine and V described it as being new the previous year, saying that it had been used to cut about 50 or 60 acres only. When the machine was delivered, W discovered that it was a very old one, so he returned it to V. V brought this action against W for the price of the machine. HELD: there was a contract of sale by description. There was a breach of the implied condition as to correspondence with description in *s.* 13 and V could not succeed in his action.

Arcos Ltd. v. *Ronaasen & Son* (1932), H.L.: There were two contracts under which A agreed to sell to R a quantity of staves $\frac{1}{2}$ in. thick. One per cent of the staves delivered were more than $\frac{5}{8}$ in. thick, and the rest were between $\frac{1}{2}$ in. thick and $\frac{5}{8}$ in. thick. R claimed to reject the staves and submitted the question to arbitration according to a term in each of the contracts. It was found in arbitration that the staves delivered were "commercially within and merchantable under the contract specification" and that the buyer was not, therefore, entitled to reject the goods.

R appealed, and the umpire's decision was reversed. A appealed to the Court of Appeal and then to the House of Lords. HELD by the House of Lords: where a contract stipulates for a certain measurement, that stipulation must be complied with. "A ton does not mean about a ton" and still less "does half an inch mean about half an inch." A was entitled to reject the goods because of the breach of the implied condition as to correspondence with description in *s.* 13.

Macpherson Train & Co. Ltd. v. *Howard Ross & Co. Ltd.* (1955): There was a contract between the parties for the sale of 5,064 cases of cans of Australian quick-frozen peaches. The contract included a clause which provided as follows: "Shipment and destination: afloat per s.s. *Morton Bay* due London approximately June 8th." The *Morton Bay* did not arrive in London until June 21st. The buyers refused to accept the goods, contending that there was a breach of condition, as "afloat per s.s. *Morton Bay* due London approximately June 8th" was part of the description of the goods. The sellers claimed that June 8th was not intended to be the delivery date. HELD: the clause was part of the description of the goods, and the sellers were in breach of contract. The buyers were entitled to refuse to accept the goods.

Wilensko Slaski, etc. v. *Fenwick & Co. Ltd.* (1938): There was a contract between the parties for the sale of a quantity of pit-props of specified lengths. The buyer undertook that he would "not reject the goods herein named or any part of them." The goods delivered did not comply with the specification and the buyer claimed to be able to reject them. HELD: notwithstanding his undertaking, the buyer was entitled to reject the goods, because they were not the goods specified in the contract.

Andrews Bros. v. *Singer & Co. Ltd.* (1933), C.A.: In a contract for a *new* Singer car there was a stipulation that "all conditions, warranties and liabilities implied by statute, common law or otherwise are excluded." After the buyer had accepted the car, he discovered that it was not new. He brought this action against the seller for breach of contract. The seller, in his defence, relied on the exemption clause. HELD: it was an express term in the contract that the sale was of a *new* Singer car. There was a breach of this express condition and the buyer was entitled to damages. The exemption clause was irrelevant, since it applied to implied conditions only.

Beale v. *Taylor* (1967), C.A.: T advertised a car for sale in the following terms: "Herald convertible, white, 1961, twin carbs." B went to T's home, saw the car and was driven in it and, as a result, bought the car for £160. B shortly discovered that the car was, in fact, made up of two cars. The rear part was from a

1961 model, the front part was from an earlier model, and the two parts were welded together. T was not aware of this fact. B brought this action, contending that there was a breach of the implied condition in *s*. 13. T denied that it was a sale by description, claiming that it was "the sale of a particular car as seen, tried and approved." HELD: there was a sale by description within *s*. 13. The implied condition as to correspondence with description was broken.

13. Fitness for a particular purpose. There is no implied warranty or condition as to the fitness for any particular purpose of the goods supplied under a contract of sale, except:

(*a*) where the buyer, expressly or by implication, makes known to the seller the particular purpose for which the goods are required, so as to show that the buyer relies on the seller's skill or judgment, and the goods are of a description which it is in the course of the seller's business to supply (whether he be the manufacturer or not), there is an implied condition that the goods shall be reasonably fit for such purpose; provided that, in the case of a contract for the sale of a specified article under its patent or other trade name, there is no implied condition as to its fitness for any particular purpose: *s*. 14 (1);

(*b*) where there is a statutory provision as to fitness for purpose (*s*. 14), *e.g.* the *Anchors and Chain Cables Act*, 1899, *s*. 2.

NOTE

(*i*) Any right, duty or liability which would arise under an implied condition as to fitness for purpose may be negatived or varied by exemption clause, or by a course of dealing between the parties: *see s*. 55 and *s*. 14 (3).

(*ii*) Where goods have a *self-evident purpose*, *e.g.* a hot water bottle or a pair of underpants, there is no need for the buyer to make known to the seller expressly the purpose for which the goods are required; the seller will be deemed to know by implication: *see Priest* v. *Last* (1903); *Grant* v. *Australian Knitting Mills* (1936); *Grenfell* v. *Meyrowitz* (1936); *Jackson* v. *Watson & Sons* (1909).

(*iii*) Where goods have no self-evident purpose, *e.g.* a ton of sand or a stack of timber, there is no implied condition as to fitness for any purpose unless it is clear from the circumstances that the seller knew the purpose for which the goods are required; *i.e. caveat emptor* applies. *See Kendall* v. *Lillico* (1968).

(*iv*) There is no implied condition as to fitness for purpose where the goods are not of a kind supplied by the seller in the course of his business, *e.g.* in the case of a private sale.

(*v*) If the buyer expressly makes known to the seller the purpose for which he needs the goods, there is an implied condition as to fitness for purpose even though the goods are bought under a patent or trade name: *see* the proviso in *s.* 14 (1); *see* also *Baldry* v. *Marshall* (1925): *Harrison & Jones* v. *Bunton & Lancaster* (1953).

(*vi*) Where goods are not fit for a particular purpose, the seller (or manufacturer) may be liable in tort, quite apart from contract, to any person injured by the goods: *Grant* v. *Australian Knitting Mills* (1936); *Moore* v. *Fox & Sons* (1956); *Vacwell Engineering Co. Ltd.* v. *B.D.A. Chemicals Ltd.* (1969).

(*vii*) It is no defence that the seller took all reasonable precautions to ensure that the goods were fit for the purpose for which they were supplied: *Frost* v. *Aylesbury Dairy* (1905); or that no defect was apparent from a casual inspection: *Priest* v. *Last* (1903).

(*viii*) The implied condition as to fitness arises in connection with goods *supplied* under a contract of sale: therefore, there may be an implied condition as to fitness in connection with a box, carton, bottle or other container which is not subject to the sale but is returnable to the seller: *Geddling* v. *Marsh* (1920).

(*ix*) Where the goods are not fit for the buyer's purpose because of some abnormal circumstances not known to the seller, there is no implied condition as to fitness for the buyer's purpose: *Griffiths* v. *Peter Conway* (1939).

(*x*) The implied condition as to fitness of purpose may take effect as a condition precedent to the passing of property: *Polar Refrigeration Service Ltd.* v. *Moldenhauer* (1967), a Canadian case.

(*xi*) An express warranty or condition as to fitness for a particular purpose does not negative a warranty or condition as to fitness for a particular purpose implied by the Act unless inconsistent therewith: *s.* 14 (4).

(*xii*) Section 14 does not apply to conditional sales agreements as defined in the *Hire-Purchase Act,* 1965.

CASES

Priest v. *Last* (1903): There was a retail sale of a hot water bottle. The bottle burst and injured the buyer's wife. The buyer brought this action to recover damages for the medical expenses incurred. HELD: the seller was in breach of the implied condition as to fitness for purpose, the purpose being self-evident.

Donoghue (or McAlister) v. *Stevenson* (1932), a Scottish appeal to the House of Lords: B bought a bottle of ginger beer from S, a retailer, who in his turn had bought it from M, the manufacturer, The bottle was opaque. B poured out a glass of ginger beer from the bottle and X drank it. When a second glass was poured out, the decomposed remains of a snail emerged from the bottle, and caused X to become very ill. X brought this action against M in negligence. HELD: M was liable to X in negligence. *Per* Lord Atkin, "A manufacturer of products, which he sells in such a form as to show that he intends them to reach the ultimate consumer in the form in which they left him with no reasonable possibility of intermediate examination, and with the knowledge that the absence of reasonable care in the preparation or putting up of the products will result in an injury to the consumer's life or property, owes a duty of care to the consumer to take reasonable care." N.B. The liability in tort is to the *consumer*, whether he be the buyer or not.

Grant v. *Australian Knitting Mills Ltd.* (1935), an appeal from the High Court of Australia to the Privy Council: G became seriously ill for a long period owing to an infection caused by a new pair of underpants which he had bought from M, a retailer. The retailer had bought the garment from the Australian Knitting Mills. G brought this action against the retailer in contract, and against the Australian Knitting Mills in tort. HELD by the Privy Council:

(*i*) the retailers were in breach of the implied conditions in *s.* 14 (1) and (2) of the *South Australia Sale of Goods Act,* 1895 (the South Australia Act of 1895, *s.* 14, is similar to the *Sale of Goods Act,* 1893, *s.* 14);

(*ii*) the manufacturer was liable in negligence: *Donoghue* v. *Stevenson* applied.

In connection with the words "*so as to show that the buyer relies on the seller's skill or judgment,*" Lord Wright said, "It is clear that the reliance must be brought home to the seller, expressly or by implication. The reliance will seldom be express: it will usually arise by implication from the circumstances; thus to take a case like that in question, or a purchase from a retailer, the reliance will be in general inferred from the fact that a buyer goes to a shop in the confidence that the tradesman has selected his stock with skill and judgment."

Manchester Liners v. *Rea* (1922), H.L.: There was a contract for the sale of a quantity of coal which the sellers knew was required by the buyers for their steamship *Manchester Importer*. The coal delivered by the sellers was quite unsuitable for the buyer's ship, which had to turn back shortly after putting out to sea. HELD: there was a breach of implied condition as to fitness for purpose under *s.* 14 (1). Lord Sumner said that the words of *s.* 14 (1) are satisfied "if the reliance is a matter of reasonable inference to the seller and to the Court."

Baldry v. *Marshall Ltd.* (1924), C.A.: B told M Ltd., who were dealers in motor cars, that he wanted a car which was "comfortable and suitable for the ordinary purpose of a touring car." The dealer told B that he thought a Bugatti car would be satisfactory for him. B thereupon entered into a contract to buy a Bugatti from M, and he paid £1,050 in purchase money. When the car was delivered to B, he discovered that it was not "comfortable and suitable for the ordinary purpose of a touring car." B claimed that the dealer was in breach of the implied condition in *s.* 14 (1) that the car was reasonably fit for the purpose he had described. HELD: although the car was bought as a Bugatti, nevertheless, the buyer made it clear that he was relying on the seller's skill and judgment. The dealer was liable for breach of the implied condition as to fitness for purpose. *Per* Bankes, L. J., "I am inclined to think that the key to the meaning of the proviso [in *s.* 14 (1)] is to see whether or not the buyer has specified an article by its trade name in such a way as to indicate that he is satisfied, at any rate, rightly or wrongly, that it will fulfil his particular purpose and that he is not relying upon the skill or judgment of the seller, however great that skill or judgment may be."

Frost v. *Aylesbury Dairy Co. Ltd.* (1905), C.A.: The defendant dairy company supplied the plaintiff with milk for the consumption of his family. The book used to record the amount supplied to the plaintiff contained a notice in which the dairy company stated the precautions taken to ensure that the milk supplied was pure. The plaintiff's wife died as a result of being infected with typhoid by milk supplied by the defendants. The plaintiff claimed damages under *s.* 14 (1). HELD: the defendants knew, by implication, the purpose for which the plaintiff bought the milk, *i.e.* for domestic consumption. The plaintiff had relied on the skill of the defendants. As the milk was not reasonably fit for domestic consumption, the defendants were in breach of the implied condition in *s.* 14 (1).

Geddling v. *Marsh* (1920): G, a retailer, bought bottles of mineral water from M, the manufacturer. The bottles were returnable to M when empty, and a penny was refunded for each bottle returned. G was injured when an empty bottle exploded. She claimed damages from M for breach of the implied condition under *s.* 14 (1). HELD: the bottle was supplied under a contract of sale, and there was breach of the implied condition as to fitness for purpose under *s.* 14 (1). It was immaterial whether the bottle —as opposed to its contents—was the subject of a sale.

Griffiths v. *Peter Conway Ltd.* (1939), C.A.: The defendants made

B

a Harris tweed coat specially for the plaintiff. The coat caused the plaintiff to suffer from dermatitis, so she brought this action to recover damages from the seller, contending that there was a breach of the implied condition in s. 14 (1). The plaintiff's skin was highly sensitive, and the coat would have been quite harmless to a normal skin. HELD: since the seller could not know, and did not know, of the buyer's idiosyncracy, s. 14 (1) did not apply and there was no breach of any implied condition.

Daniels and Daniels v. *R. White & Sons Ltd. and Tabard* (1938): The plaintiffs were husband and wife, and the defendants were the manufacturers and the retailer, respectively, of a bottle of lemonade bought by the husband for his wife. The husband asked for R. White's lemonade. The bottle of lemonade contained carbolic acid which caused the wife to become ill. The plaintiffs claimed damages against the manufacturer and also against the retailer under s. 14. The manufacturers showed that they used a fool-proof system of manufacture and bottling, and that the processes were carried out under proper supervision. HELD: (*i*) the manufacturers were not in breach of their duty to take reasonable care that their products did not cause injury to a consumer; (*ii*) the husband did not rely on the seller's skill or judgment, and so could not succeed under s. 14 (1). But the sale was a sale by description, and there was a breach of the implied condition in s. 14 (2) that the goods were of merchantable quality.

Vacwell Engineering Co. Ltd. v. *B.D.H. Chemicals Ltd.* (1969): V bought 400 glass ampoules of boron tribonide from B.D.H., each ampoule bearing a label with the words "harmful vapour." It was necessary for B.D.H. to remove the labels before the ampoules were used in their manufacturing process, and two physicists were instructed to wash them off in two adjacent sinks. While this was being done an explosion occurred, killing one of the physicists. It was overwhelmingly probable that the explosion was caused by the dropping into the sink of an ampoule which had shattered and released boron tribonide into contact with the water. V claimed damages from B.D.H. HELD: B.D.H. were liable as follows: (*i*) B.D.H. were in breach of an implied condition of fitness for purpose under s. 14 (1) inasmuch as there was no express warning of the danger of the chemical coming into contact with water; (*ii*) B.D.H. were negligent in not warning of the damages of explosion when boron tribonide came into contact with water.

Christopher Hill v. *Ashington Piggeries Ltd.* (1969), C.A.: The defendants were two mink companies concerned with the breeding of mink and with the supply of equipment and foodstuffs to other mink breeders. The plaintiffs, who manufactured compounds for animal feeding, entered an agreement with the defendants for the manufacture of a mink food to be called King Size. The formula was supplied by the defendants, and the plaintiffs had made it clear that they knew nothing about the nutritional requirements of mink. The plaintiffs did, however, suggest, as a variation in the formula, the substitution of herring meal for fish meal. For about a year King Size was used by about 100 mink farms without complaint. But in March, 1961, the plaintiffs bought a large consignment of herring meal which had been contaminated by a chemical known as D.M.N.A., toxic to mink, but harmless to other animals. The inclusion of the contaminated herring meal in the manufacture of King Size resulted in serious losses on some mink farms. The plaintiffs claimed payment for King Size containing the contaminated meal and the defendants counterclaimed for damages for breach of contract. HELD: the plaintiffs were entitled to recover payment as they were not in breach of contract because (i) it had not been shown that the King Size in question did not "correspond with description" under s. 13, and (ii) there was no implied condition of fitness for feeding to mink under s. 14 (1) because there was no reliance on the plaintiff's skill and judgment with respect to ingredients which might be toxic to mink alone. The counterclaim was dismissed.

Kendall v. *Lillico & Sons Ltd.* (1968), H.L.: G bought ground nuts from K. G's purpose was to re-sell in smaller quantities for compounding as food for cattle and poultry—this purpose being known to K. The nuts were in fact toxic and unfit for poultry. G sold some of the nuts to S, knowing that S required them for compounding into food for pigs and poultry. S compounded the nuts into food which was then bought by H, who fed it to his pheasants, which consequently died. S (who admitted liability to H) sued G, who sued K. The claim was for breach of the implied condition of fitness for purpose under s. 14 (1) and of merchantable quality under s. 14 (2). HELD: (i) *As between G and S.* The compounding into foodstuffs was a "particular purpose" within s. 14 (1) and S had relied on G's skill or judgment. G was liable to S. (ii) *As between K and G.* The purpose for which G required the goods was sufficiently "particular" to be within s. 14 (1) and K was liable for breach of the implied condition of fitness for purpose.

14. Quality of the goods. There is no implied warranty or condition as to the quality of goods supplied under a contract of sale, *i.e. caveat emptor* applies, except:

(a) where goods are bought by description from a seller who deals in goods of that description (whether he be the manufacturer or not), there is an implied condition that the goods shall be of merchantable quality; provided that if the buyer has examined the goods there shall be no implied condition as regards defects which such examination ought to have revealed: *see s.* 14;

(*b*) where there is a statutory provision as to quality, *e.g.* the *Merchandise Marks Acts*, 1887 and 1953; *Sale of Goods Act*, 1893, *ss.* 13, 14 (2) and 15; *see s.* 14.

NOTE

(*i*) Any right, duty or liability which would arise under the implied condition as to merchantable quality may be negatived or varied by exemption clause, or by a course of dealing between the parties: *see s.* 55, *s.* 14 (3) and X, **4–15**.

(*ii*) *Sale by description* is considered in **12** (*c*) above.

(*iii*) As to the meaning of *merchantable quality*: *per* LORD WRIGHT in *Grant* v. *Australian Knitting Mills* (1936), an article is not merchantable "if it has defects unfitting it for its only proper use but not apparent on ordinary examination"; *per* ATKIN, L. J., in *Niblett* v. *Confectioners' Materials Co.* (1921), "No one who knew the facts would buy them in that state or condition; in other words they were unsaleable and unmerchantable"; *per* LORD REID in *Kendall* v. *Lillico* (1968) and *Brown* v. *Craiks* (1970), "What sub-section (2) now means by 'merchantable quality' is that the goods in the form in which they were tendered were of no use for any purpose for which goods which complied with the description under which these goods were sold would normally be used, and hence were not saleable under that description. This is an objective test: 'were of no use for any purpose . . .' must mean 'would not have been used by a reasonable man for any purpose'."

(*iv*) An express warranty or condition as to quality does not negative a warranty or condition as to quality implied by the Act unless inconsistent therewith: *see s.* 14 (4).

(*v*) "Quality of goods" includes their state or condition: *s.* 62 (1).

(*vi*) Section 14 does not apply to conditional sale agreements as defined in the *Hire-Purchase Act*, 1965.

CASES

Wilson v. *Rickett, Cockerell & Co.* (1954), C.A.: W bought from the defendant coal merchants "a ton of 'Coalite'." When part of the consignment was being burnt in the grate, there was an explosion which caused damage to W's goods in the room. The explosive substance was not "Coalite" but some foreign matter which had got mixed with the "Coalite." W claimed damages under *s.* 14 of the Act. HELD: (*i*) *s.* 14 (1) did not apply because the "Coalite" was bought under its trade name; (*ii*) but there was a breach of the implied condition as to merchantability under *s.* 14 (2).

Sumner, Permain & Co. v. *Webb & Co.* (1921), C.A.: The defendants sold a consignment of "Webb's Indian Tonic" to the plaintiff buyers. The goods were to be delivered f.o.b. London and the sellers knew that they were to be shipped to the Argentine. Argentinian law prohibited the sale of tonic water because it contained a small quantity of salicylic acid. The buyers brought this action against the sellers, claiming that there was a breach of the implied conditions in *s.* 14 (1) and (2). HELD: (*i*) as to the claim under *s.* 14 (1), the buyers did not rely on the skill or judgment of the seller as to the law of the Argentine, and the proviso as to sale under a trade name applied; (*ii*) as to the claim under *s.* 14 (2), there was no breach of the implied condition as to merchantable quality: *per* Scrutton, L. J., "In my view, 'merchantable quality' means that the goods comply with the description in the contract, so that to a purchaser buying goods of that description the goods would be good tender. It does not mean that there shall be, in fact, buyers of the article . . . I do not think 'merchantable quality' means that there can legally be buyers of that article."

Godley v. *Perry* (*Burton third party, Graham fourth party*) (1959): Gy, a boy aged six, saw some plastic catapults in P's shop window, went into the shop and bought one. When Gy used the catapult to fire a stone, the plastic snapped and caused Gy to lose an eye. P had bought the catapult from B in a sale by sample, the sample being tested by pulling back the elastic. B had bought the catapult in a sale by sample from Gm. Gy claimed against P for damages for breach of the implied conditions in *s.* 14 (1) and (2) of the *Sale of Goods Act,* 1893. P claimed against B for breach of the implied condition under *s.* 15 (2) (c) of the *Sale of Goods Act,* and B claimed under the same section against Gm. HELD: (*i*) *As between Gy and P:* Gy had relied on P's skill and judgment and the catapult was not reasonably fit for its purpose; the sale was by description and the catapult was not of merchantable quality. P was, therefore, in breach of the implied conditions in *s.* 14 (1) and (2). (*ii*) *As between P and B:* B was in breach of the implied conditions in *s.* 15 (2) (c). (*iii*) *As between B and Gm:* Gm was in breach of the implied condition in *s.* 15 (2) (c).

Brown & Son Ltd. v. *Craiks Ltd.* (1970), H.L.: B gave two orders to C for the manufacture of large quantities of rayon cloth to a detailed specification. The buyer intended to use the cloth for making dresses and the seller *bona fide* thought it was for industrial use. Both orders were accepted and the agreed price was 36·25*d*. per yard. B, on discovering subsequently that the cloth was not suitable for dressmaking, wrote to C cancelling the contract. Both parties were left with a considerable amount of cloth on their hands which was eventually sold, C obtaining 30*d*. per yard and B, only 15*d*. per yard. B brought this action against C, claiming that the goods were not of merchantable quality, basing his case on *s*. 14 (2). B claimed: (*i*) that there was only one normal use for such cloth at the time of delivery, namely dressmaking, and that there was not any normal use of the cloth of the description ordered for industrial purposes, and (*ii*) that the discrepancy between the contract price (36·25*d*. per yard) and the price at which C subsequently sold the remaining cloth (30*d*. per yard) showed that the goods were not of merchantable quality. HELD: (*i*) the cloth was reasonably capable of being used, was saleable for a number of industrial purposes and was merchantable for these purposes, and (*ii*) there was not a sufficient abatement in price as to lead to the conclusion that the cloth was not of merchantable quality.

15. Sale by sample. A contract of sale is a contract of sale by sample where there is a term in the contract, express or implied, to that effect: *s*. 15 (1). In the case of a contract for sale by sample:

(*a*) there is an *implied condition* that the bulk shall correspond with the sample in quality: *s*. 15 (2) (*a*);

(*b*) there is an *implied condition* that the buyer shall have a reasonable opportunity of comparing the bulk with the sample: *s*. 15 (2) (*b*);

(*c*) there is an *implied condition* that the goods shall be free from any defect rendering them unmerchantable which would not be apparent on reasonable examination of the sample: *s*. 15 (2) (*c*);

(*d*) where there is a contract for the sale of goods by sample, as well as by description, it is not sufficient that the bulk of the goods corresponds with the sample if the goods do not also correspond with the description. There is an *implied condition* that the goods shall correspond with the description: *see s*. 13.

NOTE

(*i*) Any right, duty or liability which would arise under the implied condition as to merchantable quality may be negatived or varied by exemption clause, or by a course of dealing between the parties: *see s.* 55 and X, **4–15**.

(*ii*) Whether there is an implied term to the effect that a sale is a sale by sample will depend on the circumstances of each case.   At common law, terms may be implied:

    (1) To give effect to the presumed, but unexpressed, intentions of the parties; or

    (2) To give effect to a trade custom or usage; or

    (3) To give a contract business efficacy.

Even though a sample was exhibited at the time the parties made their contract, the sale is not necessarily a sale by sample.

(*iii*) "Quality of goods" includes their state or condition: *s.* 62 (1).

(*iv*) As to the meaning of "reasonable examination," a reasonable examination is not the most exhaustive examination possible.   Due regard must be had to the standard of knowledge of the buyer at the time of the sale.   Moreover, where the seller is a manufacturer the buyer is entitled to rely on this skill, especially where there is a confidence based on previous dealings between the parties: *Drummond* v. *Van Ingen* (1887); *Godley* v. *Perry* (1959).

(*v*) Where there is a sale by sample and the goods do not correspond with the sample, there is a breach of the implied condition, even though a simple process would restore the bulk of the goods to the quality of the sample: *E. & S. Ruben Ltd.* v. *Faire Bros. & Co. Ltd.* (1948).

(*vi*) Where a contract of sale by sample includes a term to the effect that the goods are to be taken "*with all faults and imperfections,*" the seller will not be liable if the goods contain imperfections which were also in the sample, but he will be liable for imperfections which were not contained in the sample.   That is to say, provided the bulk corresponds with the sample, the seller will be liable if the goods are unmerchantable: *Champanhac & Co. Ltd.* v. *Waller & Co. Ltd.* (1948).

(*vii*) Section 15 does not apply to conditional sale agreements as defined in the *Hire-Purchase Act*, 1965.

DELIVERY OF THE RIGHT QUANTITY

16. Seller's duty.   It is the duty of the seller to deliver the quantity of goods he agreed to sell to the buyer: *see s.* 27.

17. Stipulated quantity is part of description.   Where a contract of sale stipulates the quantity of goods to be sold, the stipulation as to quantity is part of the description of the goods. There is, therefore, an implied condition that the quantity delivered corresponds with the quantity contracted for: *see s.* 13.

NOTE
- (*i*) The implied condition as to correspondence with description may be negatived or varied by exemption clause or by a course of dealing between the parties: *see s.* 55 and X, 4–15.
- (*ii*) Where there is no term in the contract to the effect that delivery shall be made by instalments, it is the duty of the seller to deliver the goods in a single consignment: *see s.* 31 (1).
- (*iii*) Where there is a term in the contract to the effect that the goods shall be packed in containers each containing a specified quantity of goods, it is the duty of the seller to conform to this requirement. If he fails to do so, there is a breach of the implied condition as to correspondence with description: *re Moore and Landauer* (1921).

18. Delivery of too little or too much.

(*a*) *Too little.* Where the seller delivers to the buyer a quantity of goods less than he contracted to sell, the buyer may reject them, but if the buyer accepts the goods so delivered, he must pay for them at the contract rate: *s.* 30 (1).

(*b*) *Too much.* Where the seller delivers to the buyer a quantity of goods larger than he contracted to sell, the buyer may accept the goods included in the contract and reject the rest, or he may reject the whole. If the buyer accepts the whole of the goods so delivered, he must pay for them at the contract rate: *s.* 30 (2).

NOTE
- (*i*) These provisions are subject to any usage of trade, special agreement, or course of dealing between the parties: *see s.* 55.
- (*ii*) Where there is only a minute discrepancy between the quantity delivered and the quantity contracted for, the maxim *de minimis non curat lex* applies: *Shipton Anderson v. Weil Bros.* (1912).
- (*iii*) Where there is a contract for the sale of a large bulk of goods, it is usual for the seller to stipulate a margin with respect to the quantity to be delivered, *e.g.* 2% more or less.

19. Delivery of mixed goods. Where the seller delivers to the buyer the goods he contracted to sell mixed with goods of a different description, not included in the contract, the buyer may accept the goods which are in accordance with the contract and reject the rest, or he may reject the whole: *s.* 30 (3).

NOTE

(*i*) This provision is subject to any usage of trade, special agreement, or course of dealing between the parties: *see s.* 30 (4).

(*ii*) This provision does not entitle the buyer to accept the goods of a different description not included in the contract. Whether he can do so or not will depend upon the general rules of contract: upon whether the delivery of the goods of a different description can be construed as an offer to sell.

(*iii*) Do not confuse *s.* 30 (3) with *s.* 30 (2). The former deals with goods different from the goods included in the contract, whereas the latter deals with goods similar to those included in the contract.

CASES

Re Moore & Co. Ltd. and Landauer & Co. (1921), C.A.: The terms of a contract for the sale of tinned pears provided that the goods were to be packed in cases of 30 tins each. When the buyers inspected the tendered consignment they found that about half the cases contained 24 tins each, the remainder containing 30 tins each. The buyers rejected all the cases. HELD: it was part of the contract description of the goods that there should be 30 tins to the case and that, accordingly, the sellers were in breach of the implied condition in *s.* 13. Furthermore, by *s.* 30 (3), the buyer was entitled to reject the whole consignment.

Ebrahim Dawood Ltd. v. *Heath Ltd.* (1961): There was an agreement for the sale of 50 tons of steel sheets "assorted over 6, 7, 8, 9 and 10 feet long. Assorted tonnage per size." In the letter of credit the goods were described as being "equal number of sheets per each size." The seller delivered 50 tons of sheets of length 6 feet. The buyers contended that they were entitled to accept one-fifth of the sheets delivered and reject four-fifths. They claimed the recovery of four-fifths of the purchase price as money paid on a consideration that had wholly failed. HELD: (*i*) it constituted part of the description of the sheets that they should be of 6, 7, 8, 9 and 10 feet lengths, assorted equal tonnage per size; (*ii*) the buyers were entitled to reject the part of the consignment which should have consisted of sheets of 7, 8, 9 and 10 feet length; (*iii*) the buyers were entitled to recover *pro tanto* the purchase price as money had and received or paid for a consideration that had wholly failed; and (*iv*) the buyers were entitled to damages.

OFFENCES

20. The Consumer Protection Act, 1961. Quite apart from contract, this Act imposes additional obligations on the seller. By *s.* 1 of the Act, the Secretary of State is empowered to make Regulations governing the design, construction or packing of any class of goods, or requiring that goods be marked or accompanied by warning notices or instructions, the purpose of such Regulations being to prevent or reduce risk of death or personal injury. Section 2 of the Act provides that no person may sell, or have in his possession for the purpose of selling, any goods unless the Regulations governing them are complied with. Subject to certain defences specified in the Act, any person who contravenes these Regulations is guilty of an offence and liable on summary conviction to a fine not exceeding £100, or in the case of a second or subsequent offence to a fine not exceeding £250 or to imprisonment for a term not exceeding three months or to both.

Regulations have been made under this provision for the following classes of goods: oil heaters, nightdresses, stands for carry-cots and toys.

21. The Trade Descriptions Act, 1968. By *s.* 1 of this Act, any person who, in the course of a trade or business, (*a*) applies a false trade description to any goods, or (*b*) supplies or offers to supply any goods to which a false trade description is applied, is guilty of an offence. The Act also provides that it is an offence to make false or misleading indications as to the price of goods, or as to royal approval, etc., or as to the provision of services or facilities. A person found guilty of an offence under this Act is liable on summary conviction to a fine not exceeding £400, and, on conviction on indictment, to a fine or imprisonment for a term not exceeding two years or both.

PROGRESS TEST 2

1. It is the duty of the seller to deliver the goods in accordance with the terms of the contract of sale. What do you understand by "delivery"? (**2**)

2. In what ways may delivery take place? (**3**)

3. What rules govern the time at which delivery should be made? (**4**)

4. May the buyer always examine the goods before accepting them? (**5**)

5. List the implied conditions and warranties which arise by virtue of the Act. (**10–15**)

6. What is the effect where a seller is in breach of the implied condition that he has a right to sell the goods? (**10**)

7. In what circumstances is there an implied condition that the goods shall correspond with the description? (**12**)

8. Where there is an implied condition that the goods shall correspond with the description, a heavy burden is placed upon the seller. Explain this statement with the aid of decided cases. (**12**)

9. In what circumstances is there an implied condition that the goods are fit for a particular purpose? (**13**)

10. Where there is a breach of the implied condition as to fitness for purpose, is it a defence that the seller took all reasonable precautions to ensure that the goods were fit for the purpose for which they were supplied? (**13**)

11. What is the position where goods are sold under a patent or trade name? (**13**)

12. When is there an implied condition as to quality? (**14–15**)

13. What do you understand by the expression "merchantable quality"? (**14**)

14. What implied conditions arise in cases of sale by sample? (**15**)

15. In what circumstances are the implied conditions and warranties negatived? (**12–16**)

16. What are the rules affecting the quantity of goods to be delivered? (**16–19**)

17. What is the position where the seller delivers to the buyer a quantity of goods larger than he contracted to sell? (**18**)

18. Explain the position where the seller includes goods which are not in accordance with the contract description. (**19**)

19. A, a manufacturer of beer barrels, entered into a contract with B for the purchase of 10,000 staves $\frac{5}{8}$ in. thick. When the staves were delivered to A, he discovered that 120 of them were only $\frac{1}{2}$ in. thick. Is B entitled to reject the whole consignment?

20. C agreed to buy from D, a motor cycle dealer, a new "Speedster" motor cycle. The printed contract stipulated that "all conditions, warranties and liabilities implied by statute, common law or otherwise are excluded." A week after C had accepted delivery of the motor cycle from D, he discovered that it was not quite new, but had been used for demonstration purposes before the sale. C now wishes to know whether he has an action for breach of contract. Advise him.

21. E bought a "Super" drip-dry shirt from F's shop. The shirt caused E to suffer from dermatitis. E wishes to know whether he has an action for damages (*i*) against the manufacturer of "Super" shirts and (*ii*) against F.   Advise him.

Would it make any difference to your answer if E had a specially sensitive skin?

22. How may a seller incur criminal liability under the *Consumer Protection Act*, 1961, and the *Trade Descriptions Act*, 1968?

CHAPTER III

THE BUYER'S DUTIES

1. Acceptance and payment. It is the duty of the buyer to accept and pay for the goods in accordance with the terms of the contract of sale: *s.* 27.

THE DUTY TO ACCEPT THE GOODS

2. Acceptance. The buyer is deemed to have accepted the goods when he intimates to the seller that he has accepted them, or (except where *s.* 34 provides otherwise) when the goods have been delivered to him, and he does any act in relation to them which is inconsistent with the ownership of the seller, or when after the lapse of a reasonable time, he retains the goods without intimating to the seller that he has rejected them: *s.* 35.

(*a*) *Examination.* Where goods are delivered to the buyer, which he has not previously examined, he is not deemed to have accepted them unless and until he has had a reasonable opportunity of examining them for the purpose of ascertaining whether they are in conformity with the contract: *s.* 34 (1).

(*b*) *Re-sale.* Where the buyer re-sells goods before he has had a reasonable opportunity of examining them, he has performed an act inconsistent with the ownership of the seller, but will be not deemed to have accepted the goods: *s.* 4 of the *Misrepresentation Act, 1967*, reversing *Hardy & Co.* v. *Hillerns and Fowler* (1923).

3. Neglect or refusal to accept. When the seller is ready and willing to deliver the goods, and requests the buyer to take delivery, and the buyer does not within a reasonable time after such request take delivery of the goods, he is liable to the seller for any loss occasioned by his neglect or refusal to take delivery, and also for a reasonable charge for the care and custody of the goods: *s.* 37.

(*a*) *Repudiation*.   This provision does not affect the rights of the seller where the neglect or refusal of the buyer to take delivery amounts to a repudiation of the contract: *s*. 37.

(*b*) *Reasonable time*.   What is a reasonable time is a question of fact: *s*. 56.

THE DUTY TO PAY THE PRICE

4. The price.   It is the duty of the buyer to pay for the goods according to the terms of the contract: *see s*. 27.

(*a*) The price in a contract for sale may be fixed by the contract, or may be left to be fixed in a manner thereby agreed, or may be determined by the course of dealing between the parties: *s*. (1).

(*b*) Where the price is not determined in accordance with the foregoing, the buyer must pay a reasonable price: *s*. 8 (2).

NOTE

(*i*) What is a reasonable price is a question of fact dependent on the circumstances of each particular case: *s*. 8 (2).

(*ii*) Where there is an agreement to sell goods on the terms that the price is to be fixed by the valuation of a third party, and such third party cannot or does not make such a valuation, the agreement is avoided; provided that if the goods or any part thereof have been delivered to, and appropriated by, the buyer, he must pay a reasonable price therefor: *s*. 9 (1).   But where such third party is prevented from making a valuation by the fault of the seller or buyer, the party not in fault may maintain an action for damages against the party in fault: *s*. 9 (2).

5. Time of payment.   It is the buyer's duty to pay the seller at the time he agreed to pay in the contract of sale: *see s*. 27.

(*a*) *Stipulations not of the essence*.   Unless a different intention appears from the terms of the contract, stipulations as to time of payment are not deemed to be of the essence of a contract of sale: *see s*. 10 (1).

(*b*) *Payment and delivery concurrent*.   Unless otherwise agreed, payment of the price and delivery of the goods are concurrent conditions, that is to say, the buyer must be ready and willing to pay the price in exchange for possession of the goods: *see s*. 28.

(c) *Payment on delivery of documents of title.* Unless otherwise agreed, it is the duty of the buyer to pay the price on delivery of the documents of title, even though he is not yet in possession of the goods: *Clemens Horst & Co.* v. *Biddell Bros.* (1912).

PROGRESS TEST 3

1. It is the duty of the buyer to accept and pay for the goods in accordance with the terms of the contract of sale. When is the buyer deemed to have accepted the goods? (**2**)

2. What is the position where the buyer neglects or refuses to accept the goods? (**3**)

3. In what circumstances must the buyer pay a reasonable price for the goods? (**4**)

4. Are stipulations as to time of payment of the essence of a contract of sale of goods? (**4**)

5. Unless otherwise agreed, payment of the price and delivery of the goods are concurrent conditions. Explain. (**5**)

6. A sends his lorry driver to deliver a consignment of goods which he has contracted to sell to B. The driver unloads the goods in B's yard and immediately departs. On that same day B examines the goods and finds that they do not accord with the contract description. What would you advise B to do? (**5**)

CHAPTER IV

THE TRANSFER OF OWNERSHIP OF GOODS

1. Ownership and possession. It is important to distinguish between ownership and possession.

(*a*) *Transfer of ownership.* Under a contract of sale, the seller transfers, or agrees to transfer, the property in (*i.e.* the ownership of) goods to the buyer: *see s.* 1 (1).

(*b*) *Ownership.* If property passes before delivery, the buyer has ownership but not possession.

(*c*) *Ownership and possession.* If property passes concurrently with delivery, the buyer gets ownership and possession together.

(*d*) *Possession.* If property does not pass before, or concurrently with, delivery, the buyer gets possession but not ownership. The buyer will get ownership according to the terms of the contract.

THE TRANSFER OF PROPERTY AS BETWEEN SELLER AND BUYER

2. Goods must be ascertained. Where there is a contract for the sale of unascertained goods, no property in the goods is transferred to the buyer unless and until the goods are ascertained: *s.* 16. *See Laurie & Morewood* v. *Dudin & Sons Ltd.* (1925).

(*a*) *Property* means the general property in goods, and not merely a special property: *see s.* 62 (1).

(*b*) *Ascertained* probably means identified in accordance with the agreement after the time when a contract of sale is made: *see per* Atkin, L. J., in *re Wait* (1926). It would seem that "unascertained goods" means goods of a specified class, but which have not yet become identified as the goods which are to pass under the contract.

3. Property passes when intended to pass. Where there is a contract for the sale of specific or ascertained goods, the property in them is transferred to the buyer at such time as the parties to the contract intend it to be transferred: *s.* 17 (1).

NOTE

(*i*) For the purpose of ascertaining the intention of the parties, regard shall be had to the terms of the contract, the conduct of the parties, and the circumstances of the case: 17 (2).

(*ii*) Where property has already passed under an unconditional contract of sale, a subsequent stipulation to the effect that property shall not pass except upon the fulfilment of a condition shall not be valid: *Dennant* v. *Skinner* (1948).

4. Rules for ascertaining intention: s. 18. *Unless a different intention appears,* the rules contained in *s.* 18 are applied to discover the intention of the parties as to the time at which the property in the goods is to pass to the buyer. The rules are as follows:

Rule 1. Where there is an unconditional contract for the sale of specific goods, in a deliverable state, the property in the goods passes to the buyer when the contract is made, and it is immaterial whether the time of payment or the time of delivery, or both, be postponed.

Rule 2. Where there is a contract for the sale of specific goods and the seller is bound to do something to the goods, for the purpose of putting them into a deliverable state, the property does not pass until such thing be done, and the buyer has notice thereof.

Rule 3. Where there is a contract for the sale of specific goods in a deliverable state, but the seller is bound to weigh, measure, test, or do some other act or thing with reference to the goods for the purpose of ascertaining the price, the property does not pass until such act or thing be done, and the buyer has notice thereof.

Rule 4. When goods are delivered to the buyer on approval or "on sale or return" or other similar terms the property therein passes to the buyer:

(*a*) When he signifies his approval or acceptance to the seller or does any other act adopting the transaction.

(*b*) If he does not signify his approval or acceptance to the seller but retains the goods without giving notice of rejection, then, if a time has been fixed for the return of the goods, on the expiration of such time, and, if no time has been fixed, on the expiration of a reasonable time. What is a reasonable time is a question of fact.

Rule 5.

(*a*) Where there is a contract for the sale of unascertained or future goods by description, and goods of that description and in a deliverable state are unconditionally appropriated to the contract, either by the seller with the assent of the buyer, or by the buyer with the assent of the seller, the property in the goods thereupon passes to the buyer. Such assent may be express or implied, and may be given either before or after the appropriation is made.

(*b*) Where, in pursuance of the contract, the seller delivers the goods to the buyer or to a carrier or other bailee (whether named by the buyer or not) for the purpose of transmission to the buyer, and does not reserve the right of disposal, he is deemed to have unconditionally appropriated the good to the contract.

NOTE
(*i*) Section 18 applies only if the parties have not shown a different intention: *see re Anchor Line (Henderson Bros.) Ltd.* (1916); *R.* v. *Eaton* (1966); *Weiner* v. *Smith* (1906).
(*ii*) *Rules* 1–4 apply only to contract for the sale of specific goods. *Specific goods* means goods identified and agreed upon at the time a contract of sale is made: *s.* 62.
(*iii*) *Rule* 2: Goods are in a "deliverable state" when they are in such a state that the buyer would under the contract be bound to take delivery of them: *s.* 62. *See Underwood Ltd.* v. *Burgh Castle Brick and Cement Syndicate* (1921).
(*iv*) *Rule* 4: A person to whom goods have been sent on approval is not necessarily a person who has "bought or agreed to buy goods" within *s.* 25. Moreover, there is some difficulty in reconciling the use of the word "buyer" in Rule 4 with the definition in *s.* 62 ("buyer" means a person who buys or agrees to buy goods).
(*v*) *Rule* 4: Where a person to whom goods have been delivered on approval gives the goods as a pledge for a loan, he is deemed to adopt the transaction; thus the property in the goods has passed to that person as buyer, and hence to the pledgee: *Kirkham* v. *Attenborough* (1896). But note *Weiner* v. *Smith* (1906), where there was a "different intention," so that *s.* 18 did not apply.

(*vi*) *Rule* 5: The buyer's assent may be inferred from the terms
of the contract or from trade usage. *See Ross T. Smyth &
Co. Ltd.* v. *T. D. Bailey Son & Co.* (1940). It may also
be inferred from the conduct of the parties: *Pignataro* v.
Gilroy (1919).

CASES

Koppel v. *Koppel* (1966), C.A.: There was an agreement between
K and Mrs. W which was affirmed by K as follows: "This is to state
that on this date I transfer the entire contents of this house to
Mrs. W.   This is to compensate her, as agreed, for her giving up
her own and daughter's home and for disposing of her furniture in
order to look after my children permanently."   Mrs. W went to
live at K's house according to the agreement.   When a writ of
fieri facias was issued against K, Mrs. W claimed that she had
title to the contents of the house.   On the question of title it was
HELD: that property had passed to Mrs. W.   *Per* HARMAN, L. J.:
"I think that the property in the goods, this being a document
evidencing a transfer for consideration, passed under *s.* 18, *r.* 1,
of the *Sale of Goods Act*, 1893 . . .   There is no question of a gift
here.   It was money or money's worth."

Underwood Ltd. v. *Burgh Castle Brick and Cement Syndicate*
(1921), C.A.: There was an agreement for the sale, free on rail in
London, of a condensing machine.   At the time of the agreement,
the machine was bolted down and embedded in concrete.   It took
two days to detach the machine from its bed.   The sellers accidentally damaged the machine during the loading on to a railway
truck.   The buyers refused to accept the machine and the sellers
brought this action.   On the question whether property passed
at the time the contract was made, HELD: (*i*) rule 1 did not apply
because the engine was not, at the time of making the contract,
in a deliverable state inasmuch as it was affixed to the freehold
and could not be put in a state in which the buyers were bound
to accept it until it was detached: (*ii*) rule 2 applied, because the
sellers were bound to do something to the engine for the purpose of
putting it into a deliverable state—namely to detach it in order
to put it on rail.   Property did not pass at the time the contract
was made.

Nanka-Bruce v. *Commonwealth Trust* (1962), P.C.: There was an
agreement between N, the seller, and L, the buyer, for the sale
of 160 bags of cocoa at a price of 59*s.* per 60 lb.   It was understood
by N that the price would be ascertained when the cocoa was
weighed up at the premises of a third party to whom L intended
to sell the cocoa.   L sold the cocoa to the Commonwealth Trust,
who acted in good faith, but L did not subsequently pay the price
to N according to the agreement.   N brought this action against
the Commonwealth Trust for conversion of the cocoa.   On the

question whether property passed from N to L, HELD: the provision as to the weighing of the cocoa was not a condition precedent to a sale. The goods were transferred, their price was fixed, and the testing was merely to see whether the goods fitted the weights as represented by the seller, but this testing was not suspensive of the contract of sale nor a condition precedent to it. Property accordingly passed to L, who was able to pass good title to the Commonwealth Trust.

Kirkham v. *Attenborough* (1896), C.A.: There was a contract by which K, a manufacturing jeweller, delivered jewellery to W "on sale or return." W then pawned part of the jewellery with A. Subsequently, W died. He had not paid for the jewellery pledged to A, nor had he intimated to K that he did not intend to return it. K brought this action to recover the jewellery from A. HELD: the act of pawning the jewellery, being inconsistent with the return of the goods, was an act "adopting the transaction" within *s.* 18, *r.* 4 (a) and that, accordingly, property passed from K to W (K's only right being to sue for the price).

Weiner v. *Smith* (1906), C.A.: W delivered goods to H on the following written terms: "On approbation. On sale for cash only or return . . . goods had on approbation or on sale or return remain the property of W until such goods are settled for or charged." H then delivered the goods to L, who had falsely stated that he had a customer for them. L immediately pledged the goods with S, who took them in good faith. On the question whether property in the goods had passed from W to A, HELD: the terms upon which the goods were delivered to H showed a "different intention" within *s.* 18 and that, accordingly, rule 4 (a) and (b) did not apply. No property passed.

Genn v. *Winkel* (1912), C.A.: On January 4th the plaintiff delivered diamonds to the defendant on sale or return. On the same day the defendant delivered the diamonds to a third person G, on sale or return. On January 6th G delivered the diamonds to a fourth person on sale or return. This fourth person lost the diamonds. The plaintiff sued for the unpaid balance of the price. HELD: the diamonds were not returned to the plaintiff within a reasonable time and, accordingly, property passed by virtue of *s.* 18, rule 4. The defendant was liable.

London Jewellers Ltd. v. *Attenborough* (1934), C.A.: The plaintiffs delivered jewellery to W "on appro." W immediately, through his agents, pawned the jewellery with the defendants. On the question whether property had passed from the plaintiffs to W, HELD: by pawning the jewellery, W had "adopted the transaction" and, accordingly, property passed to him by virtue of *s.* 18, rule 4 (a).

R. v. *Eaton* (1966), C.C.A.: X obtained delivery of jewellery on the terms of an approbation note which provided that it remained the property of O, the jeweller, until it was paid for.   X delivered certain pieces of jewellery to A so that A could decide which to keep, but A pawned all the pieces, pretending that he was the owner.   On the question whether property had passed to A, HELD: no property passed to X because the terms of the approbation note showed a "contrary intention" within *s.* 18 so as to exclude rule 4.   Since X got no property he could pass none to A.

Pignataro v. *Gilroy* (1919): There was a contract for the sale of "140 bags of rice . . . to be taken delivery in 14 days free from date."   At the time of the contract, the goods were not ascertained, the sale being by sample.   The buyer was told that 125 bags would be delivered at a specified wharf and the remaining 15 bags at the seller's place of business.   On being paid the price, the seller, on February 28th, wrote to the buyer enclosing a delivery note for the 125 bags and stating that the 15 bags were ready for delivery.   In this letter the seller asked the buyer to send for the 15 bags at once as he was very short of room.   The buyer sent for the 15 bags on March 25th, by which time they had been stolen.   The buyers brought this action to recover the price paid for the missing bags.   On the question whether property in the 15 bags had passed to the buyer, HELD: the seller's letter of February 28th was notice to the buyer that the 15 bags had been appropriated by the seller.   The buyer's failure to act until March 25th raised the inference that the buyer had assented to the appropriation and that, accordingly, property passed to him.

Wardar's Co. Ltd. v. *W. Norwood & Sons Ltd.* (1968), C.A.: There was an agreement by telephone for the sale of 600 cartons of kidneys.   At this time the seller had 1,500 cartons in cold store.   On the same day the buyer inspected the cartons in the seller's store.   Early the following morning, the seller's agent gave the buyer's carrier a note authorising him to collect 600 cartons from the buyer's cold store.   When the carrier arrived at the store he found the cartons already taken out of store and stacked on the pavement.   Porters were then directed to load the cartons on the lorry—a process which was not completed until noon.   During the course of the loading there was a tea-break at about 10.00 a.m. when the carrier noticed that the cartons were dripping.   He then switched on the refrigeration in his lorry, although this would not become effective until about three hours later.   When the carrier signed for the kidneys before his departure at noon, he added a note that they were in a soft condition.   The carrier then drove from London to Glasgow.   Upon his arrival the next day, the kidneys were found to be unfit for human consumption.   The buyer brought this action for damages and the seller counterclaimed for the price.   HELD: (i) that, at the time of the making of the contract, the goods were unascertained and that, by s. 16, no property could pass until the goods were ascertained; (ii) by rule 5 of s. 18, the property in unascertained goods, such as these, passes when the goods are unconditionally appropriated, and in this case there was a clear unconditional appropriation when the delivery order was handed over in respect of the cartons deposited on the pavement, and by s. 20, the goods were then at the buyer's risk. The seller's counterclaim succeeded.

5. Reservation of right of disposal. Where there is a contract for the sale of specific goods or where goods are subsequently appropriated to the contract, the seller may, by the terms of the contract or appropriation, reserve the right of disposal of the goods until certain conditions are fulfilled. In each case, notwithstanding the delivery of the goods to the buyer, or to a carrier or other bailee for the purpose of transmission to the buyer, the property in the goods does not pass to the buyer until the conditions imposed by the seller are fulfilled: s. 19 (1).

NOTE

(i) Where goods are shipped, and by the bill of lading the goods are deliverable to the order of the seller or his agent, the seller is *prima facie* deemed to reserve the right of disposal: s. 19 (2).

(ii) Where the seller of goods draws on the buyer for the price, and transmits the bill of exchange and bill of lading to the buyer together to secure acceptance of the bill of exchange, the buyer is bound to return the bill of lading if he does not honour the bill of exchange, and if he wrongfully retains the bill of lading the property in the goods does not pass to him: s. 19 (3).

(iii) The right of disposal is sometimes referred to as *jus disponendi*.

6. The passing of risk. Unless otherwise agreed, the goods remain at the seller's risk until the property therein is transferred to the buyer, but when the property therein is transferred to the buyer, the goods are at the buyer's risk whether delivery has been made or not: s. 20.

(a) *May be varied or inferred.* This is a *prima facie* rule only, and may be varied according to the intention of the parties. The intention may be express, as occurred in *Sterns Ltd.* v. *Vickers Ltd.* (1922), or inferred from trade custom, as in *Bevington* v. *Dale* (1902).

(*b*) *Delay.* The *prima facie* rule as to the passing of risk may be displaced where delivery is delayed by the fault of either party. The goods will then be at the risk of the party at fault: *Demby Hamilton & Co. Ltd.* v. *Barden* (1949).

(*c*) *Insurance.* Where a party has the risk, he has an insurable interest in the goods.

(*d*) *Goods perished at the time of the contract.* Where there is a contract for the sale of specific goods, and the goods without the knowledge of the seller have perished at the time when the contract is made, the contract is void: *s.* 6. *See Barrow Lane and Ballard Ltd.* v. *Philip Phillips & Co. Ltd.* (1928).

(*e*) *Goods subsequently perished.* Where there is an agreement to sell specific goods, and subsequently the goods, without any fault on the part of the seller or buyer, perish before the risk passes to the buyer, the agreement is thereby avoided: *s.* 7.

TRANSFER OF TITLE

7. Title. Title to goods is the right of ownership with respect to them.

8. Nemo dat quod non habet. Where goods are sold by a person who is not the owner thereof, the buyer acquires no better title to the goods than the seller had: *see s.* 21. This provision is a general statement of law and is often expressed by the maxim *nemo dat quod non habet* ("no one can give what he does not possess").

9. Exceptions to the nemo dat rule. The general rule in *s.* 21 is subject to certain important exceptions:

(*a*) Sale by an agent.
(*b*) Sale by a mercantile agent without authority.
(*c*) Sale in market overt.
(*d*) Sale under a voidable title.
(*e*) Sale by seller in possession to a third person.
(*f*) Sale by buyer in possession to a third person.
(*g*) Sale under a Court order or special power.

(*h*) Disposition under Part III of the *Hire-Purchase Act*, 1964.

These eight exceptions are discussed in the following paragraphs.

10. Sale by an agent. Where goods are sold by a person who is not the owner thereof, and who sells them under the authority or with the consent of the owner, the buyer acquires good title to the goods: *see s.* 21.

NOTE
   (*i*) The essential characteristic of an agent is that he is invested with a legal power to establish legal relations between his principal and third parties. Thus, where an agent sells his principal's goods, the buyer acquires good title.
   (*ii*) The authority under which the goods are sold by an agent may be *actual* or *ostensible*. In either case the principal is bound by the sale, and the buyer gets good title.

11. Sale by a mercantile agent without authority. Where a mercantile agent is, with the consent of the owner, in possession of goods or of the documents of title to goods, any sale or other disposition of the goods made by him when acting in the ordinary course of business of a mercantile agent shall be as valid as if he were expressly authorised by the owner to make the same: *Factors Act*, 1889, *s.* 2.

(*a*) *Document of title.* The expression "document of title" includes any bill of lading, dock warrant, warehouse-keeper's certificate, and warrant or order for the delivery of goods, and any other document used in the ordinary course of business as proof of the possession of control of goods, or authorising or purporting to authorise, either by endorsement or by delivery, the possessor of the document to transfer or receive goods thereby represented: *Factors Act*, 1889, *s.* 1 (4).

(*b*) *Possession.* A person is deemed to be in possession of goods, or of the documents of title to goods, where the goods or documents are in his actual custody, or are held by any person subject to his control or for him or on his behalf: *Factors Act*, 1889, *s.* 1 (2). A mercantile agent cannot pass good title under *s.* 2 of the Factors Act unless he has been in continuous physical possession of the goods *qua* mercantile agent: *Astley Industrial Trust* v. *Miller* (1968).

(c) *Mercantile agent.* The expression "mercantile agent" means a mercantile agent having, in the customary course of his business as such agent, authority either to sell goods, or to consign goods for the purpose of sale, or to buy goods, or to raise money on the security of goods: *Factors Act, 1889, s.* 1 (1). This definition covers factors, brokers, auctioneers and dealers on a commission: but it does not cover clerks and servants of mercantile agents.

(d) *Agent's authority.* A mercantile agent acting without authority can pass a good title under *s.* 2 of the Factors Act, provided the person taking under the disposition acts in good faith, and has not, at the time of the disposition, notice that the mercantile agent has no authority: *see Factors Act,* 1889, *s.* 2.

CASE

Folkes v. *King* (1923), C.A.: The owner of a motor car delivered it to a mercantile agent, having agreed with the agent that the car should not be sold at less than the price stipulated by the owner. The agent immediately sold the car for less than the stipulated price and then misappropriated the proceeds. The purchaser from the agent bought in good faith. The car was subsequently bought by the defendant. The original owner brought this action in detinue. HELD: the agent passed good title to the car by virtue of *s.* 2 of the *Factors Act,* 1889.

12. Sale in market overt. Where goods are sold in market overt, according to the usage of the market, the buyer acquires a good title to the goods, provided he buys them in good faith and without notice of any defect or want of title on the part of the seller: *s.* 22 (1).

(a) *Market overt* obtains in all shops in the City of London, and in all markets where the usage is established.

(b) *A sale in a shop in the City of London* is deemed to be a sale in market overt when:

(i) the sale takes place in business hours on a business day;

(ii) the *entire transaction* takes place in the part of the shop which is open to the public; thus a sale by sample would appear to be excluded: *see Hargreave* v. *Spink* (1892) and *Crane* v. *London Dock Co.* (1864);

(*iii*) the goods are of the class of goods usually sold in that shop;

(*iv*) the shopkeeper is the seller, *i.e.* he must not be the buyer: *Ardath Tobacco Co.* v. *Ocker* (1931).

(*c*) *Outside the City.*   Market overt obtains outside the City of London *only in markets where the usage has been established.*

(*d*) *Good faith.*   The buyer gets good title only if he buys in good faith and without notice of any defect or want of title on the part of the seller.   A thing is deemed to be done "in good faith" when it is in fact done honestly, whether it be done negligently or not: *see s.* 62 (2).

(*e*) *Where goods have been stolen* and the offender is prosecuted to conviction, the property in the goods so stolen does not automatically revest in the person who was the owner of the goods.   But in such cases, the court has a discretionary power under *s.* 28 of the *Theft Act,* 1968, to order restitution.

(*f*) The market overt rule has been criticised as being out-dated and capricious in its application.   For reform proposals, *see* X, **5** and **6**.

13. Sale under a voidable title.   When the seller of goods has a voidable title thereto, but his title has not been avoided at the time of the sale, the buyer acquires a good title to the goods, provided he buys them in good faith and without notice of the seller's defect of title: *s.* 23.

(*a*) *Where there are two contracts.*   Section 23 applies to circumstances where there are two contracts:

(*i*) X sells and delivers goods to Y, and subsequently X discovers that he has a right to avoid the contract, *i.e.* to set it aside.

(*ii*) Y re-sells the goods to Z.   Z's title will depend on whether or not X had avoided the first contract before Y and Z made their contract.   Y can pass good title until X takes steps to avoid the first contract: *Phillips* v. *Brooks* (1919); *Car and Universal Finance Co. Ltd.* v. *Caldwell* (1963).

(*b*) *Voidable contract.*   Title to goods is voidable where the contract under which they were supplied is itself voidable, *e.g.* for misrepresentation.

(*c*) *Avoidance in case of fraud.*   Where a seller has a right to avoid a contract for fraud, there is no need for him to communicate his election to avoid the contract to the fraudulent buyer. It is fully sufficient for him to take all possible steps to recover the goods: *Car and Universal Finance Co. Ltd.* v. *Caldwell* (1963).

(d) *Void contract.* Section 23 has no application where a contract is void, for in this case, no title whatever is passed: *see Ingram* v. *Little* (1961).

CASES

Phillips v. *Brooks* (1919): The plaintiff was a jeweller. One North entered his shop and asked to see some jewellery. He chose a pearl necklace, price £2,550, and a ring, price £450. He then took out his cheque book and wrote out a cheque for £3,000. As he signed the cheque, he said "You see who I am. I am Sir George Bullough," and gave a London address, which the jeweller checked in a directory. The jeweller then asked whether he would like to take the ring. North promptly pledged the ring with the defendant, a pawnbroker, for £350. The cheque was dishonoured and the jeweller claimed to recover the ring from the pawnbroker. HELD: the jeweller intended to contract with the person present in front of him, whoever he was, *i.e.* the mistake as to the identity of the man North did not affect the formation of the contract. North got a voidable title to the ring, and since it was not avoided at the time of pledging it, the pawnbroker got a good title.

(In this case, North's title to the ring was voidable because of the fraudulent misrepresentation, but at the time of the pledge his title was still good, since by then the jeweller had done nothing to avoid his title.)

Ingram v. *Little* (1960), C.A.: Three ladies, the joint owners of a car, advertised it for sale. A swindler called at their home and agreed to buy the car for £717. He offered a cheque in payment, but it was refused. The swindler then attempted to convince the ladies that he was a Mr. Hutchinson of Stanstead Road, Caterham. One of the ladies checked the name and address in the telephone directory. The ladies decided to accept the cheque in payment. The cheque was dishonoured and the swindler disappeared (he was not Mr. Hutchinson). The swindler had sold the car to L, who bought it in good faith. The ladies sought to recover possession of the car from L. HELD: the offer to sell, with payment to be made by cheque, was made to Hutchinson only. As the swindler knew this, the offer was not one he could accept. Therefore, there was no contract for the sale of the car, and the plaintiffs were entitled to its return.

14. Seller in possession after sale. Where a person having sold goods continues or is in possession of the goods, or of the documents of title to the goods, the delivery of transfer by that person, or by a mercantile agent acting for him, of the goods or documents of title under any sale, pledge or other disposition thereof, to any person receiving the same in good faith and without notice of the previous sale, shall have the same effect as if the person making the delivery or transfer were expressly authorised by the owner of the goods to make the same: *s.* 25 (1).

(*a*) *Resale by a possessor with no property in the goods.* According to this sub-section, if X sells goods to Y, so that Y has the property in the goods, but the actual possession is retained by X, and X sells and delivers the same goods to Z, who takes them in good faith and without notice of the previous sale to Y, Z *gets good title*. Y will be left with an action for damages against X, for he cannot recover the goods from Z.

(*b*) *Document of title.* The expression "document of title" includes any bill of lading, dock warrant, warehouse-keeper's certificate, and warrant or order for the delivery of goods, and any other document used in the ordinary course of business as proof of the possession or control of goods, or authorising or purporting to authorise, either by endorsement or by delivery, the possessor of the document to transfer or receive goods thereby represented: *Factors Act,* 1889, *s.* 1.

"Documents of title to goods" has the same meaning in the Act as it has in the Factors Acts: *see s.* 62 (1).

(*c*) *Mercantile agent.* In *s.* 25, the term "mercantile agent" has the same meaning as in the Factors Acts: the expression "mercantile agent" means a mercantile agent having, in the customary course of his business as such agent, authority either to sell goods, or to consign goods for the purpose of sale, or to buy goods, or to raise money on the security of goods: *Factors Act,* 1889, *s.* 1. This definition covers factors, brokers, auctioneers and dealers on a commission; but it does not cover clerks and servants of mercantile agents.

15. Buyer in possession after sale. Where a person having bought or agreed to buy goods obtains, with the consent of the seller, possession of the goods or the documents of title to the goods, the delivery or transfer by that person, or by a mercantile agent acting for him, of the goods or documents of title, under any sale, pledge, or other disposition thereof, to any person receiving the same in good faith and without notice of any lien or other right of the original seller in respect of the goods, shall have the same effect as if the person making the delivery or transfer were a mercantile agent in possession of the goods or documents of title with the consent of the owner: *s.* 25 (2).

NOTE

   (*i*) According to this subsection, if X buys or agrees to buy goods from Y, and obtains possession of the goods or documents of title while Y retains the property in the goods and, subsequently, X sells the goods to Z, who buys in good faith and without notice of Y's rights, then Z gets good title to the goods. Y cannot recover the goods from Z, but is left with his remedy in damages against X. Also, Y cannot exercise the unpaid seller's rights against the goods: *Cahn & Meyer* v. *Pockett's Bristol Channel Steam Packet Co. Ltd.* (1899).

  (*ii*) For the purposes of *s.* 25 (2) of the *Sale of Goods Act,* 1893 (and of *s.* 9 of the *Factors Act,* 1889) the buyer under a conditional sale agreement, as defined in the *Hire-Purchase Act,* 1965, shall not be deemed to be a person who has bought or agreed to buy goods: *Hire-Purchase Act,* 1965. This provision seriously reduces the importance of *s.* 25 (2). *See* XII.

 (*iii*) The definitions set out above in **14** (*b*) and **14** (*c*) apply to *s.* 25 (2).

CASES

Cahn & Meyer v. *Pockett's Bristol Channel Steam Packet Co. Ltd.* (1899): S entered into a contract to sell to P, a German merchant, ten tons of copper c.i.f. Rotterdam. According to the agreement, P undertook to make payment by accepting a bill of exchange drawn on him. In due course, P received the bill of lading for the consignment of copper together with a bill of exchange drawn on him. By this time P was insolvent. P then forwarded the bill of lading to the plaintiff who, in good faith, had agreed to buy the copper from P. In the meantime, S learnt of P's insolvency and immediately gave notice to the carrier of his claim to stop the goods in transit (*s.* 46 (1)). The plaintiff then claimed delivery of the goods from the carrier, the defendants. HELD: the plaintiff obtained possession of the bill of lading as a *bona fide* sub-buyer and, therefore, got good title to the copper. S had no right of stoppage in transit.

Marten v. *Whale* (1917), c.a.: There was a written agreement between T and M by which M agreed to buy a plot of land, subject to his solicitor's approval of title and restrictions. The agreement further provided that in consideration of the above transaction, M agreed to sell and T agreed to purchase a motor car for £300, "completion of such sale and purchase to be carried out simultaneously with above transaction." M then allowed T to have possession of the car "on loan," none of the purchase money being paid. W then bought the car from T in good faith and without notice of M's rights. M's solicitors refused to approve the restrictions in connection with the land transaction. M sued W for possession of the car. HELD: that the agreement to buy the motor car was a conditional agreement and, by *s*. 1, within the Sale of Goods Act. Consequently *s*. 25 (2) applied and T, having "agreed to buy" the car, and W, having purchased and obtained possession of the car from him in good faith and without any notice of any right of the plaintiff thereto, had a good defence to M's action.

16. Sale under a court order or special power. Where a contract of sale of goods is made under any special common law or statutory power of sale, or under the order of a court of competent jurisdiction, the buyer acquires a good title to the goods: *see s*. 21 (2) (b).

(*a*) *Common law power of sale.* An example of a common law power of sale is the power of a pledgee to sell when the loan is not repaid according to the agreement (where the pledgee is a pawnbroker, however, the right of sale is governed by the *Pawnbrokers Acts*, 1872 and 1938).

(*b*) *Statutory power of sale.* An example of a statutory power of sale is the power of a trustee in bankruptcy to sell the goods of the debtor under the *Bankruptcy Act*, 1914.

(*c*) *Court order.* Where a sheriff or other officer of the court is charged with the enforcement of a writ of execution, the writ binds the property in the goods of the execution debtor when the writ is delivered to the sheriff: *see s*. 26. When the sheriff sells such goods, the buyer gets a good title: *see Goodlock* v. *Cousins* (1897).

17. Dispositions under Part III of the Hire-Purchase Act, 1964. Part III of the *Hire-Purchase Act*, 1964, was not affected by the Act of 1965. By *s*. 27 of the 1964 Act, if the owner of a motor vehicle lets it to a hirer on a hire-purchase agreement and the hirer then sells it to a purchaser who takes it in good faith and without notice of the hire-purchase agreement, the purchaser gets good title. This provision has no application to trade and finance purchasers. Notice that the hirer's liability, criminal or civil, is not affected by *s.* 27 of the 1964 Act.

PROGRESS TEST 4

1. What is the difference between ascertained goods and unascertained goods? What is the significance of the distinction? (**2**)

2. Where there is a contract for the sale of specific or ascertained goods, the property in them is transferred to the buyer at such time as the parties to the contract intend it to be transferred. How is the intention of the parties ascertained? (**3**)

3. The Act contains five rules for the ascertainment of intention of the parties as to the time at which property in the goods is to pass to the buyer. When should these rules be applied? State the gist of each rule. Illustrate your answer with decided cases. (**4**)

4. Rules 1–4 apply only to contracts for the sale of specific goods. What are specific goods? (**4**)

5. What is the effect where the seller reserves a right of disposal? (**5**)

6. Where the seller draws a bill of exchange on the buyer for the price of the goods, and transmits the bill together with a bill of lading, what is the effect where the buyer fails to accept the bill of exchange? (**5**)

7. What is the general rule as to the passing of risk? (**6**)

8. What is the position (*a*) where specific goods have perished at the time the contract was made, and (*b*) where specific goods perish before the risk passes to the buyer? (**6**)

9. What do you understand by the expression "title to goods"? (**7**)

10. Where goods are sold by a person who is not the owner thereof, the buyer acquires no better title to the goods than the seller had. What exceptions are there to this general rule? (**9**)

11. In what circumstances will a buyer get good title to goods where they are bought from a person who had not been given authority to sell by the owner? (**10, 11**)

12. Define "document of title" and "mercantile agent." (**11**)

13. What is market overt? What is the effect of a sale in market overt? (**12**)

14. In what circumstances is there a sale under a voidable title? (**13**)

15. Where, following a sale of goods, the property in the goods has passed to the buyer, but the seller retains possession, what is the effect of a sale by the seller to another buyer? **(14)**

16. Where a buyer has possession but not ownership of the goods, what is the effect of a sale to a third party? Mention the effect of the *Hire-Purchase Act*, 1965. **(15)**

17. A delivers a set of chairs to B "on sale or return." B immediately lends the chairs to C for use in C's house. A hears of this and claims the chairs from C. Will he succeed?

18. There is a contract between D and E under which D agrees to sell a gold watch to E, the price to be paid in five instalments. According to the agreement, property in the watch is not to pass to E until the last of the instalments is paid. If E attempts to sell the watch to F, a prospective purchaser in good faith, before the last instalment is paid, will F get good title?

CHAPTER V

RIGHTS OF THE UNPAID SELLER AGAINST THE GOODS

1. Unpaid seller's rights. Notwithstanding that the property in the goods may have passed to the buyer, the unpaid seller of goods, as such, has by *implication of law* the following rights:

(*a*) A lien on the goods for the price while he is in possession of them.

(*b*) In case of the insolvency of the buyer, a right of stopping the goods in transit after he has parted with possession of them.

(*c*) A right of re-sale: *see s.* 39 (1).

NOTE

(*i*) The seller of goods is deemed to be an *unpaid seller* within the meaning of the Act:

(1) when the whole of the price has not been paid or tendered;

(2) when a bill of exchange or other negotiable instrument has been received as conditional payment and the instrument has been dishonoured: *see s.* 39 (1).

(*ii*) The unpaid seller has these rights even though the property in the goods has passed to the buyer.

(*iii*) In the Part of the Act which deals with the rights of the unpaid seller, the term "seller" includes any person who is in the position of a seller, as, for instance, an agent of the seller to whom the bill of lading has been indorsed, or a consignor or agent who has himself paid, or is directly responsible for, the price: *see s.* 38 (2).

(*iv*) The unpaid seller's rights of lien, stoppage in transit and re-sale are rights *against the goods*: they must be distinguished from the seller's *personal* rights against the buyer for breach of contract.

(*v*) The unpaid seller's rights of lien, stoppage in transit and re-sale arise by implication of law: *see s.* 39 (1). Thus, these rights may be negatived or varied by an express or implied contractual term binding the parties: *see s.* 55.

C

2. Withholding delivery. Where the property in goods has *not* passed to the buyer, the unpaid seller has, in addition to his other remedies, a right of withholding delivery similar to and co-extensive with his rights of lien and stoppage in transit where the property has passed to the buyer: 39 (2).

UNPAID SELLER'S LIEN

3. Seller's lien. Subject to the provisions of the Act, the unpaid seller of goods who is in possession of them is entitled to retain possession of them until payment or tender of the price in the following cases, namely:

(*a*) where the goods have been sold without any stipulation as to credit;

(*b*) where the goods have been sold on credit, but the term of credit has expired;

(*c*) where the buyer becomes insolvent: *see s.* 41 (1).

NOTE

(*i*) The seller may exercise his right of lien notwithstanding that he is in possession of the goods as agent or bailee for the buyer: *s.* 41 (2).

(*ii*) The unpaid seller's right of lien is subject to the provisions of the Act: *see s.* 41 (1). It follows that the unpaid seller's right of lien will be defeated by the right of a person to whom the buyer transferred documents of title relating to the goods, provided they were received in good faith and for value: *see ss.* 47 and 25 (2). *See* also *Ant. Jurgens Margarinefabrieken* v. *Dreyfus* (1914).

(*iii*) Where an unpaid seller has made part delivery of the goods, he may exercise his right of lien on the remainder, unless such part delivery has been made under such circumstances as to show an agreement to waive the lien: *s.* 42.

(*iv*) The lien may be exercised for the price of the goods only: it may not be exercised for any other charges, *e.g.* for storage.

(*v*) Subject to the seller's right of re-sale, a contract of sale is not rescinded by the mere exercise by an unpaid seller of his right of lien: *see s.* 48 (1).

(*vi*) Where an unpaid seller who has exercised his right of lien re-sells the goods, the buyer acquires a good title thereto as against the original buyer: *see s.* 48 (2).

4. Termination of lien. The unpaid seller of goods loses his lien thereon:

(*a*) when he delivers the goods to a carrier or other bailee for the purpose of transmission to the buyer without reserving the right of disposal of the goods;

(*b*) when the buyer or his agent lawfully obtains possession of the goods;

(*c*) by waiver thereof: *see s.* 43 (1).

NOTE

(*i*) The unpaid seller of goods, having a lien thereon, does not lose his lien by reason only that he has obtained judgment for the price of the goods: *s.* 43 (2).

(*ii*) The seller ceases to have a right of lien when the price is paid or tendered: *see s.* 41 (1).

(*iii*) Where the seller has delivered the goods to a carrier for transmission to the buyer, he loses his right of lien, unless he has reserved the right of disposal. But if the buyer becomes insolvent, a right of stoppage in transit arises in favour of the seller. If the right of stoppage in transit is exercised, the seller may retain the goods until payment or tender of the price, *i.e.* the right of lien is revived: *see s.* 44.

STOPPAGE IN TRANSIT

5. The right of stoppage. Subject to the provisions of the Act, when the buyer of goods becomes insolvent, the unpaid seller who has parted with the possession of the goods has the right of stopping them in transit, that is to say, he may resume possession of the goods so long as they are in course of transit, and may retain them until payment or tender of the price: *see s.* 44.

(*a*) *Meaning of "insolvent."* The buyer becomes insolvent when he is no longer able to pay his debts as they fall due. Notice that "insolvent" does not mean the same thing as "bankrupt."

(*b*) *Effect on contract.* Subject to the seller's right of resale, a contract of sale is not rescinded by the mere exercise of the right of stoppage in transit: *see s.* 48 (1).

(*c*) *Re-sale after stoppage in transit.* Where an unpaid seller who has exercised his right of stoppage in transit re-sells the goods, the buyer acquires a good title thereto as against the original buyer: *see s.* 48 (2).

(*d*) *Transfer of documents of title by buyer.* The right of stoppage in transit is subject to the provisions of the Act:

see s. 41 (1). It follows that the right of stoppage will be defeated by the prior right of a person to whom the buyer transferred documents of title relating to the goods, provided they were received in good faith and for value: *see ss.* 47 and 25 (2). *See* also *Cahn* v. *Pockett's Bristol Channel Steam Packet Co.* (1899).

6. Duration of transit. Goods are deemed to be in course of transit from the time when they are delivered to a carrier, by land or water, or other bailee, for the purpose of transmission to the buyer, until the buyer, or his agent in that behalf takes delivery of them from such carrier or other bailee: *s.* 45'

(*a*) *No stoppage after transit.* There is no right of stoppage after transit is at an end.

(*b*) *Transit ended by delivery.* If the buyer or his agent in that behalf obtains delivery of the goods before their arrival at the appointed destination, the transit is at an end: *s.* 45 (2). *See Reddall* v. *Union Castle Mail Steamship Co.* (1914).

(*c*) *Transit ended before destination.* If, after the arrival of the goods at the appointed destination, the carrier or other bailee acknowledges to the buyer or his agent that he holds the goods on his behalf, and continues in possession of them as bailee for the buyer, or his agent, the transit is at an end, and it is immaterial that a further destination for the goods may have been indicated by the buyer: *s.* 45 (3).

(*d*) *Buyer's rejection of goods.* If the goods are rejected by the buyer, and the carrier or other bailee continues in possession of them, the transit is not deemed to be at an end, even if the seller has refused to receive them back: *s.* 45 (4).

(*e*) *Delivery to a ship.* When goods are delivered to a ship chartered by the buyer it is a question depending on the circumstances of the particular case whether they are in the possession of the master as a carrier, or as agent to the buyer: *s.* 45 (5). If the ship's master is the servant of the buyer, transit is at an end when the goods are delivered to him; otherwise, the goods are in transit while in the custody of the master: *see Berndtson* v. *Strang* (1867); *Kemp* v. *Falk* (1882); *Bethell* v. *Clark* (1888).

(*f*) *Refusal of carrier to deliver.*   Where the carrier or other bailee wrongfully refuses to deliver the goods to the buyer, or his agent in that behalf, the transit is deemed to be at an end: *s.* 45 (6).

(*g*) *Transit may be ended by part delivery.*   Where part delivery of the goods has been made to the buyer, or his agent in that behalf, the remainder of the goods may be stopped in transit, unless such part delivery has been made under such circumstances as to show an agreement to give up possession of the whole of the goods: *s.* 45 (7): *see Kemp* v. *Falk* (1882).

7. How stoppage in transit is effected.   The unpaid seller may exercise his right of stoppage in transit either:

(*a*) by taking actual possession of the goods; or

(*b*) by giving notice of his claim to the carrier or other bailee in whose possession the goods are: *see s.* 46 (1).

NOTE

(*i*) *Notice.*   Notice may be given either to the person in actual possession of the goods, or to his principal: *see s.* 46 (1).

(*ii*) *Suitable time.*   Where notice is given to the principal, the notice, to be effectual, must be given at such time and under such circumstances that the principal, by the exercise of reasonable diligence, may communicate it to his servant or agent in time to prevent a delivery to the buyer: *see s.* 46 (1).

(*iii*) *Re-delivery.*   When notice of stoppage in transit is given by the seller to the carrier, or other bailee in possession of the goods, he must re-deliver the goods to, or according to the directions of, the seller. The expenses of such re-delivery must be borne by the seller: *s.* 46 (2).   Where an unpaid seller requires the carrier to re-deliver to himself, the seller has a duty to take delivery, even though this may mean discharging the carrier's lien for charges, *e.g.*, shipowner's lien for freight: *see Booth Steamship Co. Ltd.* v. *Cargo Fleet Iron Co. Ltd.* (1916).

(*iv*) *Legal position of carrier.*   Consider the legal position of the carrier or other bailee to whom notice of stoppage in transit has been given:

(1) If he refuses to comply with a lawful notice he will be liable to the seller under *s.* 57 of the Act and also in tort.

(2) If he restores the goods to the seller by virtue of an

invalid notice of stoppage, he will be liable in tort to the buyer: *see Taylor* v. *Great Eastern Railway* (1901).

In cases of doubt, the carrier or other bailee should resolve the dilemma by resorting to an interpleader.

UNPAID SELLER'S RIGHT OF RE-SALE

8. Right of re-sale. An unpaid seller's right of re-sale may arise:

    (*a*) from an express contractual reservation; or
    (*b*) from the provisions of the Act, *s*. 48 (3); or
    (*c*) from the common law.

9. Right of re-sale by express reservation. Where the seller expressly reserves a right of re-sale in case the buyer should make default, on the buyer making default the seller may re-sell the goods: *s*. 48 (4).

    (*a*) *Rescission.* Where the seller re-sells by virtue of an express contractual reservation, the original contract is rescinded: *s*. 48 (4).
    (*b*) *Damages.* The rescission of the contract of sale in this manner does not deprive the seller of any claim for damages he may have against the original buyer: *s*. 48 (4).

10. Statutory right of re-sale. An unpaid seller may re-sell the goods in the following circumstances:

    (*a*) Where the goods are of a perishable nature; or
    (*b*) Where the unpaid seller gives notice to the buyer of his intention to re-sell, and the buyer does not, within a reasonable time, pay or tender the price: *s*. 48 (3).

    (*i*) The unpaid seller may recover damages from the original buyer for any loss occasioned by the breach of contract: *s*. 48 (3).
    (*ii*) What is a reasonable time within which the buyer must pay or tender the price is a question of fact, depending on all the circumstances of the case: *see s*. 56.
    (*iii*) Where an unpaid seller exercised his right of re-sale under *s*. 48 (3), the contract of sale is rescinded. Accordingly, the seller is entitled to retain the proceeds of the re-sale. Where the proceeds (after deduction of expenses) represent a lesser sum than the contract price, the seller may sue for the

difference as damages for non-acceptance. The buyer is discharged from his liability to pay the contract price. Consequently, after a statutory re-sale of part or all of the goods, the proper action, if any, is the seller's action for damages: *Ward* v. *Bignall* (1967).

CASE

Ward v. *Bignall* (1967), C.A.: On May 6th, B, the buyer, contracted to buy from W a Vanguard motor car and a Zodiac motor car. The contract price was £850 and B paid £25 deposit. On the same day, B repudiated the contract and W's solicitors warned him that W would try to re-sell the cars if B failed to pay the balance by May 11th. B did not pay the balance and W re-sold the Vanguard for £350 on May 24th. Being unable to sell the Zodiac, W brought this action against B for total damages of £497 10*s*., this total being made up of £475 (unpaid balance of purchase price) and £22 10*s*. (advertising expenses). HELD: the re-sale of the Vanguard amounted to an election to treat the contract as rescinded, because the unpaid seller had thereby put it out of his power to perform his primary obligation under the contract. The property in the Zodiac thereupon reverted to him, and his only remedy against the buyer was for damages for non-acceptance of the two motor cars. The *prima facie* measure is the difference between the contract price and the market value on May 24th. The total contract price was £850, against which W had received £25 deposit, £350 for the Vanguard re-sale, and the market value of the Zodiac was £450. To the computed loss of £25 must be added £22 10*s*. advertising expenses. Total damages, £47 10*s*.

11. Right of re-sale at common law. An unpaid seller may have a right of re-sale at common law where the buyer has expressly or impliedly repudiated the contract of sale.

(*a*) *Breach as repudiation.* Where the seller lawfully chooses to treat the buyer's breach of contract as a repudiation, he is absolved from further liability. *It is the discharge from further obligation to the original buyer which gives the seller a right of re-sale at common law.*

(*b*) *Buyer's repudiation.* Where the buyer has repudiated the contract, the seller may keep any deposit paid by the buyer by way of earnest of his intention to complete the sale: *see Mayson* v. *Clouet* (1924). Also, the seller may claim for damages.

(*c*) *Seller as agent of necessity.* It is possible, but very much doubted, that an unpaid seller could claim to re-sell as agent of necessity of the original buyer, *e.g.* if delivery were prevented by some emergency. The point is not finally settled, but *see Kemp* v. *Prior* (1812); *Prager* v. *Blatspiel* (1924); *Jebara* v. *Ottoman Bank* (1927); *Sachs* v. *Miklos* (1948).

PROGRESS TEST 5

1. State the three rights which an unpaid seller may have against the goods by implication of law. **(1)**

2. Define an "unpaid seller." **(1)**

3. Are the rights of the unpaid seller against the goods affected by the question as to whether property in them has passed to the buyer? **(1)**

4. May the agent of an unpaid seller exercise these rights against the goods? **(1)**

5. Is it possible for the rights against the goods to be negatived or varied by express or implied agreement to that effect? **(1)**

6. Distinguish between unpaid seller's right of withholding delivery and the rights of lien and stoppage in transit. **(2)**

7. What is the unpaid seller's lien, and in what circumstances does it arise? **(3)**

8. The unpaid seller's right of lien is subject to the provisions of the Act. Give an example of a provision to which the right of lien is subject. **(3)**

9. In what ways may an unpaid seller's lien come to an end? **(4)**

10. What is the right of stoppage in transit, and in what circumstances does it arise? **(5)**

11. Does the exercise of the right of stoppage in transit necessarily rescind the contract of sale? **(5)**

12. The right of stoppage in transit is subject to the provisions of the Act. Give an example of a provision to which the right of stoppage is subject. **(5)**

13. When are goods deemed to be in the course of transit? **(6)**

14. What is the legal position where the carrier wrongfully refuses to deliver the goods to the buyer? **(6)**

15. Where part delivery of the goods has been made to the buyer, may the seller exercise a right of stoppage in transit over the remainder? **(6)**

16. In what ways may stoppage in transit be effected? **(7)**

17. Explain the legal position of the carrier to whom notice of stoppage in transit has been given. **(7)**

18. In what ways may an unpaid seller's right of re-sale arise? **(8)**

19. Explain fully the circumstances in which a statutory right of re-sale may arise.   **(10)**

20. Does the exercise of the statutory right of re-sale necessarily rescind the contract?   **(10)**

21. Explain how a seller's right of re-sale may arise at common law.   **(11)**

22. A, who has agreed to buy a consignment of timber from B, sends his lorry driver to collect it. The lorry is loaded with the full consignment in B's yard. As the lorry is passing out of B's yard, B is informed that A is insolvent. Is B entitled to stop A's lorry and recover the timber?

23. C, a carrier, has received a notice of stoppage in transit from D, whose goods have been consigned to E. E telephones C and tells him that the notice of stoppage is not valid. Advise C.

24. State the facts and explain the decision in *Ward* v. *Bignall* (1967).

CHAPTER VI

SELLER'S PERSONAL REMEDIES FOR BUYER'S BREACH

1. Seller's remedies. The remedies available to the seller in the event of breach of contract by the buyer are:

(*a*) an action for the price of the goods: *s.* 49; or

(*b*) an action for damages for non-acceptance: *s.* 50;

according to the nature of the breach.

ACTION FOR THE PRICE

2. The right of action. The seller's right of action arises in the following circumstances:

(*a*) Where, under a contract of sale, *the property in the goods has passed to the buyer* and the buyer wrongfully neglects or refuses to pay for the goods according to the terms of the contract, the seller may maintain an action against him for the price of the goods: *s.* 49 (1).

(*b*) Where, under a contract of sale, the price is payable on a day certain irrespective of delivery, and the buyer wrongfully neglects or refuses to pay such price, the seller may maintain an action for the price, *although the property in the goods has not passed and the goods have not been appropriated to the contract*: *s.* 49 (2).

NOTE

(*i*) *Non-payment must be wrongful.* The seller's right of action arises only where the buyer's neglect or refusal to pay is *wrongful, i.e.* in breach of an express or implied term of the contract; *e.g.* where there is a credit sale under which property has passed to the buyer, the seller may not bring an action for the price until the credit period has expired.

(*ii*) *Time of payment not of the essence.* Unless a different intention appears from the terms of the contract, stipulations as to *time of payment* are not deemed to be of the essence of a contract of sale: *s.* 10 (1). Where time of

58

payment is not of the essence of the contract, the seller cannot treat the contract as repudiated by non-payment, he is left with his action for the price, or such rights against the goods as the circumstances admit.

(*iii*) *Delivery and payment concurrent conditions.* Unless otherwise agreed, delivery of the goods and payment of the price are concurrent conditions: *s.* 28. Thus, the seller's right of action for the price arises if the buyer does not pay when the goods are delivered, unless there is an express or implied contractual term to the effect that payment is to be made at some other time: *Clemens Horst & Co.* v. *Biddell* (1912).

(*iv*) *Bill as conditional payment.* Where the buyer makes payment by bill of exchange, the bill or cheque is usually taken as a conditional payment. The seller's right of action for the price is thereby suspended. If the bill is dishonoured in the hands of the seller, the right of action for the price revives, and there is an alternative action on the bill itself. If, however, the seller has negotiated the bill before it was dishonoured, he has no action for the price of the goods unless he has been made liable on the bill: but *see Davis* v. *Reilly* (1898).

3. Ascertainment of price. The price in a contract of sale may be:

(*a*) fixed by the contract: *s.* 8 (1); or

(*b*) left to be fixed in a manner agreed between the parties: *s.* 8 (1); *e.g.* an agreement to sell at a valuation: *s.* 9; or

(*c*) determined by the course of dealing between the parties: *s.* 8 (1), *i.e.* by an implied term to give effect to the presumed intentions of the parties; or

(*d*) a reasonable price, which is payable:

(*i*) when price is not determined in accordance with *s.* 8 (1): *see s.* 8 (2); or

(*ii*) where there is an agreement to sell at a valuation, and no valuation is made, and the goods have been delivered to, and appropriated by, the buyer: *s.* 9 (1).

NOTE

(*i*) *Liquidated demand.* Where the price is determined in accordance with section 8 (1), the seller's action should take the form of a *liquidated demand*.

(*ii*) *Damages.* Before the abolition of the forms of action, the seller's action for the agreed price of goods was always an action of debt. The liquidated sum claimed was properly called damages: *see Hixt* v. *Goats* (1615).

(*iii*) *Liquidated damages*. Although the action is now always called an action for the price, it is an *action for damages for breach of contract by non-payment*. But where the action is a liquidated demand for a fixed price, it would not be correct to regard it as an action for liquidated damages in view of the narrow definition of liquidated damages in *Dunlop Pneumatic Tyre Co.* v. *New Garage & Motor Co. Ltd.* (1915). Lord Dunedin's classic words, ". . . the essence of liquidated damages is a genuine covenanted pre-estimate of damage," were quoted with approval by Lord Morton in *Bridge* v. *Campbell Discount Co. Ltd.* (1962). It seems, oddly enough, that a claim for damages on a liquidated demand for the price of goods cannot be regarded as liquidated damages, for it lacks the essence referred to by Lord Dunedin in *Dunlop* v. *New Garage* (1915).

(*iv*) *Unliquidated demand*. Where the action is for a *reasonable price*, according to the circumstances of the case, the action will take the form of an unliquidated demand in the nature of the common law claim on a *quantum valebant*.

(*v*) *Loss beyond the unpaid price*. Where the buyer's breach has caused the seller to suffer *loss over and above the amount of price unpaid, e.g.* interest on the price, the seller may claim for this in addition to the price: for nothing in the Act affects the right of the seller to recover interest or special damages in any case where, by law, interest or special damages may be recoverable: *s.* 54.

ACTION FOR DAMAGES FOR NON-ACCEPTANCE

4. The right of action. Where the buyer wrongfully neglects or refuses to accept and pay for the goods, the seller may maintain an action against him for damages for non-acceptance: *s.* 50 (1).

5. The measure of damages. The measure of damages for non-acceptance is as follows:

(*a*) *Estimated natural loss*. The estimated loss directly and naturally resulting, in the ordinary course of events, from the buyer's breach of contract: *s.* 50 (2).

(*b*) *Further loss*. Any further loss due to special circumstances outside the ordinary course of events, but of which the buyer had knowledge, actual or imputed: *see s.* 54 and *Victoria Laundry* v. *Newman* (1949).

NOTE

(*i*) Section 50 (2) is a re-statement of the first part of the rule in *Hadley* v. *Baxendale* (1854).

(*ii*) The seller should take reasonable steps to mitigate the loss resulting from the buyer's non-acceptance. Generally, this means that he should sell the goods to a third person for the best price reasonably obtainable. The seller's duty to mitigate the loss is a duty to act reasonably. There is no duty to nurse the interests of the contract-breaker: *Harlow & Jones Ltd.* v. *Panex (International) Ltd.* (1967).

(*iii*) Where there is an available market for the goods in question, the measure of damages is *prima facie* to be ascertained by the difference between the contract price and the market or current price at the time or times when the goods ought to have been accepted or, if no time was fixed for acceptance, then at the time of refusal to accept: *s.* 50 (3); *i.e.* the seller should sell the goods for what he can get on the market and claim for damages to recover the difference between the market price and the contract price. But *see Campbell Mostyn (Provisions)* v. *Barnett* (1954).

(*iv*) *Available market* is a commercial expression and does not seem to have a precise legal meaning. In any case, the important question is, Could the seller reasonably have re-sold the goods immediately after the breach by non-acceptance? And if so, what price could he reasonably have got? Notice that whether the seller, in fact, re-sold the goods is not strictly relevant to the application of the *prima facie* rule in *s.* 50 (3).

(*v*) The rule in *s.* 50 (3) is a convenient rule which in most cases produces a just result. But it should be clearly seen as being auxiliary to the general rule in *s.* 50 (1). Moreover it is a *prima facie* rule, which the court can always disregard if it tends to produce a result which is not just in any particular case: *see Thompson Ltd.* v. *Robinson Ltd.* (1955); *cf. Charter* v. *Sullivan* (1957).

(*vi*) The rule in *Hadley* v. *Baxendale*, refined in the light of later authorities, was re-stated in *Victoria Laundry Ltd.* v. *Newman Industries Ltd.* (1949). In that case there was a single judgment which contained a summary of the law relating to causation and remoteness of loss. The summary took the form of six propositions:

(1) The governing purpose of damages is to put the party

whose rights have been violated in the same position, so far as money can do so, as if his rights had been observed.

(2) The aggrieved party is entitled to recover only such part of the loss actually resulting as was at the time of the contract reasonably foreseeable as liable to result from the breach.

(3) What is reasonably foreseeable depends on the knowledge possessed by the parties.

(4) Knowledge "possessed" is of two kinds:

   (a) *Imputed* knowledge.—Everyone is taken to know the ordinary course of things and what loss is liable to result from a breach of that ordinary course.

   (b) *Actual* knowledge.—An actual knowledge of special circumstances may make an additional loss recoverable.

(5) It is not necessary that the contract-breaker should actually have asked himself what loss is liable to result from the breach.

(6) To make the particular loss recoverable, it need not be proved that on a given state of knowledge the defendant could, as a reasonable man, foresee that a breach must necessarily result in that loss. It is enough if he could foresee that the particular loss was likely to result.

Propositions (2) and (3) must now be regarded as somewhat amended by the House of Lords decision in the *Heron II* by substituting the concept of reasonable contemplation for reasonable foreseeability.

CASES

Campbell Mostyn v. *Barnett* (1954), c.a.: The buyer agreed to buy from the seller 500 tons of tinned ham. The seller attempted to deliver 350 tons and the buyer refused to accept. The seller then sold the 350 tons at a price higher than that which the original buyer had agreed to pay. But at the date of the buyer's refusal to accept delivery, the market price was below the contract price. The seller brought this action for damages against the buyer. HELD: the measure of damages should be the difference between the contract price and the *market price at the time of refusal to accept*. The subsequent rising of the market price was immaterial.

Thompson Ltd. v. *Robinson Ltd.* (1955): There was a written agreement for the purchase of a new Standard "Vanguard" motor car. On the day following the agreement, the buyers told the sellers that they were not prepared to accept delivery of the car after all. At the time of the agreement, the local demand for cars of this type was not great enough to absorb all Standard "Vanguard" cars available there for sale. HELD: the sellers were entitled to damages to compensate them for the loss of their bargain, *i.e.* the measure of damages was the profit the sellers would have made on the sale.

Charter v. *Sullivan* (1957): After agreeing to buy a Hillman "Minx" motor car, the buyer wrote to the seller telling him that he no longer intended to complete the purchase. About a week later, the seller sold the car to another buyer. At the time of the agreement, the local demand was such that the seller was able to sell all Hillman "Minx" cars he could get. HELD: the seller was entitled to nominal damages only. The seller in this case had not lost any profit.

PROGRESS TEST 6

1. What are the main remedies available to the seller in the event of a breach of contract by the buyer? **(1)**

2. In what circumstances does the seller have a right of action against the buyer for the price of the goods? **(2)**

3. "Unless otherwise agreed, delivery of the goods and payment of the price are concurrent conditions." Explain. **(2)**

4. What ways may the price in a contract of sale of goods be ascertained? **(3)**

5. May the seller claim special damages over and above the price of the goods? **(3)**

6. When has the seller an action for damages for non-acceptance? **(4)**

7. What is the measure of damages for non-acceptance? Illustrate your answer with decided cases. **(5)**

8. A agreed to buy from B, a motor dealer, an Italian sports car of a specified make and style. B made all the necessary arrangements to obtain the required model and notified A when it was ready for delivery. In reply, A wrote to B, saying that he no longer wanted the car. Advise B.

9. A contracts to sell B a consignment of Tunisian dates for an agreed price. A attempts to effect delivery according to the contract but B refuses to accept the dates. At the time of B's refusal to take delivery, the market price of dates had fallen considerably and A decided to store the consignment of dates in his warehouse in the hope that the market price would later rise. Three months later, the market price of dates having fallen still further, A asks you to advise him as to his remedies, if any. Advise him.

CHAPTER VII

BUYER'S PERSONAL REMEDIES FOR SELLER'S BREACH

1. Buyer's remedies. The remedies which may be available to the buyer in the event of breach of contract by the seller are:

(*a*) an action for damages for non-delivery; or

(*b*) to reject the goods and treat the contract as repudiated; or   *if breach of condition*

(*c*) an action for damages for breach of warranty; or

(*d*) to set up breach of warranty as a defence to an action for the price; or

(*e*) an action for money paid on a consideration which has wholly failed; or

(*f*) specific performance; *& for specific or ascertained goods*

according to the circumstances. *Discretionary.*

DAMAGES FOR NON-DELIVERY

2. The right of action. Where the seller wrongfully neglects or refuses to deliver the goods to the buyer, the buyer may maintain an action against the seller for damages for non-delivery: *s.* 51 (1). The duty of the seller to deliver the goods is considered in II.

3. The measure of damages. The measure of damages for non-delivery is as follows:

(*a*) *Estimated natural loss.* The estimated loss directly and naturally resulting, in the ordinary course of events, from the seller's breach of contract: *s.* 51 (2); and

(*b*) *Further loss.* Any further loss due to special circumstances outside the ordinary course of events, of which the seller had knowledge, actual or imputed: *see s.* 54 and the six propositions in *Victoria Laundry* v. *Newman* (1949): VI, **5**.

NOTE

(*i*) Section 51 (2) is a re-statement of the first part of the rule in *Hadley* v. *Baxendale* (1854).

(*ii*) The buyer should take reasonable steps to mitigate the loss resulting from the seller's non-delivery. Generally, this means that he should buy similar goods from a third person for a reasonable price.

(*iii*) Where there is an available market for the goods in question, the measure of damages is *prima facie* to be ascertained by the difference between the contract price and the market or current price of the goods at the time or times when they ought to have been delivered or, if no time was fixed, then at the time of the refusal to deliver: *s.* 51 (3); *i.e.* the buyer should buy the goods at the current price obtaining, and claim for damages to recover the difference between the current price and the contract price.

(*iv*) *Available market* is a commercial expression and does not seem to have a precise legal meaning. In any case, the important question is, Could the buyer reasonably have bought similar goods elsewhere immediately after the breach by non-delivery? And if so, what price should he reasonably have paid? Notice that whether the buyer, in fact, bought the goods elsewhere is not strictly relevant to the application of the *prima facie* rule in *s.* 51 (3).

(*v*) The rule in *s.* 51 (3) corresponds to the rule in *s.* 50 (3). It is a rule which is generally both just and convenient. But it is auxiliary to the general rule in *s.* 51 (2). Moreover, it is a *prima facie* rule which the court may disregard if it so wishes in any particular case.

(*vi*) Where a buyer has entered a contract of sale with the view to *re-selling* the goods to a third party, he may be forced to break his contract with the third party and thus be liable to him in damages, as a result of non-delivery by the seller. The question arises as to whether the buyer's loss of profits on the sub-sale should affect the measure of damages awarded against the original seller.

In *The Arpad* (1934), Maugham, L. J., said, "I suppose most vendors of goods and most carriers might be taken to know that if the purchaser or consignee is a trader the goods will probably be sold, or are bought for sub-sale, but the authorities seem to show conclusively that something more than that is necessary to enable the damages to be assessed by reference to a contract of sub-sale entered into before the date of delivery."

It seems that the buyer cannot maintain a claim for damages to the extent of a loss on a sub-sale, unless the seller was aware of some special circumstances, *e.g.* an unusually large profit to be made on the sub-sale. The right of the buyer to recover special damages of this kind is saved by *s.* 54 of the Act.

BUYER'S RIGHT TO TREAT THE CONTRACT AS REPUDIATED

4. The right of rejection. Where the seller is in breach of a *condition*, express or implied, the buyer may reject the goods and treat the contract as repudiated: *see s.* 11.

NOTE

- (*i*) The Act does not define "condition." For discussion as to what is meant by "a condition," *see* general works on contract law.
- (*ii*) Briefly, a condition is a term which is identified with the main purpose of a contract. Notice that "warranty" is defined in *s.* 62 (1) as being *collateral* to the main purpose of a contract.
- (*iii*) Whether a stipulation in a contract of sale is a condition or a warranty depends in each case on the construction of the contract: *s.* 11 (1) (b).
- (*iv*) A stipulation may be a condition although called a warranty in the contract: *s.* 11 (1) (b).
- (*v*) Breach of an implied condition has the same legal consequences as breach of an express condition.
- (*vi*) Unless otherwise agreed, where goods are delivered to the buyer and he refuses to accept them having the right to do so, he is not bound to return them to the seller, but it is sufficient if he intimates to the seller that he refuses to accept them: *s.* 36.

5. Loss of the right of rejection. The buyer loses the right of rejection where the contract is not severable and he has accepted the goods, or part of them: *s.* 11 (1) (c). By *s.* 35, as amended by the *Misrepresentation Act*, 1967, the buyer is deemed to have accepted the goods when he intimates to the seller that he has accepted them, or, except where *s.* 34 applies (buyer's right of examining the goods), when the goods have been delivered to him, and he does any act in relation to them which is inconsistent with the ownership of the seller, or when, after the lapse of a reasonable time, he retains the goods without intimating to the seller that he has rejected them.

NOTE

(*i*) A contract is not severable when there is either a single
delivery of goods, or a series of deliveries under a single
contract. Whether a contract is severable or otherwise
depends on the terms of the contract and the circumstances
of the case: *see s.* 31 (2). *See Taylor* v. *Oakes, Roncoroni
& Co.* (1922); *Cargo Carriers* v. *Citati* (1957); *Jackson* v.
Rotax (1910); *Claddagh Steamship Co.* v. *Stevens* (1919).

(*ii*) What is a reasonable time within which the buyer must
intimate to the seller that he has rejected the goods is a
question of fact, to be determined according to the circumstances of each case: *s.* 56. Notice that it is not necessary
for the buyer to reject immediately on delivery: *Fisher,
Reeves & Co.* v. *Armour & Co.* (1920).

(*iii*) Where a buyer exercises his right to treat the seller's
breach of condition as a repudiation of the contract, he is
absolved from further performance and may, in addition,
bring an action for damages.

(*iv*) The *Sale of Goods Act, s.* 11 (1) (c), originally provided that
the buyer's right of rejection was lost where the property
in specific goods had passed to him. This provision is now
omitted by virtue of the amendment contained in *s.* 4 (1)
of the *Misrepresentation Act,* 1967. The result is that the
buyer of specific goods is not compelled to treat a breach
of condition as a breach of warranty merely because property in those goods has passed to him.

ACTION FOR DAMAGES FOR BREACH OF WARRANTY

6. The right of action. Where there is a breach of warranty
by the seller, or where the buyer elects, or is compelled, to
treat any breach of condition on the part of the seller as a
breach of warranty, the buyer may maintain an action for
damages for the breach of warranty: *s.* 53.

(*a*) *Warranty* means an agreement with reference to goods
which are the subject of a contract of sale, but collateral
to the main purpose of such contract: *s.* 62 (1).

(*b*) *Condition or warranty?* Whether a stipulation in a
contract of sale is a condition or a warranty depends in
each case on the construction of the contract: *s.* 11 (1) (b).

(*c*) *Rejection.* A breach of warranty by the seller does not
give the buyer the right to reject the goods: *see ss.* 53 and
62 (1).

(*d*) *Buyer's choice of action.* The buyer may elect to treat the seller's breach of condition as a breach of warranty, *i.e.* he may elect not to treat the contract as repudiated, accept delivery of the goods, and bring an action for damages for breach of warranty *ex post facto.*

(*e*) *Breach of condition as breach of warranty.* Where a contract of sale is not severable, and the buyer has accepted the goods, or part thereof, the breach of any condition to be fulfilled by the seller can only be treated as a breach of warranty, and not as a ground for rejecting the goods and treating the contract as repudiated, unless there be a term of the contract, express or implied, to that effect: *s.* 11 (1) (c).

(*f*) *Defective instalments.* Where there is a contract for the sale of goods to be delivered by stated instalments, which are to be separately paid for, and the seller makes defective deliveries in respect of one or more instalments, it is a question in each case depending on the terms of the contract and the circumstances of the case, whether the breach of contract is a repudiation of the whole contract or whether it is a severable breach giving rise to a claim for compensation but not to a right to treat the whole contract as repudiated: *see s.* 31 (2) and *Howell* v. *Evans* (1926).

(*g*) *Misrepresentation.* Before the *Misrepresentation Act,* 1967, came into force, a claim in damages for breach of contract would fail if the defendant could show that the false statement complained of was not a term of the contract, but a mere representation. At common law, no action for damages will lie for innocent misrepresentation, *i.e.*, where no fraud is proved. But by *s.* 2 of the *Misrepresentation Act,* 1967, where a person has entered into a contract after a misrepresentation has been made to him by the other contracting party, that party will be liable in damages as if the representation was made fraudulently. It is a defence for the defendant to prove that he had reasonable grounds to believe and did believe up to the time the contract was made that the facts represented were true.

7. The measure of damages. The measure of damages for breach of warranty is as follows:

(*a*) *Estimated natural loss.* The estimated loss directly

and naturally resulting in the ordinary course of events, from the breach of warranty: *s.* 53 (2); and

(*b*) *Further loss.* Any further loss due to special circumstances outside of the ordinary course of events, of which the seller had knowledge, actual or imputed: *see s.* 54 and the six propositions in *Victoria Laundry* v. *Newman* (1949): VI, 5.

NOTE

(*i*) Section 53 (2) is a re-statement of the first part of the rule in *Hadley* v. *Baxendale* (1854).

(*ii*) The buyer should take reasonable steps to mitigate the loss resulting from the seller's breach of warranty.

(*iii*) Where there is a breach of warranty as to the profit-earning capacity of the goods sold, the buyer may claim *either*:

(1) to recover his capital loss, *i.e.* the difference between the contract price and the actual value of the goods; *or*

(2) to recover loss of profits resulting from the breach of warranty.

An allowance may be made for depreciation in computing the loss under (1) above, but not in (2) above, for depreciation has nothing to do with a claim in this form: *Cullinane* v. *British "Rema" Manufacturing Co. Ltd.* (1953).

CASES

Victoria Laundry Ltd. v. *Newman Industries Ltd.* (1949), C.A.: The defendants agreed to sell a large boiler to a laundry company, but the defendants did not know that, at the time of contracting, the laundry company intended to use the boiler to expand its business by embarking upon certain lucrative government work. The boiler was delivered some five months after the contractual delivery date. The laundry sued for damages for breach of contract, the claim including the loss attributable to the company's inability to expand its business during the five months' delay. HELD: damages for loss of business profits were recoverable, but only to the extent of what the defendants knew or must be taken to know at the material time.

Heskell v. *Continental Express Ltd.* (1950): H had contracted to sell goods to X, an importer in Persia. There was a breach of this contract by H, owing to failure of the carriers, C.E., to deliver the goods. Accordingly, H paid £1,319 damages to X, the amount being the assessment of X's loss of profits. H now sought to recover damages from C.E. HELD: the measure of damages was £175, being the loss of profit on a sub-sale at the wholesale level of trade. Knowledge of the abnormally high retail prices obtaining temporarily in Persia could not be imputed to the carrier, C.E.

SELLER'S BREACH OF WARRANTY AS BUYER'S DEFENCE OR COUNTERCLAIM

8. The defence or counterclaim. Where there is a breach of warranty by the seller, or where the buyer elects, or is compelled, to treat any breach of a condition on the part of the seller as a breach of warranty, the buyer may set up against the seller the breach of warranty in diminution or extinction of the price: *s.* 53 (1).

(a) *Loss to buyer.* Where a buyer suffers loss through the breach of warranty, or breach of warranty *ex post facto*, on the part of the seller, and he has not paid the full purchase price, he should deduct the amount of his loss from the price, and pay this reduced amount to the seller. If the seller subsequently brings an action for the full price, the buyer, in his defence, must prove the breach and loss which flowed from it.

(b) *Rules for reduction of price.* The amount by which the buyer may thus reduce the price is governed by the rules relating to the measure of damages, *i.e.* the estimated loss directly and naturally resulting in the ordinary course of events, from the breach of warranty: *s.* 53 (2), together with special damages, if any, as allowed by *s.* 54.

(c) *Action for breach of warranty.* The buyer may, if he so wishes, pay the price in full and then bring an action against the seller for the breach of warranty.

ACTION FOR MONEY PAID ON A CONSIDERATION WHICH HAS WHOLLY FAILED

9. The right of action. Where the buyer has paid money to the seller under a contract of sale, and there has been a total failure of consideration moving from the seller, the buyer may maintain an action for the recovery of the money paid: *see Rowland* v. *Divall* (1923).

NOTE

(i) This rule is based on the general rule of quasi-contract that where money is paid on a total failure of consideration, the sum may be recovered.

(*ii*) The action is an alternative to an action for damages for breach of contract.

SPECIFIC PERFORMANCE

10. The statutory position. In any action for breach of contract to deliver *specific* or *ascertained* goods, the court may, *if it thinks fit*, on the application of the plaintiff, by its judgment direct that the contract shall be performed specifically, without giving the defendant the option of retaining the goods on payment of damages. The judgment may be unconditional, or upon such terms and conditions as to damages, payment of the price, and otherwise, as to the court may seem just, and the application by the plaintiff may be made at any time before judgment: *s.* 52.

11. An equitable remedy. Specific performance is an equitable remedy and the court's discretion to award it will be exercised only on certain well-established principles. In particular, the remedy is not available when damages would be an adequate remedy. It may, therefore, be a useful remedy to the buyer in cases where the seller refuses to deliver specific or ascertained goods which are not available on the market.

PROGRESS TEST 7

1. List the remedies which may be available to the buyer in the event of a breach by the seller. (**1**)

2. Where the seller wrongfully neglects or refuses to deliver the goods to the buyer, the buyer may maintain an action against the seller for damages for non-delivery. What is the measure of damages for non-delivery? Explain fully. (**3**)

3. When may the buyer treat the contract as repudiated by the seller? (**4**)

4. In what circumstances does the buyer lose his right to reject the goods? (**5**)

5. When may the buyer bring an action for damages against the seller for damages for breach of warranty? (**6**)

6. In what circumstances may the buyer claim damages under the *Misrepresentation Act*, 1967? What statutory defence may be raised by the seller? (**6**)

7. What is the measure of damages for breach of warranty by the seller? (**7**)

8. What is the legal position where the seller brings an action

for the price of the goods, but the buyer claims that the seller is in breach of warranty? **(8)**

9. When has the buyer an action for money paid on a consideration which has wholly failed? **(9)**

10. A, who has contracted to sell certain goods to B at a specified price, is in breach of his contract by reason of his inability to deliver the goods according to his promise. In consequence, B is forced to break a contract with C, who had agreed to buy part of these goods from B. If B brings an action for damages against A, will his contract with C and his consequent loss of profits be taken into account when damages are assessed by the court?

11. D, who has agreed to buy goods from E, examines the goods shortly after delivery and finds that they do not accord with the contract description. D immediately telephones E and tells him this and, further, that he does not accept delivery of the goods and that E should make arrangements to collect them from D's premises. E, who has made no attempt to collect the goods, now sues D for the price. Advise D, who still has the goods in his possession.

CHAPTER VIII

SALE OF GOODS AT PUBLIC AUCTIONS

AUCTION SALES

1. The fall of the hammer. A sale by auction is complete when the auctioneer announces its completion by the fall of the hammer, or in other customary manner: *s.* 58 (2).

NOTE

    (*i*) Until such announcement is made, any bidder may retract his bid: *s.* 58 (2).

    (*ii*) This sub-section gives statutory form to the rule in *Payne* v. *Cave* (1790).

CASE

    Dennant v. *Skinner* (1948): D, an auctioneer, knocked down a van to the highest bidder, who falsely gave his name as King, claiming to be the son of a well-known and reputable motor dealer. D then knocked down five more vehicles to this bidder. After the sale, D, with some reluctance, accepted payment by cheque, taking from the bidder a signed statement in the following terms: "I hereby certify my cheque No. —— will be met on presentation at my bank. Furthermore, I agree that the ownership of the vehicles will not pass to me until such time as the proceeds of my cheque have been credited to the South London Motor Auction account at Lloyds Bank." D permitted the bidder to remove the vehicles, one of which was subsequently sold to C, who later sold it to S. The cheque given to D was dishonoured and he brought this action against S for the return of the car or its value. HELD: (*i*) there was no question of mistaken identity at the time the sale was made, *i.e.* by *s.* 58 (2) at the fall of the hammer; (*ii*) this was an unconditional contract for the sale of specific goods to which *s.* 18, rule 1, applied and, accordingly, property passed at the fall of the hammer; (*iii*) the signed certificate given by the bidder after the sale could have no effect, for property had already passed to the bidder; (*iv*) by allowing the bidder to remove the vehicles, D lost his right to retain possession until payment of the price under *s.* 39 (1) (a); and (*v*) property in the car in question passed from the bidder to C and subsequently to S.

2. Sale of lots. Where goods are put up for sale by auction in lots, each lot is *prima facie* deemed to be the subject of a separate contract of sale: *s.* 58 (1).

3. Seller's right to bid. A right to bid may be expressly reserved by or on behalf of the seller: *s.* 58 (4). Where a right to bid is expressly reserved, but not otherwise, the seller, or any one person on his behalf, may bid at the auction: *s.* 58.

(*a*) *Must be expressly reserved.* The seller's right to bid must be *expressly* reserved.

(*b*) *One bidder on seller's behalf.* Only *one* person may be authorised to bid on the seller's behalf.

(*c*) *Where seller may not bid.* Where a sale by auction is not notified to be subject to a right to bid on behalf of the seller, it shall not be lawful for the seller to bid himself or to employ any person to bid at such sale, or for the auctioneer knowingly to take any bid from the seller or any such person. Any sale contravening this rule may be treated as fraudulent by the buyer: *s.* 58 (3).

4. Reserve price. A sale by auction may be notified to be subject to a reserve price: *s.* 58 (4).

(*a*) Where a sale by auction is notified to be subject to a reserve price, every bid is "a conditional offer subject to its being up to the reserve price." *See* Sir Richard Henn Collins, M.R., in *McManus* v. *Fortescue* (1907).

(*b*) Where an auctioneer inadvertently knocks down to a bidder who has bid less than the reserve price, there is no contract of sale, for the auctioneer has no authority to sell below the reserve price: *McManus* v. *Fortescue* (1907).

(*c*) It is sufficient that the bidders have been notified that there is a reserve price: it is not necessary that they be notified what that reserve price is.

ILLEGAL BIDDING AGREEMENTS

5. "Knockouts." A "knockout," *i.e.* an agreement by which an intending bidder undertakes to abstain from bidding, is not illegal at common law.

6. Auctions (Bidding Agreements) Act, 1927. If any dealer agrees to give, or gives, or offers any gift or consideration to any other person as an inducement or reward for abstaining, or for having abstained, from bidding at a sale by auction either generally, or for any particular lot, or if any person agrees to accept any such gift or consideration, he shall be guilty of a criminal offence: *see s.* 1 (1) of the 1927 Act.

NOTE
  (*i*) *Dealer* means a person who in the normal course of his business attends sales by auction for the purpose of purchasing goods with a view to reselling them: *s.* 1 (2) of the 1927 Act.
  (*ii*) No prosecution under this Act may be instituted without the consent of the Attorney-General or the Solicitor-General.
  (*iii*) Where there is a prosecution and a conviction under the 1927 Act, the vendor may, as against a purchaser who has been a party to the illegal knockout, treat the sale as induced by fraud.

MOCK AUCTIONS ACT, 1961

7. Definition. A sale of goods by way of competitive bidding is a *mock auction* if during the course of the sale:

(*a*) any lot is sold to a person bidding for it, and either it is sold to him at a price lower than the amount of his highest bid for that lot, or part of the price at which it is sold to him is repaid or credited to him or is stated to be so repaid or credited; or

(*b*) the right to bid for any lot is restricted, or is stated to be restricted, to persons who have bought or agreed to buy one or more articles; or

(*c*) any articles are given away or offered as gifts.

8. Mock Auctions Act, 1961. This Act provides that it shall be a criminal offence to promote or conduct, or to assist in the conduct of, a mock auction at which one or more lots of certain prescribed articles are offered for sale.

(*a*) *The prescribed articles* to which the 1961 Act applies are any plate, plated articles, linen, china, glass, books, pictures, prints, furniture, jewellery, articles of household or personal use or ornament or any musical or scientific instrument or apparatus.

(*b*) *Defect or damage.* A sale is not a mock auction where the price has been reduced from the amount of the highest bid on account of a defect or damage discovered or sustained after the bid was made.

PROGRESS TEST 8

1. At what point is a sale by auction complete?   (1)

2. In what circumstances may a seller make a bid for his own goods?   (3)

3. What is the legal position where a sale by auction is notified to be subject to a reserve price and the auctioneer inadvertently knocks a lot down at a price below the reserve price?   (4)

4. What is a "knockout"?   (5)

5. Explain the effect of the *Auctions (Bidding Agreements) Act*, 1927, on agreements to abstain from bidding.   (6)

6. What is a mock auction?   (7)

7. What is the main provision of the *Mock Auctions Act*, 1961? (8)

8. Explain carefully the decision in *Dennant* v. *Skinner* (1948).

Ex ship. (Transit at seller's risk)
(Tho' not bound to insure them, (so ') usually does)
Buyer not bound to pay for goods until they are unloaded
from the ship + all freightage charges paid.

CHAPTER IX

INTERNATIONAL TRADING CONTRACTS

COMMERCIAL PRACTICE

1. C.i.f., f.o.b., etc. In international commercial practice
it is usual to divide international trading contracts into the
following classes:

(*a*) C.i.f. (cost, insurance and freight).
(*b*) F.o.b. (free on board).
(*c*) F.a.s. (free alongside ship).

2. Commercial expressions. The expressions c.i.f., f.o.b.,
etc., are generally used in commerce, and are useful in that they
give a general indication as to the terms of the contract they
describe. But they do not indicate with precision any detailed
contractual terms. Indeed, the International Chamber of
Commerce advises the use of "incoterms 1953," which are
standardised interpretations of these expressions, so as to
avoid misunderstandings between contraction parties.

C.I.F. CONTRACTS

3. Seller's duties. Under a c.i.f. contract, the duties of the
seller usually include the following:

(*a*) To obtain any export licence required.
(*b*) To arrange for the carriage of the goods to the port of
destination and to pay freight charges.
(*c*) To arrange for the loading of the goods at the port of
shipment at the time required by the contract.
(*d*) To procure a policy of insurance to cover the goods
during transit. The benefit of the policy is to be transfer-
able to the buyer or his assignee.
(*e*) To furnish the buyer with a bill of lading, the invoice of
the goods, and the insurance policy, within a reasonable
time from the date of the shipment.

4. Buyer's duties.   Under a c.i.f. contract, the duties of the buyer usually include the following:

(*a*) To pay the contract price on delivery of the documents: *Clemens Horst* v. *Biddell* (1912).

(*b*) To pay any outstanding charges in respect to the carriage of the goods, with the exception of freight and insurance.

(*c*) To pay all unloading, lighterage and wharfage charges.

(*d*) To pay all customs and import duties.

(*e*) To procure any licence or permit needed to import the goods.

Risk *passes to buyer once goods delivered to ship. Property passes too,*

F.O.B. CONTRACTS *(unless rt. of disposal reserved.)*

5. Seller's duties.   Under an f.o.b. contract, the duties of the seller usually include the following:

(*a*) To deliver the goods on board the ship named by the buyer at the agreed time.

(*b*) To notify the buyer immediately the goods have been delivered on board.

6. Buyer's duties.   Under an f.o.b. contract, the duties of the buyer usually include the following:

(*a*) To arrange for a contract of affreightment of the goods.

(*b*) To give the seller sufficient notice of the name of the ship, its loading berth, and the time for delivery on the ship.

(*c*) To pay all charges from the time the goods have passed the ship's rail.

(*d*) To bear all risks after the goods have passed the ship's rail.   *property passes too, usually.*

F.A.S. CONTRACTS

7. Seller's duties.   Under an f.a.s. contract, the duties of the seller usually include the following:

(*a*) To deliver the goods alongside the ship named by the buyer at the agreed time.

(*b*) To notify the buyer immediately the goods have been delivered alongside.

8. Buyer's duties. Under an f.a.s. contract, the duties of the buyer usually include the following:

(*a*) To arrange for a contract of affreightment of the goods.

(*b*) To give the seller sufficient notice of the name of the ship, its loading berth, and the time for delivery alongside.

(*c*) To pay all charges from the time the goods are delivered alongside.

(*d*) To bear all risks after the goods have been delivered alongside according to the contract.

UNIFORM LAWS ON INTERNATIONAL SALES ACT, 1967

9. The Hague Conference, 1964. Two international Conventions drawn up at the Hague in 1964 have since been incorporated into English law by means of the *Uniform Laws on International Sales Act*, 1967. The first Convention contains a set of rules known as the Uniform Law on the International Sale of Goods (*see* **10** below). The second Convention contains the Uniform Law on the Formation of Contracts for the International Sale of Goods (*see* **11** below).

10. The Uniform Law on the International Sale of Goods. This law is designed to apply to contracts of sale of goods whose parties carry on business in different states. The law specifies the obligations of the seller and buyer under such a contract, but leaves the parties to contract out if they so wish.

11. The Uniform Law on the Formation of Contracts for the International Sale of Goods. This law specifies the rules governing offer and acceptance where the contract, if concluded, would be governed by the Uniform Law on the International Sale of Goods.

PROGRESS TEST 9

1. Have the expressions c.i.f., f.o.b., etc., any precise legal meaning? **(2)**

2. What are "incoterms"? **(2)**

3. List the usual duties of buyer and seller under the following kinds of contract: (*i*) f.o.b., (*ii*) c.i.f., (*iii*) f.a.s. **(3–8)**

4. What is the general purpose of the Uniform Laws on *International Sales Act*, 1967? **(9–11)**

CHAPTER X

PROPOSALS FOR REFORM

1. General need for reform. The Malony Report, 1962 (para. 473), contains the following observations on the *Sale of Goods Act*, 1893:

> "This Act enjoys a special position in English jurisprudence. It has been long regarded as an outstandingly successful codification of an important branch of law—indeed almost a unique example which has been widely adopted, with modification, in the English-speaking world. In the near 70 years of its life it has only been amended once; this was by deletion of a provision which had its roots in 1677. [Section 4, re-enacting Section 17 of the *Statute of Frauds*, 1677, was repealed by the *Law Reform (Enforcement of Contracts) Act*, 1954.] The Act has given clarity and certainty to the law affecting transactions of everyday occurrence. As against this, it has precluded the judicial development that has advanced most branches of the law since Victorian days. While the law has stood still, new selling methods have been introduced and an infinity of new types of complex goods have appeared on the market. The modern retail purchaser may find himself on his perplexity and ignorance at grave disadvantage."

In this chapter, the more important proposals contained in the Reports of the Molony Committee (Cmnd. 1781), 1962, the Law Reform Committee on Transfer of Title (Cmnd. 2958), 1966, and the Law Commission (Law Com. No. 24), 1969, will be considered.

THE MALONY COMMITTEE REPORT, 1962

2. Scope. The Malony Committee was appointed "to review the working of the existing legislation relating to merchandise marks and certification trade marks, and to consider and report what changes if any in the law and what other measures, if any, are desirable for the further protection of the consuming public." The wide scope of these terms of reference clearly included much of sale of goods law and also the law of hire-purchase. But the Committee was clearly restricted to dealing with the law relating to goods acquired for private use or consumption. For the purposes of this report, a *consumer* is "one who purchases (or hire-purchases) goods for private use or consumption."

3. Implied terms. The Committee found that there is a widespread practice among sellers to "contract out" of the implied terms in *ss.* 12–15 of the 1893 Act. The Committee felt "compelled to view the practice as a general threat to consumer interests, in the sense that heavy and irrevocable loss may fall on the consumer who is unlucky enough to get a defective article."

4. "Contracting out." The Report compares the law of sale of goods with the statutory provisions against "contracting out" which are to be found in hire-purchase law. The Committee thought that these provisions ought generally to be followed in the law of sale of goods, but that separate consideration should be given to each implied condition. The recommendations with respect to "consumer sales" were as follows:

(*a*) *Merchantable quality.* The Committee recommended that the condition of merchantable quality should be irrevocably implied, save as regards defects of which the buyer should have become aware if he had examined the goods, and as regards secondhand or imperfect goods clearly described in writing as such and goods offered by auction.

(*b*) *Fitness for purpose.* The Committee recommended that the condition of reasonable fitness for such purpose as the buyer expressly or by implication makes known to the seller should be implied subject to avoidance orally by retention of the requirement that the buyer must show that he relies on the seller's skill and judgment.

(*c*) *Title.* The Committee recommended that the statutory conditions and warranties as to title, quiet possession, freedom from encumbrance, and correspondence with sample, etc., should be irrevocably implied.

(*d*) *Description.* The Committee recommended that the condition of correspondence with description should be irrevocably implied, save in respect of auctioneer's descriptions.

D

THE LAW REFORM COMMITTEE REPORT, 1966

5. Market overt. The Law Reform Committee Report on Transfer of Title, 1966 (Cmnd. 2958), contained a recommendation for the modification of *s.* 22 of the *Sale of Goods Act*, 1893. This section contains the rule that, where goods are sold in market overt according to the usage of the market, the buyer will acquire a good title provided he buys in good faith and without notice of any defect or want of title on the part of the seller. The Committee considered the rule to be capricious in its application and that it should either be abolished or else be extended so as to cover all retail sales at trade premises as well as sales by auction. The Committee pointed out that which solution is adopted depends on whether it is thought better to protect property rights or to facilitate commercial transactions.

6. Recommendation. The majority of the Committee recommended that *s.* 22 of the *Sale of Goods Act*, 1893, should be replaced by a provision that a person who buys goods by retail at trade premises or by public auction acquires a good title provided he buys in good faith and without notice of any defect or want of title on the part of the apparent owner. By "trade premises," the Committee meant premises open to the public at which goods of the same or a similar description to those sold are normally offered for sale by retail in the course of business carried on at those premises. A street market would not be included. This recommendation provided that the onus of proving good faith and lack of notice should rest on the purchaser, who should not acquire a good title if he had actual knowledge of any facts or circumstances which should have led him to infer the existence of some defect of title or to make inquiries which would have revealed the existence of such a defect.

7. Finance companies as buyers. The Committee went on to recommend that where goods are exposed for sale at trade premises by a dealer whose customer wishes to take the goods on hire-purchase terms, and the goods are first sold to a finance company, the finance company should get good title to the goods notwithstanding any defect of title on the part of the dealer. This recommendation was subject to the proviso that the finance company is able to discharge the onus of proof mentioned in **6** above in relation both to itself and to the would-be purchaser.

THE LAW COMMISSION REPORT, 1969: AMENDMENTS TO THE SALE OF GOODS ACT

8. The Law Commission. The Law Commission was set up by *s.* 1 of the *Law Commissions Act*, 1965, for the purpose of promoting the reform of the law. The Exemption Clauses in Contracts, First Report: Amendments to the Sale of Goods Act, 1893 (Law Com. No. 24), is concerned with the implied terms in *ss.* 12–15 of the 1893 Act, and the practice of "contracting out." Draft clauses designed to give effect to the Law Commission's recommendations are set out in an appendix to the Report: *see* Appendix II. This is a First Report, and is part of a wider study of exemption clauses in contracts; a subsequent report will be concerned partly with exemption clauses in contracts for the supply of services and partly with certain problems common to contracts for the sale of goods and contracts for the supply of services.

9. Title and quiet possession. The Law Commission recommended that the exclusion or variation of the condition and warranties implied by *s.* 12 of the Sale of Goods Act should be possible only where it is clear that the seller is purporting to sell a limited title; and that, even where the seller does make this clear, he should not be permitted to exclude in their entirety the warranties of quiet possession and of freedom from charges or encumbrances in favour of third parties.

10. Description. The Law Commission recommended that, in view of the growing importance of self-service stores, *s.* 13 should be amended so as to make it quite clear that sales in such stores rank as sales "by description."

11. Fitness for purpose. In connection with the statutory condition of fitness for purpose in *s.* 14 (1), the Report contains the following recommendations:

(*a*) The condition should no longer be confined to sales where the goods are "of a description which it is in the course of the seller's business to supply," but that it should be extended to cover all sales in which the seller is acting in the course of business.

(b) The proviso for sales under a patent or trade name should be repealed.

(c) The provision in s. 14 (1) to the effect that the condition of fitness will be implied in a contract of sale only where the buyer makes known the particular purpose for which he requires the goods so as to show that he relies on the seller's skill and judgment should be replaced by a provision whereby the condition of fitness will be implied unless the circumstances are such as to show that the buyer did not rely, or that it was unreasonable for him to rely, on the seller's skill and judgment.

(d) It should be made clear that the words "particular purpose" in s. 14 (1) cover not only an unusual or special purpose for which goods are bought but also a normal or usual purpose.

12. Merchantable quality. The Report contains the following recommendations with regard to the condition of merchantable quality in s. 14 (2):

(a) The following definition should be included in s. 62: "Goods of any kind are of merchantable quality within the meaning of this Act if they are as fit for the purpose or purposes for which goods of that kind are commonly bought as it is reasonable to expect having regard to their price, any description applied to them and all the other circumstances; and any reference in this Act to unmerchantable goods shall be construed accordingly."

(b) The implication of the condition of merchantable quality into a contract of sale should cease to be dependent on the sale being a sale "by description."

(c) The condition of merchantable quality in s. 14 (2) should no longer be confined to sales in which the seller is a dealer in goods of the relevant description, but should be extended to all sales where the seller is acting in the course of business.

(d) There should be no implied condition of merchantable quality under s. 14 (2) as regards such specific defects of which notice was given to the buyer before the contract was made.

13. Sample. The Report contains no recommendation for the amendment of *s.* 15 except that it should be made clear that the proposed definition of "merchantable quality" applies to *s.* 15 as well as *s.* 14 (2).

14. Position of third parties. The Report notes that, as the law now stands, the donee or user of goods bought by someone else has in general no right of action against the seller for any breach of condition or warranty, as there is no privity of contract between him and the seller. If such a person is injured or his property is damaged because the goods are defective, he may obtain redress only if he can show that the seller or manufacturer was negligent. His action, if any, lies in tort and not in contract. The Report notes that even though the plaintiff's burden of proof is lightened by the doctrine of *res ipsa loquitur,* there is no room for doubt that the law's strict observance of the boundaries between the fields of contractual and tortious liability can and does lead to anomalies and hardship in individual cases. The Law Commission was, accordingly, in some sympathy with the tentative proposal to give to users of goods a remedy which would no longer be dependent upon their ability to establish a claim in negligence. Simply stated, the proposal was that any user of goods sold, regardless of whether he is the actual buyer or a donee or a person otherwise entitled to use the goods, should have a direct remedy against the seller for any breach of the statutory conditions or warranties. The Report does not recommend the adoption of this proposal, but that its further consideration should await a full study of what the Americans call "products liability."

15. Contracting out. In considering the question of contracting out of the conditions implied by *ss.* 13–15 of the 1893 Act, the Law Commission distinguished between sales to private purchasers and sales to business buyers:

(*a*) *Private purchasers.* The Report contains the recommendation that these conditions should apply to any sale of consumer goods to a private consumer, notwithstanding any term of the contract to the contrary. But the ban on contracting out ought not to apply to sales by auction.

(*b*) *Business buyers.* Although the Commissioners were

agreed that business buyers should receive some protection from the sellers' practice of contracting out, they were divided as to what the extent of that protection should be. The Report, therefore, contains two alternative recommendations:

Alternative A. The ban on contracting out should be extended to certain limited classes of sales of consumer goods to business buyers. This proposal would operate with a definition of "consumer sale" which would include sales of consumer goods to business buyers except where the buyer can according to certain specified criteria be said to be in the business of dealing in or dealing with the goods bought. The court would have the power to exclude from the ban any transaction where to do so would be reasonable, having regard to the size and terms of the transaction and other relevant circumstances.

Alternative B. Protection against contracting out should be made available to all business buyers, by empowering the court to render unenforceable any contracting-out provisions in the business sale to the extent that it considered reliance on them not to be fair or reasonable in all the circumstances. The onus of establishing this would fall on the buyer. The Report contains a number of principles to guide the court in applying the test of reasonableness.

PROGRESS TEST 10

1. Do you regard the law of sale of goods as standing in general need of reform? (**1**)

2. Do you think that the Malony Report might have been more useful if the adopted definition of "consumer" had been wide enough to include all users of goods? (**2**)

3. What were the recommendations with regard to contracting out in the Malony Report? (**4**)

4. Does the law of market overt stand in need of reform? (**5**)

5. Outline the recommendations of the Law Commission for the amendment of the Sale of Goods Act. (**8–15**)

6. The Commissioners were divided as to the right of business buyers to contract out of the terms implied by *ss.* 12–15. Which of the alternative proposals in this connection would you support? Give reasons. (**15**)

7. Do you agree with the Commissioners that a private purchaser should have a greater right of contracting out of the implied terms than a business buyer? (**15**)

8. How did the Commissioners deal with the question of "products liability"? (**14**)

CHAPTER XI

HIRE-PURCHASE CONTRACTS AT COMMON LAW

THE NATURE OF HIRE-PURCHASE

1. Definition. A contract of hire-purchase is a bailment of goods coupled with an option to purchase.

(a) *The option.* The option to purchase may or may not be exercised, and there is no contract of sale unless and until the option is exercised.

(b) *Incentive to purchase.* Although the hirer has a mere option to purchase and is, therefore, not bound to purchase, he has a strong incentive to purchase because hire-purchase charges are higher than mere hiring charges.

(c) *The parties* to a contract of hire-purchase are:

(i) the owner, who undertakes to let out the goods on hire with an option to purchase;

(ii) the hirer, who undertakes to pay the hire-purchase charges according to the agreement.

2. The aim of hire-purchase. The object of a hire-purchase contract is to evade the *Sale of Goods Act, s.* 25 (2). The hirer is not a "person who has agreed to buy goods." Therefore the hire-purchase contract is not a contract of sale of goods. Thus, the hirer cannot pass title to a third party.

The first hire-purchase agreement to come before the courts was in *Helby* v. *Matthews* (1895). In that case the House of Lords examined the nature of hire-purchase and differentiated it clearly from sale of goods.

CASE

Helby v. *Matthews* (1895), H.L.: O gave possession of a piano to B under an agreement in writing by which B, "*the hirer,*" agreed to pay O, "*the owner,*" a rent or hire instalment of 10s. 6d. a month, and to keep the instrument in his, B's, own custody at the address named in the agreement, and not to remove it without

O's consent in writing. The agreement provided that B might terminate the hiring by delivering up the instrument to O, and further that, if B should punctually pay the full sum of eighteen guineas by instalments according to the agreement, the instrument should become the absolute property of B. The agreement provided that, until the full sum of eighteen guineas was duly paid, the piano should continue to be the property of O. B pledged the piano with X, a pawnbroker. O brought this action against X for its recovery. HELD: B was not a person who had "bought or agreed to buy" the piano within *s*. 9 of the *Factors Act*, 1889 (*s*. 9 is equivalent to *s*. 25 (2) of the *Sale of Goods Act*, 1893). Consequently, no property passed, and O was entitled to recover the piano. *Per* LORD HERSCHELL, L.C.: "An agreement to buy imports a legal obligation to buy. If there was no such legal obligation there cannot, in my opinion, properly be said to have been an agreement to buy. Where is any such legal obligation to be found? B might buy or not just as he pleased. He did not agree to make thirty-six or any number of monthly payments. All that he undertook was to make the monthly payment of 10*s*. 6*d*. so long as he kept the piano. He had an option, no doubt, to buy it by continuing the stipulated payments for a sufficient length of time. If he had exercised that option he would have become the purchaser. I cannot see, under these circumstances, how he can be said either to have bought or agreed to buy the piano. The terms of the contract did not, upon its execution, bind him to buy, but left him free to do so or not as he pleased, and nothing happened after the contract was made to impose that obligation."

3. The modern hire-purchase transaction. The usual commercial procedure is for the dealer to sell the goods to a finance company, which then enters into the hire-purchase agreement with the customer. This procedure gives rise to a triangular relationship between the three parties: finance company, dealer and hirer. Consider the three limbs of this relationship:

(*a*) *Between finance company and dealer* there is a sale of goods contract.

(*b*) *Between finance company and hirer* there is a hire-purchase contract.

(*c*) *Between dealer and hirer* there may or may not be a collateral contract: see *Andrews* v. *Hopkinson* (1956). But in no event is there a contract of sale between these two parties.

CASE

Drury v. *Victor Buckland Ltd.* (1941), C.A.: The defendant's
salesman persuaded D to enter a hire-purchase agreement with the
E.T. Co., a finance company, for an ice-cream refrigerator, cash
price £105, on May 11th, 1938.   On the same date, the defendant's
salesman signed a document by which the refrigerator was
"invoiced" to D, crediting her with a deposit of £10 10s. and
computing a total liability of £113 17s. "payable by thirty-six
monthly instalments of £3 3s. 0d.   The hire-purchase agreement
between D and the E.T. Co. provided that the monthly instalments should be paid to the E.T. Co.   The refrigerator proved
unsatisfactory and D brought this action against the defendants,
contending that there was a sale of goods agreement and breach of
the implied condition in *s.* 14 (1) of the *Sale of Goods Act.*   HELD:
there was no sale of goods agreement between D and the defendants.   *Per* SCOTT, L. J.: "I think that the document called the
hire-purchase agreement was the reality, and that the use of the
invoice form by the defendant company was not any evidence,
in the circumstances, that there had been a sale by them.   Being
merchants, they would naturally send out an invoice, and very
likely they would not think that the word 'invoice' at the top of
the document made any difference.   That they realised what the
nature of the transaction was, however, appears from the contents
of the invoice, to which I have referred—namely, that there was
to be a deduction of the amount of the first payment, and that the
balance was to be the subject of a hire-purchase agreement, including interest charges payable to the finance company, out of which
it made its profits, and that there was to be payment to them, or to
somebody, by thirty-six monthly instalments, which in fact were
instalments covered by the hire-purchase agreement of even date.
It was a sale by the Buckland company to the hire-purchase
company.   The property passed to them on the terms that they
would get paid by the hire-purchase company, as no doubt they
were in fact.   Therefore, the claim against them for damages for
breach of warranty is a cause of action unsupported by any contract of sale which would carry it."

4. The nature of hire-purchase.   In *Bridge* v. *Campbell
Discount Co. Ltd.* (1962), a House of Lords case concerning the
hire-purchase of a motor car, Lord Denning began his speech
with an examination of the nature of hire-purchase.

He said, "It [a hire-purchase transaction] is in effect, though
not in law, a mortgage of goods.   Just as a man who buys
land may raise part of the price by a mortgage of it, so, also,
a man who buys goods may raise part of the price by hire-
purchase of them.   And just as the old mortgage of land was

not what it appeared to be, so, also, the modern hire-purchase of goods is not what it seems to be.   One might well say of a hire-purchase transaction what MAITLAND said of a mortgage deed: 'That is the worst of our mortgage deed . . . it is one long suppressio veri and suggestio falsi': see his *Lectures on equity* (2nd edn., 1949), p. 182.   Take this present transaction. If you were able to strip off the legal trappings in which it has been dressed and see it in its native simplicity, you would discover that the appellant agreed to buy a car from a dealer for £405 but he could only find £105 towards it.   So he borrowed the other £300 from a finance house and got them to pay it to the dealer, and he gave the finance house a charge on the car as security for repayment.   But if you tried to express the transaction in those simple terms, you would soon fall into troubles of all sorts under the Bills of Sale Acts, the Sale of Goods Act, and the Money-lenders Acts.   In order to avoid these legal obstacles, the finance house has to discard the role of a lender of money on security and it has to become an owner of goods who lets them out on hire: *see re Robertson, ex. p. Crawcour, McEntire* v. *Crossley Brothers Ltd.*   So it buys goods from the dealer and lets them out on hire to the appellant. The appellant has to discard the role of a man who has agreed to buy goods, and he has to become a man who takes them on hire with only an option to purchase: *see Helby* v. *Matthews*. And when these new roles have been assumed, the finance house is not a money-lender but a hire-purchase company free of the trammels of the Money-lenders Acts: *see Transport & General Credit Corporation Ltd.* v. *Morgan.*   So you arrive at the modern hire-purchase transaction whereby (*i*) the dealer sells the goods to a finance house for cash; and (*ii*) the finance house lets them out on hire to a hirer in return for rentals which are so calculated as to ensure that the finance house is eventually repaid the cash with interest; and (*iii*) when the finance house is repaid, the hirer has the option of purchasing the car for a nominal sum.   The dealer is the intermediary who arranges it all.   The finance house supplies him with the printed forms, and he gets them signed.   In the result, the finance house buys a car it has never seen and lets it to a hirer it has never met, and the dealer seemingly drops out."

Where there is a dispute as to whether a transaction is one of purchase or whether it is a loan on the security of a chattel, it is the duty of the court to look through or behind the document to see what was the real transaction.

CASE

Polsky v. *S. and A. Services* (1951), c.a. P bought a motor car for which he gave the seller a cheque for £895. He knew that there were insufficient funds in his account to meet the cheque, and so he entered into the following transaction with S.A.S. to obtain the sum he needed. S.A.S. purported to buy the car from P and to let it out to him under a hire-purchase agreement. A standard hire-purchase agreement form was used and was signed by P. According to this form, an initial payment of £495 had been made, leaving a balance of £400 owed by P. To this balance was added £50 for charges. The total amount owed by P was to be paid by eighteen instalments of £25. P now brought this action, claiming that the transaction was not one of hire-purchase but was, in reality, an assurance of a chattel as security for a debt, and that, as it was not registered under the *Bills of Sale Act* (1878) *Amendment Act*, 1882, it was void. HELD: there was no genuine sale followed by a hiring. The true nature of the transaction was a loan on the security of the car. The purported hire-purchase agreement was an unregistered bill of sale and was, accordingly, void.

5. Implied terms. In any contract of hire-purchase the following terms are implied at common law unless the circumstances show that the parties intended otherwise:

(*a*) *That the goods are reasonably fit for their purpose* where the hirer has relied on the seller's skill of judgment: *Astley Industrial Trust* v. *Grimley* (1963), c.a.

(*b*) *That the goods are of merchantable quality.* It must be admitted that there is no case in direct support of the proposition that this is an implied term at common law, but it is highly unlikely that the courts would not recognise its existence in appropriate circumstances as analagous with the implied term in *s.* 14 (2) of the *Sale of Goods Act*, 1893: see *Young & Marten* v. *McManus Childs* (1968), H.L.

(*c*) *That the goods correspond with the contract description:* *Karflex* v. *Pool* (1933).

POSITION OF THE DEALER

6. Owner and hirer are principal parties. The owner of the goods, *i.e.* the finance company, and the hirer, *i.e.* the customer, are the principal parties to the contract of hire-purchase. The dealer is not a party. Nevertheless, it is necessary to consider the position of the dealer in the transaction. The dealer may:

    (a) incur personal liability under an implied collateral contract with the customer; or

    (b) be deemed at common law to be the agent of the finance company in his dealings with the customer.

7. Implied collateral contract. Where a dealer gives an express undertaking with respect to the goods, and there is a breach of this undertaking, this may amount to a breach of an implied collateral contract between the dealer and the customer: *Andrews* v. *Hopkinson* (1956).

    (a) *Implied contract is collateral.* The implied contract between the dealer and customer is collateral to the contract of hire-purchase. It is collateral because the customer is deemed to have entered the hire-purchase contract in consideration for the express undertaking by the dealer.

    (b) *Dealer's liability.* It seems that the dealer is liable only upon his express undertaking. He is not liable on any implied term under the *Sale of Goods Act*, 1893, for the contract is not one of sale of goods.

    (c) *The practical significance* of the implied collateral contract is that the customer may be able to sue the dealer in circumstances where he cannot sue the finance company, *e.g.* where the finance company is effectively protected by an exemption clause.

CASES

    Andrews v. *Hopkinson* (1956): H, a car dealer, induced A to enter a hire-purchase contract with a finance company by praising a second-hand car which he wished to supply to A. H said "It's a good little bus. I would stake my life on it." A week later the car was wrecked and A was injured in an accident caused by the faulty steering mechanism of the car. HELD: there was a contract between A and H collateral to the hire-purchase contract. H was in breach of this collateral contract.

    Yeoman Credit Ltd. v. *Odgers* (1962): V, a car dealer, induced O to enter a hire-purchase contract with Y by stating that a second-hand car which he wished to supply to O was in perfect condition. The car proved to be quite unroadworthy. At O's suggestion, Y took possession of the car and resold it. Y then sued O for damages for breach of the hire-purchase contract. O joined V as defendant, claiming an indemnity on the grounds of his undertaking that the car was in perfect condition. HELD: O was liable to Y for breach of the hire-purchase contract, but O's loss directly and naturally resulted from V's breach of warranty. O was entitled to an indemnity from V.

8. Dealer as agent. Can the dealer bind the finance company contractually by his statements to the hirer? May the finance company be made liable for a misrepresentation made by the dealer to the hirer? These questions are important and the answers depend, of course, on whether the dealer acts as agent for the finance company. In order to protect themselves from liability, many finance companies insert a clause in their standard-form hire-purchase agreements to the effect that the dealer is not the agent of the company. Such clauses give the company no protection where the facts show that the dealer has acted with authority, express or implied, as the company's agent.

In *Northgran Finance Ltd.* v. *Ashley* (1962), ORMEROD, L. J., said, ". . . this [the agency of the dealer] is not a matter in which decided cases can be of much assistance. The extent and nature of the authority must be decided on the facts of each case." In an earlier case, LORD DENNING, M.R., said that "if we take, as we should, a realistic view of the position, the dealer is in many respects and for many purposes the agent of the finance company. I am aware, of course, that the finance companies often put clauses into their forms in which they say that the dealer is not their agent. But these clauses are often not worth the paper they are written on. Nobody can make an assertion of that kind in an agreement so as to bind the courts if it is contrary to the facts of the case": *Financings Ltd.* v. *Stimson* (1962).

It is clear, then, that the court will look at the facts of each case—at the true role of the dealer—to discover whether he has acted as agent of the finance company. It is unlikely that the courts will be deflected by the insertion of a clause in the hire-purchase agreement providing that the dealer is not the company's agent. The position is that a finance company must accept liability for the statements and acts of the dealer where it can be shown that he has the express or implied authority of the company to act for any purpose. Indeed, the position of the dealer as intermediary between the hirer and the finance company may involve him in acting as agent for either, or both, of these parties. In *Mercantile Credit Co. Ltd.* v. *Hamblin* (1964), C.A., PEARSON, L. J. said: "There is no rule of law that in a hire-purchase transaction the dealer never is, or always is, acting as agent for the finance company or as agent for the customer. In a typical hire-purchase transaction the dealer is a party in his own right, selling his car to the finance company, and he is acting primarily on his own behalf and not as a general agent for either of the other two parties. There is no need to attribute to him an agency in order to account for his participation in the transaction. Nevertheless the company and he may well have in a particular case some *ad hoc* agencies to do particular things on behalf of one or the other or it may be both of those two parties."

PROGRESS TEST 11

1. Define a contract of hire-purchase. **(1)**

2. Is a hirer under a contract of hire-purchase a person who has bought or agreed to buy goods? Give reasons for your answer. **(1, 2)**

3. What is the commercial aim of the contract of hire-purchase? **(2)**

4. What part does the dealer play in a modern complex hire-purchase transaction? **(3)**

5. Compare hire-purchase with mortgage of goods. **(4)**

6. What terms may be implied at *common law* in a contract of hire-purchase? **(5)**

7. How may a dealer be liable *at common law* to a hirer? **(6, 7)**

8. Is the dealer the agent of the finance company *at common law*? **(8)**

CHAPTER XII

THE HIRE-PURCHASE ACT, 1965

1. Introductory. Until the *Hire-Purchase Act*, 1938, hire-purchase agreements were governed by the common law and, accordingly, the parties were theoretically free to contract in any lawful terms they wished, without restriction. Because of the dominant position of the owner (the finance company), it became usual for standard-form agreements to contain terms which were very much against the interest of the hirer. For example, agreement forms usually provided for the owner to have a right of entry into the hirer's home to recover possession of the goods in the event of minimal default on the part of the hirer. And so it could, and did, happen that a hirer who had paid almost all of the required instalments would yet lose the goods and all rights in them by default in payment of one or two instalments, the default being perhaps due to sickness or unemployment. Further, it was common practice to exclude all implied conditions and warranties relating to the goods. Moreover, the hirer was seldom given a copy of the agreement he had signed and was often not told of the difference between the cash price and the hire-purchase price. In the 1930s hire-purchase was not the fashionable and socially respectable transaction that it is today. In fact it carried a social stigma and the finance companies and dealers had only the poorer and less educated section of the population to deal with when carrying out this kind of business. By the middle 1930s, hire-purchase had almost reached the proportions of a social evil and the 1938 Act was passed to protect the hirer from the most unfair practices of the finance companies and dealers.

The Act provided broadly as follows:

(*a*) That certain of the harsher contractual provisions were void.

(*b*) That the hirer was entitled to require from the owner a statement showing the amount paid, the amount which is to become payable and the date and amount of each future instalment.

(*c*) That the terms as to title, merchantable quality and fitness should, in general, be implied notwithstanding any agreement to the contrary.

(*d*) That the owner's right to recover possession could be enforced by legal action only (*i.e.* not by self-help) where the hirer had paid one-third or more of the hire-purchase price.

The 1938 Act worked well and was subjected to certain minor amendments and additions by the *Hire-Purchase Act*, 1954. The 1954 Act was followed by the *Hire-Purchase Act*, 1964, which contained some new and far-reaching provisions which were the result of the growing interest in consumer protection. The position in 1964 was that hire-purchase law was governed by the principal Act of 1938 and amended and added to by the Acts of 1954 and 1964. The Act of 1965 virtually consolidated the three previous Acts, with the exception of Part III of the 1964 Act, which is concerned with motor vehicle transactions.

2. Scope of the 1965 Act. The *Hire-Purchase Act*, 1965, applies to hire-purchase agreements, credit-sale agreements and conditional sale agreements, each of which is defined in *s.* 1 (1) as follows:

(*a*) "*Hire-purchase agreement*" means an agreement for the bailment of goods under which the bailor may buy the goods, or under which the property in the goods will or may pass to the bailee.

(*b*) "*Credit-sale agreement*" means an agreement for the sale of goods under which the purchase price is payable by five or more instalments, not being a conditional sale agreement.

(*c*) "*Conditional sale agreement*" means an agreement for the sale of goods under which the purchase price or part of it is payable by instalments, and the property in the goods is to remain in the seller (notwithstanding that the buyer is to be in possession of the goods) until such conditions as to the payment of instalments or otherwise as may be specified in the agreement are fulfilled.

NOTE

(*i*) Where by virtue of two or more agreements, none of which by itself constitutes a hire-purchase agreement as defined in *s*. 1(1), there is a bailment of goods and either the bailee may buy the goods, or the property therein will or may pass to the bailee, the agreements are to be regarded for the purpose of the Act as a single agreement made at the time when the last of the agreements was made: *s*. 1(2).

(*ii*) The statutory definition of a hire-purchase agreement is wider than the *Helby* v. *Matthews* situation. Where property "will or may pass to the bailee," it could include, for example, an agreement whereby the bailor binds himself to buy the goods.

3. Limits of value. Hire-purchase agreements and conditional sale agreements are governed by the Act only where the total hire-purchase price or total purchase price, as the case may be, does not exceed £2,000: *s*. 2 (2). Credit-sale agreements are governed by the Act only where the total purchase price exceeds £30 but does not exceed £2,000: *s*. 2 (3). Thus the stringent and costly requirements for documentation do not apply to credit-sales of goods of small value.

NOTE

(*i*) "*Hire purchase price*" (subject to *s*. 58(2)) means the total sum payable by the hirer under a hire-purchase agreement in order to complete the purchase of goods to which the agreement relates, exclusive of any sum payable as a penalty or as compulsion or damages for a breach of the agreement: *s*. 58(1).

(*ii*) "*Total purchase price*" (subject to *s*. 58(2)) means the total sum payable by the buyer under a credit-sale agreement or a conditional sale agreement, exclusive of any sum payable as a penalty or as compensation or damages for a breach of the agreement: *s*. 58(1).

(*iii*) *Deposits under s*. 58(2). Any sum payable by the hirer under a hire-purchase agreement, or by the buyer under a conditonal sale agreement, by way of deposit or other initial payment, or credited or to be credited to him under the agreement on account of any such deposit or payment, whether that sum is to be or has been paid to the owner or seller or to any other person or is to be or has been discharged by a payment of money or by the transfer or delivery of goods or by any other means, shall form part of the hire-purchase price or total purchase price, as the case may be: *s*. 58(2).

4. Power to increase the upper limit. If it appears to Her Majesty in Council that the upper limit of £2,000 should be raised, Her Majesty may by Order in Council direct that *s.* 2 be amended so as to substitute a larger sum: *s.* 3 (1).

5. Corporations as hirers. The Act does not apply where the hirer or buyer, as the case may be, is a corporation: nor where the hirer or buyer is an agent acting for a corporation: *s.* 4. Presumably the policy of consumer protection is intended for the benefit of individual consumers and not for corporations, which have less need of the kind of protection afforded by the Act. Nevertheless, it should be noticed that *s.* 4 does not preclude a company from taking an assignment of the benefit of a hire-purchase agreement from an individual hirer. For, although by *s.* 58 (1) "hirer" includes a person to whom the hirer's rights have passed by assignment, *s.* 4 excludes agreements "made by or on behalf of a body corporate as the hirer." Section 4 is concerned with the point in time when the contract was made, and not with any subsequent time, *e.g.*, with any assignment of the hirer's rights.

PROGRESS TEST 12

1. Give a brief outline of the history and scope of hire-purchase legislation. **(1, 2)**

2. What are the statutory definitions of the following: "hire-purchase agreement," "credit-sale agreement," "conditional sale agreement"? Comment on the difference between a credit-sale agreement and a conditional sale agreement. **(2, 3)**

3. What are the "limits of value" in the case of hire-purchase, conditional sale and credit-sale. To what extent may these be varied? **(3, 4)**

4. May a corporation take the benefit of an assignment by a hirer of his rights under a hire-purchase agreement? **(5)**

CHAPTER XIII

FORMALITIES: HIRE-PURCHASE AND CONDITIONAL SALE AGREEMENTS

1. Introductory. Sections 5 to 10 of the *Hire-Purchase Act*, 1965, set out the requirements in connection with making agreements. The policy of consumer protection is further served by requirements of the *Hire-Purchase* (*Documents*) (*Legibility and Statutory Statements*) *Regulations*, 1965 (S.I. 1965/1646), made by the Board of Trade in pursuance of the powers conferred by the *Hire-Purchase Act*, 1965. The overall effect of *ss.* 5–10 and the Regulations of 1965 is to place upon the owner under a hire-purchase agreement, or the seller under a conditional sale agreement, the burden of satisfying specified formal requirements during the negotiation and making of the agreement. Where the owner (or seller) fails to comply with the requirements, the agreement is unenforceable by him and he runs the risk of being unable to recover the goods in the event of default on the part of the hirer (or buyer).

Where the hirer (or buyer) signs an agreement elsewhere than at trade premises, the Act provides a special protection in the form of a right of cancellation and, at the same time, imposes additional formal requirements on the owner (or seller).

The requirements set out in *ss.* 5–10 and the Regulations of 1965 are broadly as follows:

(*a*) That the cash price be brought to the attention of the customer before the agreement is made: *s.* 6.

(*b*) That the agreement be signed by the hirer (or buyer) and by or on behalf of all other parties: *s.* 5.

(*c*) That certain specified express terms be contained in the agreement: *s.* 7.

(*d*) That the lettering of the agreement is clearly legible: *s.* 7 and S.I. 1965/1646.

(*e*) That the hirer's (or buyer's) signature be placed in a box containing a warning not to sign unless he wishes to be legally bound: *s.* 7 and S.I. 1965/1646.

(*f*) That the hirer (or buyer) be provided with a copy, or, in certain cases, two copies, of the agreement: *ss.* 8 and 9.

THE REQUIREMENTS

2. The cash price. The effect of *s.* 6 is that the price at which the goods may be purchased for cash must be brought to the attention of the hirer or buyer, either by written statement, by a price label or by advertisement or catalogue.

The section requires that *before the agreement is made*:

(*a*) the cash price of the goods must have been stated in writing to the hirer (or buyer) by the owner (or seller) otherwise than in the agreement; *or*

(*b*) if the hirer (or buyer) has inspected the goods or like goods, then, at the time of his inspection, tickets or labels must have been attached to or displayed with the goods clearly stating the cash price, either of the goods as a whole or of all the different articles or sets of articles comprised therein; *or*

(*c*) the hirer or buyer must have selected the goods by reference to a catalogue, price list or advertisement which clearly stated the cash price, either of the goods as a whole or of all the different articles comprised therein.

NOTE

(*i*) One or other of the three alternatives (*a*), (*b*) or (*c*) above must be complied with before the contract is made. To determine the time of making the contract, the ordinary rules of offer and acceptance are applied. When the usual standard forms are adopted, it is the hirer who makes the offer. The contract is made when the owner accepts.

(*ii*) When the owner relies on alternative (*a*) above, he must show that the statement of the cash price was in a document other than the agreement itself. It is not sufficient for the cash price to be shown in the agreement alone except where the hirer has seen the cash price on a price label or in a catalogue or advertisement.

(*iii*) Section 6(1)(*a*) requires that the written statement of the cash price be made by the owner (or seller). The statement will normally be made by the dealer as agent for the owner or seller. The dealer's statement would clearly fall within *s.* 16(1) as a representation "with respect to the goods" made "in the course of any antecedent negotiations."

3. Written agreement. Section 5 (1) (a) provides that the agreement is unenforceable by the owner (or seller) unless it is signed by the hirer (or buyer), and by or on behalf of all other parties. Thus, although the Act nowhere expressly requires that the agreement must be in writing, *s.* 5 (1) (a) gives rise to an inescapable implication that writing is required.

4. Contents of the agreement. Section 7 provides that the agreement must contain the following:

(*a*) A statement of the hire-purchase price (or total purchase price), the cash price, the amount of each instalment, and the date, or the mode of determining the date on which each instalment is payable.

(*b*) A list of the goods sufficient to identify them.

(*c*) A notice, which is at least as prominent as the rest of the agreement, in the terms set out in Schedule 1 (or Schedule 2) to the Act explaining the right of the hirer (or buyer) to terminate the agreement and the restrictions on the hirer's (or buyer's) right to recover the goods. (*See* Appendix III.)

5. Legibility of documents. Section 7 (1) (d) requires that the agreement complies with Regulations made by the Board of Trade under the power conferred by *s.* 32 to secure easy legibility.

In pursuance of this power, the Board has made the *Hire-Purchase* (*Documents*) (*Legibility and Statutory Statements*) *Regulations,* 1965, Part I, which provides broadly as follows:

(*a*) The paper must be white and the lettering must be black or dark grey.

(*b*) The lettering must be clear.

(*c*) Only certain specified parts of the document, *e.g.* personal particulars and particulars of goods, may be in handwriting.

(*d*) The lettering must be roman or upright sanserif of a size not less than a specified minimum.

The Regulations are set out in full in Appendix IV.

6. Hirer's signature box. Section 7 (1) (c) requires that the agreement complies with Regulations made by the Board of Trade under the power conferred by *s.* 7 (2) concerning the placing of the signature of the hirer (or buyer) so as to secure that any specified words come to his attention. In pursuance of this power, the Board has made the *Hire-Purchase* (*Documents*) (*Legibility and Statutory Statements*) *Regulations*, 1965, Part II, which provides that the signature of the hirer (or buyer) must be inserted in a red "box" in which are words in red print warning him to sign only if he wishes to be legally bound by the hire-purchase (or conditional sale) agreement. The requirements are set out in full in Appendix IV.

7. Requirements as to copies. The Act contains complicated requirements as to the delivery of copies of the agreement by the owner (or seller) to the hirer (or buyer). The requirements vary according to whether or not the hirer (or buyer) signed the agreement at "appropriate trade premises." Each case must be considered separately.

By *s.* 58 (1), "appropriate trade premises" are either:

(*a*) premises at which the owner (or seller) normally carries on a business; or

(*b*) premises at which goods of a description to which the agreement relates are normally offered or exposed for sale in the course of business.

So far as hire-purchase agreements are concerned, the finance company's office and the dealer's shop are both "appropriate trade premises."

8. Signature at trade premises. The requirements as to delivery of copies where the hirer (or buyer) signs the agreement at appropriate trade premises are set out in *s.* 8. There are two possibilities to consider:

(*a*) *Where the contract is made immediately after the hirer's (or buyer's) signature is put on the document: s.* 8 (2). This will happen either:

(*i*) where the agreement is signed by or on behalf of the owner (or seller) immediately after it is signed by the hirer (or buyer); or

(*ii*) where the signature of the owner (or seller) or his agent is already on the agreement when the hirer (or buyer) signs it.

(*b*) *Where the contract is not made immediately after the hirer's (or buyer's) signature is put on the document: s.* 8 (3). This will happen either:

(*i*) if the agreement was presented, and not sent, to the hirer (or buyer) for signature, and immediately after he signed it there was delivered to him a copy of the agreement in the form in which it then was; or

(*ii*) if the agreement was sent to the hirer (or buyer) for signature.

Where the case is as in (*a*) above, and the hirer (or buyer) is given a copy of the agreement immediately it has been signed by himself and by, or on behalf of, the owner (or seller), the requirements of *s*. 8 are satisfied. The contract is complete and the hirer (or buyer) has his copy. There would be no good purpose served by giving him a second copy. The position is different, however, when the case is as in (*b*) above, and *s*. 8 requires that the hirer (or buyer) be given a copy of the agreement in the form it takes when he signs it, and, *in addition*, a copy of the agreement in the form it takes when it is signed by, or on behalf of, the owner (or seller). The second copy must be delivered or sent to the hirer (or buyer) within seven days of making the agreement. The hirer (or buyer) is thus protected from any possibility that the document might be altered during the time elapsing between his own signature and the signature by, or on behalf of, the owner (or seller).

9. Signature elsewhere. The requirements as to delivery of copies where the hirer (or buyer) signs the agreement elsewhere than at appropriate trade premises are set out in *s*. 9, which provides that two copies must be supplied to the hirer (or buyer) as follows:

(*a*) *The "first statutory copy."* There are two possibilities to consider:

(*i*) If the agreement is presented, and not sent, to the hirer (or buyer) for signature, a copy in the form in which it then is must be delivered to him immediately after he signs it.

(*ii*) If the agreement is sent to the hirer (or buyer) for signature, a copy of the agreement in the form in which it then is must be sent to him at the same time: *s*. 9(2).

(*b*) *The "second statutory copy."* Within seven days of the making of the agreement another copy of the agreement known as the "second statutory copy" must be sent by post to the hirer (or buyer).

10. Notice of right of cancellation. Section 9 (4) requires compliance with any Regulations made by the Board of Trade under the power conferred by that sub-section. In pursuance of this power, the Board has made the *Hire-Purchase (Documents) (Legibility and Statutory Statements) Regulations,* 1965, Part III, which provides that the first statutory copy and the second statutory copy must each contain a notice in red letters, in prescribed boxed form, explaining to the hirer (or buyer) that he has a legal right to cancel the agreement and to recover any money paid. The full text of the notices is to be found in Appendix IV.

The right of cancellation after a "cooling-off period" was introduced in the 1965 Act following the recommendation of the Molony Committee. Its purpose is to protect the hirer (or buyer) against the high-pressure techniques of door-to-door salesmen.

NON-COMPLIANCE WITH REQUIREMENTS

11. Owner's right to enforce. By *s*. 5 (1), the owner (or seller) is not entitled to enforce the agreement unless:

(*a*) the agreement is signed by the hirer (or buyer) and by or on behalf of all other parties to the agreement; and

(*b*) the requirements of *s*. 6 (cash price) and *s*. 7 (contents and form), and the requirements of *s*. 8 (copies) or, as the case may be, *s*. 9 (copies), are complied with.

12. Owner's loss of rights. Where the owner (or seller) becomes disentitled to enforce the agreement because of his non-compliance with any of *ss*. 5, 6, 7, 8 or 9, he becomes subject to the following disabilities by virtue of *s*. 5 (2):

(*a*) He is not entitled to enforce any contract of guarantee relating to the agreement.

(*b*) He is not entitled to enforce any right to recover the goods from the hirer (or buyer).

Where the owner loses his right to recover the goods, the result will be that the hirer may become entitled to enjoy indefinite possession of goods for which he has not paid. Section 5 (2) provides him with a defence against the owner's action for convertion or detinue. But the hirer will lose this protection if he parts with possession of the goods to a third party: *see*

Eastern Distributors Ltd. v. *Goldring* (1957). Clearly, the rigid application of *s.* 5 (2) could lead to a grossly unfair result against the interest of the owner (or seller) in circumstances in which the hirer does not stand in need of any protection. It is for this reason that *s.* 10 endows the court with powers to dispense with certain requirements of the Act (*see* **14** below).

13. Unenforceable securities. By *s.* 5 (2) (b), where the owner (or seller) becomes disentitled to enforce the agreement, any security:

(*a*) given by the hirer (or buyer) in respect of money payable under the agreement, or

(*b*) given by a guarantor in respect of money payable under a contract of guarantee relating to the agreement,

ceases to be enforceable.

14. Court's powers under s. 10. If in any action the court is satisfied that a failure to comply with any of the requirements specified in *ss.* 6–9 has not prejudiced the hirer (or buyer), and that it would be just and equitable to dispense with the requirement, the court may, subject to any conditions that it thinks fit to impose, dispense with that requirement for the purposes of the action: *s.* 10 (1). But, by *s.* 10 (2) and (3), the court's power is not exercisable:

(*a*) in relation to the requirement of sending the second statutory copy (*s.* 9 (3)) except where it has been sent to the hirer (or buyer) but not within the period of seven days of the making of the agreement; and

(*b*) in relation to the requirement in *s.* 9 (4) that the first statutory copy and the second statutory copy must contain the notice of the right of cancellation.

The effect of this section is to protect the owner (or seller) and any security holder from the effects of a mistake or oversight leading to a failure to comply with any of *ss.* 6–9, but which does not cause loss, harm or unfairness to the hirer (or buyer).

PROGRESS TEST 13

1. State where the law governing the formalities required for hire-purchase agreements is to be found. Are the requirements

in the case of conditional sale agreements the same as those for hire-purchase agreements? **(1)**

2. What are the requirements as to the price of goods? **(2)**

3. Must a hire-purchase agreement be in writing? **(3)**

4. What statutory provision governs the requirements as to contents of a conditional sale agreement? **(4)**

5. Is the hirer made aware of any warning at the time he signs the hire-purchase agreement? **(6)**

6. What are appropriate trade premises? **(7)**

7. What are the requirements as to delivery of copies where the agreement is signed (*a*) at appropriate trade premises, and (*b*) elsewhere? **(7, 8, 9)**

8. How is the buyer under a conditional sale agreement protected against high-pressure door-to-door salesmen? **(10)**

9. Give a careful account of the position where the statutory requirements are not complied with. **(11, 12, 13)**

10. In what circumstances may the court dispense with the formal requirements? **(14)**

CHAPTER XIV

CANCELLATION: HIRE-PURCHASE AND CONDITIONAL SALE AGREEMENTS

1. The hirer's right. By *s.* 11 of the 1965 Act, the right of cancellation arises when the agreement is signed at any place elsewhere than appropriate trade premises. The purpose is to give protection against high-pressure door-to-door salesmen who induce people to sign agreements in their own homes. It should be noticed that the right of cancellation arises in *all* cases where the hirer (or buyer) signs the agreement elsewhere than in trade premises. The right would arise, for example, where the dealer gives the agreement form to a customer who then takes it home, signs it and then takes it back to the dealer.

2. Notice of the right. The first statutory copy and the second statutory copy must each contain a notice of the right of cancellation (*see* XIII, **10**). The notice, which must conform to the Regulations (S.1. 1965/1646) as to size and style, is headed: "NOTICE TO CUSTOMER: RIGHT OF CANCELLATION." The text of the notice in the first statutory copy is as follows:

"You have for a short time a legal right to cancel this agreement. You can do this by writing, saying that you are cancelling the agreement, to . . .

If you do cancel this agreement, any money you have already paid must be returned to you. If you have given any property in part exchange, the property—or its value—must also be returned to you. If you have got the goods, you need take no action to return them but can wait for them to be collected. You need not hand them over unless you have received a written request to do so and have had your money and property back. If you wish, however, you may yourself take or send the goods to the person named above."

The notice in the second statutory copy must be in identical form with the addition of the following sentence: "You must post your letter (concerning the agreement) before the end of the third day on which you receive this copy of the agreement." (*See* Appendix IV.)

3. Service of notice of cancellation.   In any case where the validity of notice of cancellation is in dispute, any of the following matters may be relevant:

(*a*) *Form.*   The Act and the Regulations (S.I. 1965/1646) envisage that a customer wishing to avail himself of the right to cancel will serve notice in writing. (It is doubtful whether oral notice would be effective.)   A notice of cancellation is effective, no matter how expressed, provided it indicates the intention to withdraw from the transaction: *s.* 11 (3).

(*b*) *Postal service.*   Notice of cancellation is deemed to be served on the owner (or seller) if it is sent by post to the person specified in either the first statutory copy or the second statutory copy.   Service takes place when the notice is posted.

(*c*) *Time limit.*   The prospective hirer (or buyer) may serve notice of cancellation at any time after he has signed the agreement and before the end of the period of four days beginning with the day on which he receives the second statutory copy: *s.* 11 (2).

(*d*) *To whom addressed.*   By *s.* 11 (2), the notice of cancellation must be served on either (*i*) the owner (or seller) or (*ii*) any person who is the agent of the owner (or seller) for the purpose of receiving the notice. The effect of *s.* 12 (3) is that the dealer will always be deemed to be the agent of the owner (or seller) for the purpose of receiving a notice of cancellation.

4. Legal position after cancellation.   The immediate effect of the service of a valid notice of cancellation on the relationship between the hirer (or buyer) and the owner (or seller) depends upon whether or not the contract was made by the time of cancellation.   By *s.* 11 (4):

(*a*) if, at the time when the notice is served, the agreement is made, the service of notice operates to rescind the agreement; and

(*b*) in any other case, the service of notice operates as a withdrawal of any offer to enter into an agreement.

5. Effect of rescission. Where a notice of cancellation operates so as to rescind an agreement, then by *s.* 14 (1):

(*a*) that agreement, and any contract of guarantee relating thereto, is deemed never to have had effect; and

(*b*) any security given by the prospective hirer (or buyer) in respect of money payable under the agreement, or given by a guarantor in respect of money payable under such a contract of guarantee, shall be deemed never to have been enforceable.

6. Recovery of money and goods. The effect of cancellation on goods delivered to the hirer (or buyer), on money paid by the hirer (or buyer) and on goods given by the hirer (or buyer)in part exchange, is set out in *ss.* 13, 14 and 15.

(*a*) *Re-delivery of goods.* After cancellation, the "prospective hirer" (or buyer) is under no obligation to deliver the goods except at his own premises and upon a written request signed by the dealer or the owner (or seller): *s.* 13 (2). If the "prospective hirer" (or buyer) delivers the goods to an authorised person or sends them at his own expense to an authorised person he shall be taken to have done so with that person's consent and be discharged accordingly.

(*b*) *Care of the goods.* The "prospective hirer" (or buyer) is under an obligation to take reasonable care of the goods until the end of the period of twenty-one days beginning with the date of service of the notice of cancellation: *s.* 13 (4). But the obligation ceases when the goods are re-delivered: *s.* 13 (5). Any breach by the hirer (or buyer) of his obligation to take reasonable care of the goods is actionable as a breach of statutory duty: *s.* 13 (7).

(*c*) *Hirer's lien.* The prospective hirer's (or buyer's) obligation to deliver the goods to the person entitled to possession (*s.* 13 (2)) is subject to any lien which he may have under *s.* 14 (2) in respect of money paid as part of the hire-purchase price (or total purchase price).

(*d*) *Recovery of money.* Any sum which has been paid by the prospective hirer (or buyer) in respect of the goods to which the agreement related and is comprised in the hire-purchase price (or total purchase price) is recoverable from the person to whom it has been paid: *s.* 14 (2). Until repayment, the prospective hirer (or buyer) may exercise his right of lien.

(e) *Goods given in part-exchange.* Unless goods given in part-exchange are returned by the dealer to the prospective hirer (or buyer) before the end of the period of ten days beginning with the date of service of notice of cancellation, and in substantially as good a condition as when they were delivered to the dealer, the prospective hirer (or buyer) is entitled to recover from the dealer a sum equal to the agreed part-exchange allowance: s. 15 (2). If no sum was agreed, then a reasonable sum is taken to be allowed: s. 15 (6) (b). Where the prospective hirer (or buyer) recovers from the dealer the sum allowed, title vests in the dealer if it has not already done so: s. 15 (5).

PROGRESS TEST 14

1. In what circumstances does the right of cancellation arise? (1)

2. What notice must be contained in the first statutory copy and the second statutory copy? (2)

3. Mention some ways in which the service of notice of cancellation may not be valid. (3)

4. Give a careful account of the legal effect of cancellation. (4, 5, 6)

CHAPTER XV

IMPLIED TERMS IN HIRE-PURCHASE AND CONDITIONAL SALE AGREEMENTS

1. Introductory. The 1965 Act provides for the implication of the following terms:

(*a*) That the hirer (or buyer) shall have good title and quiet possession.

(*b*) That the goods are of merchantable quality.

(*c*) That the goods are fit for their prupose.

(*d*) That the goods correspond with their contract description.

(*e*) Where goods are let or agreed to be sold by reference to a sample:

(*i*) that the bulk will correspond with the sample in quality; and

(*ii*) that the hirer (or buyer) will have a reasonable opportunity of comparing the bulk with the sample.

These implied terms are broadly similar to those implied by virtue of *ss.* 12–15 of the *Sale of Goods Act*, 1893. There is, however, a very important difference between the terms implied under that Act and the terms implied under the *Hire-Purchase Act*, 1965, namely that, whereas the implied terms may be excluded in the case of the Sale of Goods Act, they cannot be freely excluded in the case of those arising under the Act of 1965. The implied terms and the governing rules as to exclusionary clauses should be considered separately. By *s.* 20 (3) of the 1965 Act, a conditional sale agreement is not to be treated as a contract of sale for the purposes of *ss.* 12–15 of the *Sale of Goods Act*, 1893.

2. Title and quiet possession. By *s.* 17 (1), in every hire-purchase agreement and in every conditional sale agreement, there is implied:

(*a*) a condition on the part of the owner (or seller) that he will have a right to sell the goods at the time when property is to pass;

(*b*) a warranty that the hirer (or buyer) will have and enjoy quiet possession of the goods; and

(*c*) a warranty that the goods shall be free from any charge or encumbrance in favour of any third party at the time when the property is to pass.

The condition and the warranties specified in *s*. 17 (1) cannot be excluded and will be implied notwithstanding any agreement to the contrary: *s*. 18 (3).

3. Merchantable quality.   In every hire-purchase agreement and every conditional sale agreement there is implied a condition that the goods will be of merchantable quality: *s*. 17 (2). But this is a general rule subject to certain exceptions:

(*a*) Where the hirer (or buyer) has examined the goods, or a sample of them, the condition will not be implied in respect of defects which the examination ought to have revealed: *s*. 17 (3).

(*b*) Where the goods are second-hand and the agreement contains a statement to that effect (*i.e.* an exclusionary clause) which was brought to the attention of the hirer (or buyer) and its effect made clear to him, the condition may be excluded: *s*. 18 (1).

(*c*) Where defects are specified in the agreement and before the contract was made, those defects were brought to the notice of the hirer (or buyer) and an exclusionary clause specifying the defects and its effect was made clear to him, the condition will not be implied in respect to those defects: *s*. 18 (2).

4. Fitness for purpose.   Where the hirer (or buyer), whether expressly or by implication:

(*a*) has made known to the owner or seller, or to a servant or agent of the owner or seller, the particular purpose for which the goods are required, or

(*b*) in the course of any antecedent negotiations has made that purpose known to any other person by whom those negotiations were conducted, or to a servant or agent of such a person,

there is implied a condition that the goods will be reasonably fit for the purpose: *s*. 17 (4).   This implied condition may be excluded by an exclusionary clause, but the owner (or seller) may not rely on such a clause unless he proves that, before the agreement was made, the clause was brought to the attention of the hirer (or buyer) and its effect made clear to him: *s.* 18 (4); *see Lowe* v. *Lombank Ltd.* (1960), C.A.

5. Correspondence with description. Where goods are let (or agreed to be sold) by description, there is implied in the agreement a condition that the goods will correspond with the description: *s.* 19 (2). Any provision which purports to exclude or modify this condition is void: *s.* 29 (3).

6. Sample. Where goods are let (or agreed to be sold) by reference to a sample, there is implied in the agreement:

(*a*) a condition that the bulk will correspond with the sample in quality; and

(*a*) a condition that the hirer (or buyer) will have a reasonable opportunity of comparing the bulk with the sample: *s.* 19 (1).

Where the goods are let (or agreed to be sold) by sample and by description as well, the goods must correspond with the description as also with the sample. It is not sufficient if the bulk of the goods corresponds with the sample if the goods do not also correspond with the description: *s.* 19 (2).

Any provision in an agreement which purports to exclude or modify these conditions is void: *s.* 29 (3).

7. Other implied terms. Nothing in *ss.* 17 and 18 will prejudice the operation of any term implied at common law or by virtue of any other statute: *s.* 17 (5). There is, for example, an implied term at common law in any hire-purchase that the owner is capable of giving good title to the hirer at any time he might decide to exercise his option to purchase: *Karflex* v. *Poole* (1933). In practice, the standard-form agreements used for hire-purchase and conditional sale almost invariably exclude all implied terms apart from those which the 1965 Act insists upon.

PROGRESS TEST 15

1. List the terms implied by virtue of the 1965 Act. (**1**)

2. Are conditional sale agreements governed by *ss.* 12–15 of the *Sale of Goods Act,* 1893? (**1**)

E

3. Explain carefully the exceptions to the condition of merchantable quality in hire-purchase agreements. **(3)**

4. Are conversations between dealer and hirer of any possible relevance in deciding whether there is an implied term as to fitness for a particular purpose? **(4)**

5. What conditions are implied where there is a conditional sale agreement for goods to be sold by reference to a sample? **(6)**

6. Does anything in the 1965 Act prejudice the operation of implied terms at common law? **(7)**

7. Give a detailed account of the limitations on the owner's right to contract out of the implied terms. **(2, 3, 4, 5, 6)**

8. Do you think that the law of sale of goods should be reformed so as to give all buyers the same advantages as the 1965 Act gives buyers under conditional sale agreements? *(See X)*

CHAPTER XVI

TERMINATION AND REPOSSESSION: HIRE-PURCHASE AND CONDITIONAL SALE AGREEMENTS

TERMINATION BY HIRER

1. Right to terminate. By *s.* 27 (1), the hirer (or buyer) has a right to terminate the agreement by giving notice of termination in writing to any person entitled or authorised to receive the sums payable under the agreement. This provision does not prejudice any other right which the hirer (or buyer) might have to terminate the agreement, *e.g.* by virtue of a term in the agreement: *s.* 27 (4).

In the case of a conditional sale agreement, where the property in the goods, having become vested in the buyer, is transferred to a person who does not become the buyer under the agreement, the buyer is not thereafter entitled to terminate the agreement under *s.* 27. And, subject to this last provision, where a buyer terminates the agreement under *s.* 27 after property in the goods has vested in him, the property will thereupon vest in the previous owner: *s.* 27 (2) and (3).

A hirer (or buyer) may give notice of termination under *s.* 27 at any time before the final payment falls due: *s.* 27 (1).

2. Hirer's financial obligations. Where a hirer (or buyer) terminates the agreement under *s.* 27, he remains liable for outstanding contractual obligations, *e.g.* unpaid instalments due before the date of termination. In addition, by *s.* 28 (1), he is liable:

(a) *in the case of a hire-purchase agreement*, to pay the amount, if any, by which one half of the hire-purchase price exceeds the total of the sums paid and the sums due in respect of the hire-purchase price immediately before the termination; or

(b) *in the case of a conditional sale agreement*, to pay the amount (if any) by which one half of the total purchase price exceeds the total of the sums paid and the sums due in respect of the total purchase price immediately before the termination;

or, if (in either case) the agreement specifies a lesser amount, the hirer (or buyer) is liable to pay that lesser amount: *s*. 28 (1).

Where in any action the court is satisfied that a sum less than the amount specified in (*a*) and (*b*) above (as the case may be) would be equal to the loss sustained by the owner (or seller) in consequence of the termination of the agreement, the court may make an order for the payment of that lesser sum in lieu of the amount specified: *s*. 28 (2).

Any provision purporting to add to the hirer's (or buyer's) obligations under *s*. 28 is void: *s*. 29 (2).

3. Possession and care of goods. Section 28 makes the following further provisions:

(*a*) *Possession*. Where a hirer (or buyer) having terminated an agreement under *s*. 27, wrongfully retains possession of the goods, then, in any action brought to recover possession, the court, unless it is satisfied that having regard to the circumstances it would not be just and equitable to do so, must order the goods to be delivered to the owner (or seller) without giving the hirer (or buyer) an option to pay the value of the goods.

(*b*) *Care of goods*. Where an agreement has been terminated under *s*. 27, the hirer (or buyer) is liable to pay damages if he has failed to take care of the goods.

Any provision purporting to add to the hirer's (or buyer's) obligations under *s*. 28 is void: *s*. 29 (2).

TERMINATION BY OWNER

4. Right to terminate. The Act does not give to the owner (or seller) an express right to terminate the agreement in any particular circumstances; nor does the Act attempt to control or restrict any other right to terminate which the owner (or seller) may have. Most standard-form agreements provide explicitly that the owner (or seller) should be entitled to terminate in specified circumstances. The agreement may, for example, provide that the owner (or seller) may terminate if the hirer (or buyer) fails to insure the goods, fails to keep them in a good state of repair, commits an act of bankruptcy or dies. In none of these cases does the Act interfere. The position is determined by the terms of the agreement. But where the owner (or seller) terminates the agreement by virtue of clause enabling him to do so on default in payment by the hirer (or buyer), the provisions of *s.* 25 operate to give protection to the defaulting hirer (or buyer). With regard to the owner's (or seller's) right to terminate by virtue of a clause in the agreement, a clear distinction must therefore be drawn between termination on the grounds of default in payment and termination on other grounds.

5. Defaults in payment. By *s.* 25, the owner (or seller) may not terminate the agreement unless he serves on the hirer (or buyer) a *notice of default* stating the amount which has become due, but remains unpaid. The notice of default must require this stated amount to be paid within a specified period which must not be less than seven days beginning with the date of service of the notice. The owner (or seller) may then terminate the agreement if the amount remains unpaid. If he so wishes, the owner (or seller) may include in the notice of default a conditional notice of termination to take effect at the end of the seven-day period if the amount due remains unpaid.

RECOVERY OF POSSESSION

6. Owner's right to possess. At common law the owner's (or seller's) right to recover possession of the goods rests on the contract and, in any event, could arise only after termination. In the case of hire-purchase agreements the owner's common law right to re-possess may be founded on the termination of a bailment where the hirer deals with the goods in a manner inconsistent with the bailment: *Jelks* v. *Hayward* (1905); *North Central Wagon and Finance Co. Ltd.* v. *Graham* (1950). Where the owner has vested in him the bailor's right to repossession he immediately is in a position to bring an action for detinue against any third party into whose hands the goods may have come. He may also sue the defaulting hirer for conversion, quite apart from any claim he may have for breach of contract. This is a useful remedy where, for some reason, *e.g.* illegality, it is not possible to maintain an action for breach of contract: *see Bowmakers Ltd.* v. *Barnet Instruments Ltd.* (1945).

Where the agreement is governed by the 1965 Act, the owner's (or seller's) right to recover possession of the goods is restricted in the case of "protected goods" as defined in *s.* 33.

7. Protected goods. By *s.* 33, goods are "protected goods" if:

(*a*) one-third of the hire-purchase price (or total purchase price) has been paid or tendered; and

(*b*) the hirer (or buyer) has not terminated the agreement or the bailment.

Evasion by the owner (or seller) of the restriction on recovery of possession of protected goods by the device of making a new agreement after one-third of the hire-purchase price (or total purchase price) has been paid is prevented by *s.* 47. This section provides, in effect, that in such cases the goods are protected goods, regardless of the proportion paid, provided that the hirer (or buyer) has not terminated the agreement or the bailment. This rule is applicable where the subsequent agreement relates to the whole or any part of the original goods, with or without other goods. Thus there can be no evasion by the additional device of adding to the goods under the previous agreement, or leaving something out.

8. Restriction on recovery. By *s.* 34, the owner (or seller) may not enforce any right to recover possession of protected goods otherwise than by action. That is to say, he cannot exercise any contractual or "self-help" right to recover possession of protected goods.

Where the owner (or seller) recovers possession in contravention of this provision, the agreement is terminated, and:

(*a*) the hirer (or buyer) is released from all liability under the agreement and becomes entitled to recover all money paid under it; and

(*b*) any guarantor becomes entitled to recover from the owner (or seller) all sums paid by him.

NOTE

(*i*) This provision (*ss.* 33 and 34) replaces *s.* 11 of the 1938 Act.

(*ii*) The words "enforce any right to recover possession" imply some active step being taken and are not apt to describe the passive conduct of one who merely accepts the delivery of goods surrendered by consent: *Mercantile Credit Co. Ltd.* v. *Cross* (1965).

(*iii*) Where the owner, finding the protected goods abandoned by the hirer, took them into "protective custody," it was held that there was a contravention of *s.* 11 of the 1938 Act and the owner could not recover the unpaid balance: *United Dominions Trust (Commercial) Ltd.* v. *Kesler* (1963).

(*iv*) Where the owner returned the goods to the hirer after recovering them in contravention of *s.* 11 of the 1938 Act, and the hirer made further use of the goods, it was held that the agreement had determined and was not revived by the subsequent conduct of the parties: *Capital Finance Co. Ltd.* v. *Bray* (1964).

ACTION BY OWNER (OR SELLER) FOR POSSESSION

9. Parties. All parties to the agreement and any guarantor must be made parties to the action: *s.* 35 (2).

10. Protection of the goods. Pending the hearing of the action the court has power, on the application of the owner (or seller), to make such orders as it thinks just for the purpose of protecting the goods from damage or depreciation, including orders restricting or prohibiting the use of the goods or giving directions as to their custody: *ss.* 35 (3) and 45.

11. Court's powers on the hearing. On the hearing of an action by the owner (or seller) for the recovery of the goods from the hirer (or buyer), by *ss.* 35 (4) and 45, the court may:

(*a*) make an order for the specific delivery of all the goods to the owner; or

(*b*) make an order for the specific delivery of all the goods to the owner (or seller) and postpone the operation of the order on condition that the hirer (or buyer) or any guarantor pays the unpaid balance of the hire-purchase price (or total purchase price) at such times and in such amounts as the court thinks just; or

(*c*) make an order for the specific delivery of a part of the goods to the owner (or seller) and for the transfer of title to the remainder to the hirer (or buyer).

12. Postponed order. A postponed order for the return of goods to the owner (or seller) will not be made unless the hirer satisfies the court that the goods are in his possession or control: *ss.* 36 (1) and 45. By *ss.* 38 (2) and 45 no further sum becomes payable by the hirer (or buyer) except in accordance with the terms of the order. And, further, the court may modify any of the terms of the agreement as may be necessary, having regard to the variation of the terms of payment.

13. General effect of postponed order. The effect of a postponed order for the specific delivery of goods varies according to whether it is addressed to a hirer or a buyer:

(*a*) While the operation of an order for the specific delivery of goods to the owner is postponed, *the hirer is deemed to be a bailee of the goods under and on the terms of the agreement: s.* 38 (1).

(*b*) While the operation of an order for the specific delivery of goods to the seller is postponed, *the buyer is deemed to be in possession of the goods under and on the terms of the agreement*, other than any term providing for the property in the goods to vest in the buyer at any time before the payment of the whole of the total purchase price: *s.* 45 (3).

14. Non-compliance with postponed order. If the hirer (or buyer) fails to comply with any condition of postponement, or with any term of the agreement as varied by the court, or wrongfully disposes of the goods, the owner (or seller) must not take proceedings against the hirer (or buyer) otherwise than by making an application to the court which made the order. Provided that, in the case of a breach relating to payment of the unpaid balance, it is not necessary for the owner (or seller) to apply to the court for leave to execute the order unless the court has so directed: *ss.* 38 (4) and 45.

PROGRESS TEST 16

1. How may the buyer under a conditional sale agreement exercise his right to terminate the agreement? Mention any statutory limitation on this right. **(1)**

2. Where the right to terminate has been exercised, what are the financial obligations of (*a*) the hirer and (*b*) the buyer (under a conditional sale agreement)? **(2)**

3. What provisions are made to cover the case where an agreement has been terminated and either (*a*) the hirer refuses to return the goods to the owner, or (*b*) the hirer has failed to take proper care of the goods before returning them? (**3**)

4. Does the 1965 Act give the seller under a conditional sale agreement an express right to terminate the agreement? (**4**)

5. Would you expect to find express terms in a standard-form hire-purchase agreement giving the owner the right to terminate in any circumstances? (**4**)

6. Where there is an express term in a conditional sale agreement providing that the seller may terminate on the grounds of default in payment on the part of the buyer, does the Act give any protection to the defaulting buyer? (**4, 5**)

7. What are "protected goods"? (**7**)

8. What is the position where the owner recovers possession of goods from the hirer in contravention of the provision in *s.* 34 of the 1965 Act? (**8**)

9. Where the seller under a conditional sale agreement brings an action for possession of the goods, what are the powers of the court (*a*) pending the hearing, and (*b*) on the hearing? (**11**)

10. What is a postponed order? In what circumstances will it be made? What is its general effect? (**13**)

11. What is the effect of non-compliance with a postponed order? (**14**)

CHAPTER XVII

MISCELLANEOUS PROVISIONS: HIRE-PURCHASE AND CONDITIONAL SALES AGREEMENTS

1. Scope of chapter. This chapter deals briefly with the most important of the remaining statutory provisions, namely, the position of the dealer, void terms, the obligation to give information and the special provisions governing motor vehicles.

POSITION OF THE DEALER

2. Dealer as agent. By *s.* 16 (1), where the owner (or seller) lets, sells or agrees to sell, goods, any representations with respect to the goods which were made to the hirer (or buyer) by a person other than the owner (or seller) in the course of any antecedent negotiations conducted by that other person are deemed to have been made by him as agent of the owner (or seller). In other words, if the dealer makes any statement about the goods, that statement is deemed to be made by the dealer as agent for the owner (or seller). This provision does not operate to excuse any person from liability: *s.* 16 (2). The expressions "representation" and "antecedent negotiations" bear the following meanings respectively:

(*a*) "*Representations*" includes any statement or undertaking whether constituting a condition or a warranty or not: *s.* 16 (4). "Representations," for the purposes of the Act, includes statements which are, and statements which are not, terms of the contract. The word covers statements for which there may be a liability in damages under the *Misrepresentation Act*, 1967, and also statements for which there may be liability for breach of contract.

(*b*) "*Antecedent negotiations*" means any negotiations or arrangements with the buyer (or hirer) whereby he was induced to make the agreement or which otherwise promoted the transaction to which the agreement relates: *s.* 16 (3).

3. Owner's liability. The effect of *s.* 16 is that the owner (or seller) is liable in damages under *s.* 2 of the *Misrepresentation Act*, 1967, or for breach of contract, as the case may be, where the dealer makes a false statement concerning the goods. Liability is, of course, to the hirer (or buyer), who can sue the finance company direct, as the principal of the dealer. This is a "deeming" provision and it is, therefore, no defence to show that no agency in fact existed, *e.g.* by a term to that effect in the agreement. The finance company is liable as if it were the principal and the dealer the agent. Any attempt to contract out of this provision is void: *s.* 29 (3) (b).

4. Agency for receiving notices. The dealer is deemed to be the agent of the owner (or seller) for the purpose of receiving notices as follows:

(a) *Notice of withdrawal.* Where a prospective hirer (or buyer) wishes to withdraw his offer to enter the agreement before that offer is accepted, the dealer is deemed to be the agent of the owner (or seller) for the purpose of receiving notice that the offer is withdrawn: *s.* 31 (1). It should be noticed that this provision has nothing to do with the statutory right of cancellation: it is concerned with the offeror's common law right to withdraw his offer at any time before acceptance has taken place.

(b) *Notice of rescission.* Where the hirer (or buyer) claims to have a right to rescind the agreement, the dealer is deemed to be the agent of the owner (or seller) for the purpose of receiving any notice rescinding the agreement: *s.* 31 (2).

(c) *Notice of cancellation.* Where a prospective hirer (or buyer) serves notice of cancellation under *s.* 11 (cooling-off period in cases where the agreement was signed otherwise than at appropriate trade premises) the dealer is deemed to be the agent of the owner (or seller) for the purpose of receiving the notice of cancellation: *s.* 12 (3).

AVOIDANCE OF TERMS

5. Void contracts. Any contract oral or in writing which purports to take effect as a contract to enter into a hire-purchase or conditional sale agreement (as distinct from a contract constituting such an agreement) is void: *s.* 29 (4).

6. Void terms. By *s.* 29, any of the following terms are void:

(*a*) A provision whereby an owner (or seller) or his agent is authorised to enter upon any premises for the purpose of taking possession of goods which have been let or agreed to be sold, or is relieved from liability for any such entry: *s.* 29 (2) (a).

(*b*) A provision whereby the right conferred by *s.* 27 to terminate an agreement is excluded or restricted: *s.* 29 (2) (b).

(*c*) A provision whereby any liability, in addition to the liability imposed by *s.* 28, is imposed on a hirer (or buyer) by reason of the termination of an agreement under *s.* 27: *s.* 29 (2) (b).

(*d*) A provision whereby a hirer (or buyer), after the termination in any manner whatsoever of an agreement is (apart from any liability which has accrued before the termination) subject to a liability to pay an amount which exceeds whichever is the lesser of the two following amounts:

(*i*) The amount needed to bring the total payments up to half the hire-purchase price (or total purchase price).

(*ii*) An amount equal to the loss sustained by the owner (or seller) in consequence of the termination of the agreement: *s.* 29(2)(c). The position is the same where, in the case of hire-purchase, a bailment, as distinct from an agreement, is terminated: *s.* 29(2)(c).

(*e*) A provision whereby any person acting on behalf of an owner (or seller) in connection with the formation of an agreement is deemed to be the agent of the hirer (or buyer): *s.* 29 (2) (d).

(*f*) A provision whereby an owner (or seller) is relieved from liability for the acts or defaults of his agent in connection with the formation or conclusion of an agreement: *s.* 29 (2) (e).

(*g*) A provision excluding or modifying any condition implied by virtue of *s.* 19 (sample or description): *s.* 29 (3) (c).

INFORMATION

7. Owner's duty to hirer. By *s.* 21 (1), at any time before the final payment has been made, the owner (or seller) must, within four days of receiving a written request from the hirer (or buyer) and the sum of 2*s.* 6*d.* (£12½p) for expenses, supply a copy of the agreement, together with a statement signed by the owner (or seller), or his agent showing:

(*a*) the amount already paid;

(*b*) the amount due but unpaid, and the date on which each unpaid instalment became due, and the amount of each unpaid instalment;

(*c*) the amount of each future instalment, the dates on which each becomes payable and the total amount to become payable.

8. Non-compliance by owner. By *s*. 21 (2), where the owner (or seller) fails to comply with the requirement to supply information under *s*. 21 (1) without reasonable cause, then, while the default continues:

(*a*) the agreement is unenforceable against the hirer (or buyer);

(*b*) any contract of guarantee relating to the agreement is unenforceable;

(*c*) any right to recover the goods from the hirer (or buyer) is unenforceable; and

(*d*) no security given by the hirer (or buyer) or guarantor is unenforceable.

In addition, if the default continues for a period of one month, the owner (or seller) becomes liable on summary conviction to a fine not exceeding £25.

9. Owner's duty to guarantor. A guarantor is entitled by *s*. 23 to obtain a copy of the agreement and of the note or memorandum of the contract of guarantee and a signed statement showing the information specified in *s*. 21 (1). In the event of failure without reasonable cause on the part of the owner (or seller) to comply with a guarantor's request for information, the guarantee is unenforceable while the default continues.

10. Hirer's duty to owner. Where a hirer (or buyer) is under a duty to keep the goods in his possession or control, he must, on receipt of a written request, inform the owner (or seller) where the goods are: *s*. 24 (1). If a hirer (or buyer) fails without reasonable cause to give this information within fourteen days of the receipt of the notice, he will be liable on summary conviction to a fine not exceeding £25: *s.* 24 (2).

MOTOR VEHICLES

11. The Hire-Purchase Act, 1964. Part III of the Act of 1964 was not consolidated by the 1965 Act. Part III remains in force, operating to pass good title to an innocent purchaser of a motor vehicle subject to a hire-purchase or conditional sale agreement. In the case of goods other than motor vehicles, the innocent purchaser cannot acquire good title to the goods and can be compelled to return the goods to the owner (or seller). The rule *nemo dat* operates and the hirer (or buyer) is unable to give title. Part III of the 1964 Act (*s.* 29 (2)) draws a distinction between the "trade or finance purchaser" and the "private purchaser":

(*a*) A *"trade or finance purchaser"* is a purchaser who, at the time of the disposition made to him, carries on a business which consists, wholly or partly:

(*i*) of purchasing motor vehicles for the purpose of offering or exposing them for sale, or

(*ii*) of providing finance by purchasing motor vehicles for the purpose of letting them under hire-purchase agreements or agreeing to sell them under conditional sale agreements.

(*b*) A *"private purchaser"* is a purchaser who, at the time of the disposition made to him, does not carry on any such business.

12. Private purchasers. Where a disposition of a motor vehicle is made to a private purchaser, who takes in good faith and without notice of the hire-purchase (or conditional sale) agreement, that disposition takes effect as if the title of the owner (or seller) had been vested in the hirer (or buyer) immediately before that disposition: *s.* 27 (2) of the 1964 Act.

13. Trade or finance purchasers. Where a hirer (or buyer) disposes of the vehicle to a trade or finance purchaser, the *nemo dat* rule applies and property does not pass. But where such a transaction is followed by a disposition of the same vehicle to a private purchaser taking in good faith that private purchaser gets good title by virtue of *s.* 27 (3) and (4) of the 1964 Act. This provision is designed to afford the private purchaser the protection which is denied to the trade or finance purchaser even where he obtains the vehicle after there has been a series of transactions before it comes into his hands.

PROGRESS TEST 17

1. By *s.* 16 of the *Hire-Purchase Act,* 1965, where a dealer makes any statement about the goods, that statement is deemed to be made by the dealer as agent for the owner or seller, as the case may be. In what ways could the owner or seller be made liable as principal? **(2, 3)**

2. What are the three provisions by which the dealer is deemed to be the agent of the owner or seller for the purpose of receiving notices? **(4)**

3. X and Y conclude a written contract by which X agrees to enter a conditional sale agreement for the sale of his motor car in six months time. After the contract is signed by both parties, Y pays a "deposit" to X according to the agreement. Five months after the conclusion of this contract, the motor car is destroyed in a road accident. Y now threatens to sue X: (*a*) for breach of the contract to enter into a conditional sale agreement; and (*b*) for the recovery of his "deposit." Advise X.

4. List the provision which would be struck out of a hire-purchase agreement as being void. **(6)**

5. What information may the owner be bound to give to the hirer? What steps must the hirer take to obtain this information? What is the legal position where the owner improperly refuses or neglects to supply this information? **(8)**

6. Has a guarantor any rights of obtaining information? **(9)**

7. What information may the owner insist on obtaining from the hirer? **(10)**

8. In what respect do the rules governing motor vehicles differ from the rules governing other goods? **(11)**

9. Which statute contains the rules applicable only in the case of motor vehicles **(11)**

10. With respect to motor vehicles, what is a "trade or finance purchaser"? **(11)**

11. Where a disposition of a motor vehicle is made to a private purchaser, who takes in good faith and without notice of any hire-purchase agreement, that disposition takes effect as if the title of the owner had been vested in the hirer immediately before that disposition. Why should this advantage be conferred on private purchasers and not on trade purchasers?

CHAPTER XVIII

CREDIT-SALE AGREEMENTS

1. Definition. In the *Hire-Purchase Act*, 1965, a credit-sale agreement is an agreement under which the purchase price is payable by five or more instalments, and which is not a conditional sale agreement: *s.* 1 (1). A credit-sale agreement is, then, quite distinct from a hire-purchase agreement and a conditional sale agreement in that the property in the goods passes at the time of making the agreement. A credit-sale agreement, like a conditional sale agreement, is basically a sale of goods agreement and, as such is governed by the *Sale of Goods Act*, 1893. But the *Hire-Purchase Act*, 1965, which applies equally to hire-purchase and conditional sale agreements, applies to credit-sale agreements only to a limited extent.

By *s.* 2 (3) of the 1965 Act, the rules governing credit-sale agreements apply where the total purchase price exceeds £30 but does not exceed £2,000; and, by *s.* 4, the rules do not apply where the buyer is a body corporate.

2. No right to terminate. The buyer under a credit-sale agreement has no statutory right to terminate the agreement equivalent to that given by *s.* 27 to hirers and buyers under hire-purchase and conditional sale agreements respectively. It follows that the notice setting out the right to terminate the agreement which is required by *s.* 7 in the case of hire-purchase and conditional sale agreements is not required in the case of a credit-sale agreement.

3. Implied terms. The *Hire-Purchase Act* does not provide for implied terms as to title, quality, fitness for purpose or correspondence with description, in the case of credit-sale agreements. The terms implied by virtue of *ss.* 12–15 of the *Sale of Goods Act*, 1893, will apply, however, unless excluded under *s.* 55 of the 1893 Act.

4. Formalities and information. The provisions as to formalities and the right to require information apply to credit-sale agreements, except that the Act does not impose on the buyer any obligation to give information.

5. Cancellation. The provisions giving the right of cancellation in the case of agreements signed elsewhere than at appropriate trade premises apply fully to credit-sale agreements.

6. The dealer. The position of the dealer as agent for certain purposes is the same as in the case of hire-purchase agreements and conditional sale agreements.

PROGRESS TEST 18

1. Define a credit-sale agreement and show clearly how it differs from (a) a hire-purchase agreement and (b) a conditional sale agreement. **(1)**

2. Has the buyer under a credit-sale agreement a statutory right to terminate the agreement? **(2)**

3. Which statutory implied terms, if any, arise in the case of credit-sale agreements? What are the rules with regard to contracting out? **(3)**

4. In the case of credit-sale agreements, how do the statutory rules governing formalities and the supply of information compare with those obtaining in the case of hire-purchase agreements? **(2, 4)**

5. May the buyer under a credit-sale agreement have a right of cancellation in any circumstances? If so when? **(5)**

6. How does the position of the dealer who has brought about a credit-sale agreement compare with that of the dealer who has brought about a conditional sale agreement? **(6)**

(In this appendix, the words in square brackets are technical terms of Scots Law and may be ignored by students preparing for examination in English Law of Sale.)

SALE OF GOODS ACT, 1893

PART I

FORMATION OF THE CONTRACT

Contract of Sale

1. *Sale and agreement to sell*

(1) A contract of sale of goods is a contract whereby the seller transfers or agrees to transfer the property in goods to the buyer for a money consideration, called the price. There may be a contract of sale between one part owner and another.

(2) A contract of sale may be absolute or conditional.

(3) Where under a contract of sale the property in the goods is transferred from the seller to the buyer the contract is called a sale; but where the transfer of the property in the goods is to take place at a future time or subject to some condition thereafter to be fulfilled the contract is called an agreement to sell.

(4) An agreement to sell becomes a sale when the time elapses or the conditions are fulfilled subject to which the property in the goods is to be transferred.

2. *Capacity to buy and sell.* Capacity to buy and sell is regulated by the general law concerning capacity to contract, and to transfer and acquire property:

Provided that where necessaries are sold and delivered to an infant, [or minor,] or to a person who by reason of mental incapacity or drunkenness is incompetent to contract, he must pay a reasonable price therefor.

Necessaries in this section mean goods suitable to the condition in life of such infant [or minor] or other person, and to his actual requirements at the time of the sale and delivery.

Formalities of the contract

3. *Contract of sale, how made.* Subject to the provisions of this Act and of any statute in that behalf, a contract of sale may be made in writing (either with or without seal), or by word of mouth, or partly in writing and partly by word of mouth, or may be implied from the conduct of the parties.

Provided that nothing in this section shall affect the law relating to corporations.

4. *Repealed.*

Subject-matter of contract

5. *Existing or future goods.*

(1) The goods which form the subject of a contract of sale may be either existing goods, owned or possessed by the seller, or goods to be manufactured or acquired by the seller after the making of the contract of sale, in his Act called "future goods."

(2) There may be a contract for the sale of goods, the acquisition of which by the seller depends upon a contingency which may or may not happen.

(3) Where by a contract of sale the seller purports to effect a present sale of future goods, the contract operates as an agreement to sell the goods.

6. *Goods which have perished.* Where there is a contract for the sale of specific goods, and the goods without the knowledge of the seller have perished at the time when the contract is made, the contract is void.

7. *Goods perishing before sale but after agreement to sell.* Where there is an agreement to sell specific goods, and subsequently the goods, without any fault on the part of the seller or buyer, perish before the risk passes to the buyer, the agreement is thereby avoided.

The price

8. *Ascertainment of price*

(1) The price in a contract of sale may be fixed by the contract, or may be left to be fixed in manner thereby agreed, or may be determined by the course of dealing between the parties.

(2) Where the price is not determined in accordance with the foregoing provisions the buyer must pay a reasonable price. What is a reasonable price is a question of fact dependent on the circumstances of each particular case.

9. *Agreement to sell at valuation.*

(1) Where there is an agreement to sell goods on the terms that the price is to be fixed by the valuation of a third party, and such

third party cannot or does not make such valuation, the agreement is avoided; provided that if the goods or any part thereof have been delivered to and appropriated by the buyer he must pay a reasonable price therefor.

(2) Where such third party is prevented from making the valuation by the fault of the seller or buyer, the party not in fault may maintain an action for damages against the party in fault.

Conditions and warranties

10. *Stipulations as to time.*

(1) Unless a different intention appears from the terms of the contract stipulations as to time of payment are not deemed to be of the essence of a contract of sale. Whether any other stipulation as to time is of the essence of the contract or not depends on the terms of the contract.

(2) In a contract of sale "month" means *primâ facie* calendar month.

11. *When condition to be treated as warranty.*

(1) In England or Ireland:

(*a*) Where a contract of sale is subject to any condition to be fulfilled by the seller, the buyer may waive the condition, or may elect to treat the breach of such condition as a breach of warranty, and not as a ground for treating the contract as repudiated:

(*b*) Whether a stipulation in a contract of sale is a condition, the breach of which may give rise to a right to treat the contract as repudiated, or a warranty, the breach of which may give rise to a claim for damages but not to a right to reject the goods and treat the contract as repudiated, depends in each case on the construction of the contract. A stipulation may be a condition, though called a warranty in the contract:

(*c*) Where a contract of sale is not severable, and the buyer has accepted the goods, or part thereof, the breach of any condition to be fulfilled by the seller can only be treated as a breach of warranty, and not as a ground for rejecting the goods and treating the contract as repudiated, unless there be a term of the contract, express or implied, to that effect. (As amended by the *Misrepresentation Act*, 1967.)

(2) In Scotland, failure by the seller to perform any material part of a contract of sale is a breach of contract, which entitles the buyer either within a reasonable time after delivery to reject the goods and treat the contract as repudiated, or to retain the goods

and treat the failure to perform such material part as a breach which may give rise to a claim for compensation or damages.

(3) Nothing in this section shall affect the case of any condition or warranty, fulfilment of which is excused by law by reason of impossibility or otherwise.

12. *Implied undertaking as to title, &c.* In a contract of sale, unless the circumstances of the contract are such as to show a different intention, there is—

   (1) An implied condition on the part of the seller that in the case of a sale he has a right to sell the goods, and that in the case of an agreement to sell he will have a right to sell the goods at the time when the property is to pass:

   (2) An implied warranty that the buyer shall have and enjoy quiet possession of the goods:

   (3) An implied warranty that the goods shall be free from any charge or encumbrance in favour of any third party, not declared or known to the buyer before or at the time when the contract is made.

13. *Sale by description.* Where there is a contract for the sale of goods by description, there is an implied condition that the goods shall correspond with the description; and if the sale be by sample, as well as by description, it is not sufficient that the bulk of the goods corresponds with the sample if the goods do not also correspond with the description.

14. *Implied conditions as to quality or fitness.* Subject to the provisions of this Act and of any statute in that behalf, there is no implied warranty or condition as to the quality or fitness for any particular purpose of goods supplied under a contract of sale, except as follows:

   (1) Where the buyer, expressly or by implication, makes known to the seller, the particular purpose for which the goods are required, so as to show that the buyer relies on the seller's skill or judgement, and the goods are of a description which it is in the course of the seller's business to supply (whether he be the manufacturer or not), there is an implied condition that the goods shall be reasonably fit for such purpose, provided that in the case of a contract for the sale of a specified article under its patent or other trade name, there is no implied condition as to its fitness for any particular purpose:

   (2) Where goods are bought by description from a seller who deals in goods of that description (whether he be the manufacturer or not), there is an implied condition that the goods shall be of merchantable quality; provided that if the

buyer has examined the goods, there shall be no implied
condition as regards defects which such examination ought
to have revealed:

(3) An implied warranty or condition as to quality or fitness for
a particular purpose may be annexed by the usage of trade:

(4) An express warranty or condition does not negative a
warranty or condition implied by this Act unless inconsistent therewith.

Sale by sample

15. *Sale by sample.*

(1) A contract of sale is a contract for sale by sample where
there is a term in the contract, express or implied, to that
effect.

(2) In the case of a contract for sale by sample:

(a) There is an implied condition that the bulk shall correspond with the sample in quality:

(b) There is an implied condition that the buyer shall have
a reasonable opportunity of comparing the bulk with
the sample:

(c) There is an implied condition that the goods shall be
free from any defect, rendering them unmerchantable,
which would not be apparent on reasonable examination
of the sample.

PART II

EFFECTS OF THE CONTRACT

Transfer of property as between seller and buyer

16. *Goods must be ascertained.* Where there is a contract for
the sale of unascertained goods no property in the goods is
transferred to the buyer unless and until the goods are ascertained.

17. *Property passes when intended to pass.*

(1) Where there is a contract for the sale of specific or ascertained goods the property in them is transferred to the buyer at
such time as the parties to the contract intend it to be transferred.

(2) For the purpose of ascertaining the intention of the parties
regard shall be had to the terms of the contract, the conduct of
the parties, and the circumstances of the case.

18. *Rules for ascertaining intention.* Unless a different intention
appears, the following are rules for ascertaining the intention
of the parties as to the time at which the property in the goods is
to pass to the buyer.

Rule 1.—Where there is an unconditional contract for the sale of specific goods, in a deliverable state, the property in the goods passes to the buyer when the contract is made, and it is immaterial whether the time of payment or the time of delivery, or both, be postponed.

Rule 2.—Where there is a contract for the sale of specific goods and the seller is bound to do something to the goods, for the purpose of putting them into a deliverable state, the property does not pass until such thing be done, and the buyer has notice thereof.

Rule 3.—Where there is a contract for the sale of specific goods in a deliverable state, but the seller is bound to weigh, measure, test, or do some other act or thing with reference to the goods for the purpose of ascertaining the price, the property does not pass until such act or thing be done, and the buyer has notice thereof.

Rule 4.—When goods are delivered to the buyer on approval or "sale or return" or other similar terms the property therein passes to the buyer:

(a) When he signifies his approval or acceptance to the seller or does any other act adopting the transaction:

(b) If he does not signify his approval or acceptance to the seller but retains the goods without giving notice of rejection, then, if a time has been fixed for the return of the goods, on the expiration of such time, and, if no time has been fixed, on the expiration of a reasonable time. What is a reasonable time is a question of fact.

Rule 5.—(1) Where there is a contract for the sale of unascertained or future goods by description, and goods of that description and in a deliverable state are unconditionally appropriated to the contract, either by the seller with the assent of the buyer, or by the buyer with the assent of the seller, the property in the goods thereupon passes to the buyer. Such assent may be express or implied, and may be given either before or after the appropriation is made.

(2) Where, in pursuance of the contract, the seller delivers the goods to the buyer or to a carrier or other bailee [or custodier] (whether named by the buyer or not) for the purpose of transmission to the buyer, and does not reserve the right of disposal, he is deemed to have unconditionally appropriated the goods to the contract.

19. *Reservation of right of disposal.*

(1) Where there is a contract for the sale of specific goods or where goods are subsequently appropriated to the contract, the seller may, by the terms of the contract or appropriation, reserve the right of disposal of the goods until certain conditions are ful-

filled. In such case, notwithstanding the delivery of the goods to the buyer, or to a carrier or other bailee or custodier for the purpose of transmission to the buyer, the property in the goods does not pass to the buyer until the conditions imposed by the seller are fulfilled.

(2) Where goods are shipped, and by the bill of lading the goods are deliverable to the order of the seller or his agent, the seller is *primâ facie* deemed to reserve the right of disposal.

(3) Where the seller of goods draws on the buyer for the price, and transmits the bill of exchange and bill of lading to the buyer together to secure acceptance or payment of the bill of exchange, the buyer is bound to return the bill of lading if he does not honour the bill of exchange, and if he wrongfully retains the bill of lading the property in the goods does not pass to him.

20. *Risk* primâ facie *passes with property.* Unless otherwise agreed, the goods remain at the seller's risk until the property therein is transferred to the buyer, but when the proprety therein is transferred to the buyer, the goods are at the buyer's risk whether delivery has been made or not.

Provided that where delivery has been delayed through the fault of either buyer or seller the goods are at the risk of the party in fault as regards any loss which might not have occurred but for such fault.

Provided also that nothing in this section shall affect the duties or liabilities of either seller or buyer as a bailee [or custodier] of the goods of the other party.

Transfer of title

21. *Sale by person not the owner.*

(1) Subject to the provisions of this Act, where goods are sold by a person who is not the owner thereof, and who does not sell them under the authority or with the consent of the owner, the buyer acquires no better title to the goods than the seller had, unless the owner of the goods is by his conduct precluded from denying the seller's authority to sell.

(2) Provided also that nothing in this Act shall affect:

(a) The provisions of the Factors Acts, or any enactment enabling the apparent owner of goods to dispose of them as if he were the true owner thereof;

(b) The validity of any contract of sale under any special common law or statutory power of sale or under the order of a court of competent jurisdiction.

22. *Market overt.*

(1) Where goods are sold in market overt, according to the

usage of the market, the buyer acquires a good title to the goods, provided he buys them in good faith and without notice of any defect of title on the part of the seller.

(2) Nothing in this section shall affect the law relating to the sale of horses.

(3) The provisions of this section do not apply to Scotland.

23. *Sale under voidable title.* When the seller of goods has a voidable title thereto, but his title has not been avoided at the time of the sale, the buyer acquires a good title to the goods, provided he buys them in good faith and without notice of the seller's defect of title.

24. *Repealed.*

25. *Seller or buyer in possession after sale.*

(1) Where a person having sold goods continues or is in possession of the goods, or of the documents of title to the goods, the delivery or transfer by that person, or by a mercantile agent acting for him, of the goods or documents of title under any sale, pledge, or other disposition thereof, to any person receiving the same in good faith and without notice of the previous sale, shall have the same effect as if the person making the delivery or transfer were expressly authorised by the owner of the goods to make the same.

(2) Where a person having bought or agreed to buy goods obtains, with the consent of the seller, possession of the goods or the documents of title to the goods, the delivery or transfer by that person, or by a mercantile agent acting for him, of the goods or documents of title, under any sale, pledge, or other disposition thereof, to any person receiving the same in good faith and without notice of any lien or other right of the original seller in respect of the goods, shall have the same effect as if the person making the delivery or transfer were a mercantile agent in possession of the goods or documents of title with the consent of the owner.

(3) In this section the term "mercantile agent" has the same meaning as in the Factors Acts.

26. *Effect of writs of execution.*

(1) A writ of *fieri facias* or other writ of execution against goods shall bind the property in the goods of the execution debtor as from the time when the writ is delivered to the sheriff to be executed; and, for the better manifestation of such time, it shall be the duty of the sheriff, without fee, upon the receipt of any such writ to endorse upon the back thereof the hour, day, month and year when he received the same.

Provided that no such writ shall prejudice the title to such goods acquired by any person in good faith and for valuable consideration, unless such person had at the time when he acquired his title notice that such writ or any other writ by virtue of which the goods of the execution debtor might be seized or attached had been delivered to and remained unexecuted in the hands of the sheriff.

(2) In this section the term "sheriff" includes any officer charged with the enforcement of a writ of execution.

(3) The provisions of this section do not apply to Scotland.

Part III

PERFORMANCE OF THE CONTRACT

27. *Duties of seller and buyer.*   It is the duty of the seller to deliver the goods, and of the buyer to accept and pay for them, in accordance with the terms of the contract of sale.

28. *Payment and delivery are concurrent conditions.*   Unless otherwise agreed, delivery of the goods and payment of the price are concurrent conditions, that is to say, the seller must be ready and willing to give possession of the goods to the buyer in exchange for the price and the buyer must be ready and willing to pay the price in exchange for possession of the goods.

29. *Rules as to delivery.*

(1) Whether it is for the buyer to take possession of the goods or for the seller to send them to the buyer is a question depending in each case on the contract, express or implied, between the parties.   Apart from any such contract, express or implied, the place of delivery is the seller's place of business, if he have one, and if not, his residence: Provided that, if the contract be for the sale of specific goods, which to the knowledge of the parties when the contract is made are in some other place, then that place is the place of delivery.

(2) Where under the contract of sale the seller is bound to send the goods to the buyer, but no time for sending them is fixed, the seller is bound to send them within a reasonable time.

(3) Where the goods at the time of sale are in the possession of a third person, there is no delivery by seller to buyer unless and until such third person acknowledges to the buyer that he holds the goods on his behalf; provided that nothing in this section shall affect the operation of the issue or transfer of any document of title to goods.

(4) Demand or tender of delivery may be treated as ineffectual

unless made at a reasonable hour. What is a reasonable hour is a question of fact.

(5) Unless otherwise agreed, the expenses of an incidental to putting the goods into a deliverable state must be borne by the seller.

30. *Delivery of wrong quantity.*

(1) Where the seller delivers to the buyer a quantity of goods less than he contracted to sell, the buyer may reject them, but if the buyer accepts the goods so delivered he must pay for them at the contract rate.

(2) Where the seller delivers to the buyer a quantity of goods larger than he contracted to sell, the buyer may accept the goods included in the contract and reject the rest, or he may reject the whole. If the buyer accepts the whole of the goods so delivered he must pay for them at the contract rate.

(3) Where the seller delivers to the buyer the goods he contracted to sell mixed with goods of a different description not included in the contract, the buyer may accept the goods which are in accordance with the contract and reject the rest, or he may reject the whole.

(4) The provisions of this section are subject to any usage of trade, special agreement, or course of dealing between the parties.

31. *Instalment deliveries.*

(1) Unless otherwise agreed, the buyer of goods is not bound to accept delivery thereof by instalments.

(2) Where there is a contract for the sale of goods to be delivered by stated instalments, which are to be separately paid for, and the seller makes defective deliveries in respect of one or more instalments, or the buyer neglects or refuses to take delivery of or pay for one or more instalments, it is a question in each case depending on the terms of the contract and the circumstances of the case, whether the breach of contract is a repudiation of the whole contract or whether it is a severable breach giving rise to a claim for compensation but not to a right to treat the whole contract as repudiated.

32. *Delivery to carrier.*

(1) Where, in pursuance of a contract of sale, the seller is authorised or required to send the goods to the buyer, delivery of the goods to a carrier, whether named by the buyer or not, for the purpose of transmission to the buyer is *primâ facie* deemed to be a delivery of the goods to the buyer.

(2) Unless otherwise authorised by the buyer, the seller must make such contract with the carrier on behalf of the buyer as may be reasonable having regard to the nature of the goods and

the other circumstances of the case. If the seller omit so to do, and the goods are lost or damaged in course of transit, the buyer may decline to treat the delivery to the carrier as a delivery to himself, or may hold the seller responsible in damages.

(3) Unless otherwise agreed, where goods are sent by the seller to the buyer by a route involving sea transit, under circumstances in which it is usual to insure, the seller must give such notice to the buyer as may enable him to insure them during their sea transit, and, if the seller fails to do so, the goods shall be deemed to be at his risk during such sea transit.

33. *Risk where goods are delivered at distant place.* Where the seller of goods agrees to deliver them at his own risk at a place other than that where they are when sold, the buyer must, nevertheless, unless otherwise agreed, take any risk of deterioration in the goods necessarily incident to the course of transit.

34. *Buyer's right of examining the goods.*
(1) Where goods are delivered to the buyer, which he has not previously examined, he is not deemed to have accepted them unless and until he has had a reasonable opportunity of examining them for the purpose of ascertaining whether they are in conformity with the contract.

(2) Unless otherwise agreed, when the seller tenders delivery of goods to the buyer, he is bound, on request, to afford the buyer a reasonable opportunity of examining the goods for the purpose of ascertaining whether they are in conformity with the contract.

35. *Acceptance.* The buyer is deemed to have accepted the goods when he intimates to the seller that he has accepted them, or (except where section 34 of this Act otherwise provides) when the goods have been delivered to him, and he does any act in relation to them which is inconsistent with the ownership of the seller, or when after the lapse of a reasonable time, he retains the goods without intimating to the seller that he has rejected them. (As amended by the *Misrepresentation Act,* 1967.)

36. *Buyer not bound to return rejected goods.* Unless otherwise agreed, where goods are delivered to the buyer, and he refuses to accept them having the right so to do, he is not bound to return them to the seller, but it is sufficient if he intimates to the seller that he refuses to accept them.

37. *Liability of buyer for neglecting or refusing delivery of goods.* When the seller is ready and willing to deliver the goods, and requests the buyer to take delivery, and the buyer does not within reasonable time after such request take delivery of the goods, he

is liable to the seller for any loss occasioned by his neglect or refusal to take delivery, and also for a reasonable charge for the care and custody of the goods: Provided that nothing in this section shall affect the rights of the seller where the neglect or refusal of the buyer to take delivery amounts to a repudiation of the contract.

PART IV

RIGHTS OF UNPAID SELLER AGAINST THE GOODS

38. *Unpaid seller defined.*

(1) The seller of goods is deemed to be an "unpaid seller" within the meaning of this Act:

(a) When the whole of the price has not been paid or tendered;

(b) When a bill of exchange or other negotiable instrument has been received as conditional payment, and the condition on which it was received has not been fulfilled by reason of the dishonour of the instrument or otherwise.

(2) In this Part of this Act the term "seller" includes any person who is in the position of a seller, as, for instance, an agent of the seller to whom the bill of lading has been indorsed, or a consignor or agent who has himself paid, or is directly responsible for, the price.

39. *Unpaider's sell rights.*

(1) Subject to the provisions of this Act, and of any statute in that behalf, not withstanding that the property in the goods may have passed to the buyer, the unpaid seller of goods, as such, has by implication of law:

(a) A lien on the goods or right to retain them for the price while he is in possession of them;

(b) In case of the insolvency of the buyer, a right of stopping the goods in transitu after he has parted with the possession of them;

(c) A right of re-sale as limited by this Act.

(2) Where the property in goods has not passed to the buyer, the unpaid seller has, in addition to his other remedies, a right of withholding delivery similar to and co-extensive with his rights of lien and stoppage in transitu where the property has passed to the buyer.

40. *Attachment by seller in Scotland.* In Scotland a seller of goods may attach the same while in his own hands or possession by arrestment or poinding; and such arrestment or poinding shall have the same operation and effect in a competition or otherwise as an arrestment or poinding by a third party.

Unpaid seller's lien

41. *Seller's lien.*

(1) Subject to the provisions of this Act, the unpaid seller of goods who is in possession of them is entitled to retain possession of them until payment or tender of the price in the following cases, namely:

- (*a*) Where the goods have been sold without any stipulation as to credit;
- (*b*) Where the goods have been sold on credit, but the term of credit has expired;
- (*c*) Where the buyer becomes insolvent.

(2) The seller may exercise his right of lien notwithstanding that he is in possession of the goods as agent or bailee [or custodier] for the buyer.

42. *Part delivery.* Where an unpaid seller has made part delivery of the goods, he may exercise his right of lien [or retention] on the remainder, unless such part delivery has been made under such circumstances as to show an agreement to waive the lien [or right of retention].

43. *Termination of lien.*

(1) The unpaid seller of goods loses his lien [or right of retention] thereon:

- (*a*) When he delivers the goods to a carrier or other bailee [or custodier] for the purpose of transmission to the buyer without reserving the right of disposal of the goods;
- (*b*) When the buyer or his agent lawfully obtains possession of the goods;
- (*c*) By waiver thereof.

(2) The unpaid seller of goods, having a lien [or right of retention] thereon, does not lose his lien [or right of retention] by reason only that he has obtained judgment [or decree] for the price of the goods.

Stoppage in transitu

44. *Right of stoppage in transitu.* Subject to the provisions of this Act, when the buyer of goods becomes insolvent, the unpaid seller who has parted with the possession of the goods has the right of stopping them in transitu, that is to say, he may resume possession of the goods as long as they are in course of transit, and may retain them until payment or tender of the price.

45. *Duration of transit.*

(1) Goods are deemed to be in course of transit from the time

when they are delivered to a carrier by land or water, or other bailee [or custodier for] the purpose of transmission to the buyer, until the buyer, or his agent in that behalf, takes delivery of them from such carrier or other bailee [or custodier].

(2) If the buyer or his agent in that behalf obtains delivery of the goods before their arrival at the appointed destination, the transit is at an end.

(3) If, after the arrival of the goods at the appointed destination, the carrier or other bailee [or custodier] acknowledges to the buyer, or his agent, that he holds the goods on his behalf and continues in possession of them as bailee or custodier for the buyer, or his agent, the transit is at an end, and it is immaterial that a further destination for the goods may have been indicated by the buyer.

(4) If the goods are rejected by the buyer, and the carrier or other bailee [or custodier] continues in possession of them, the transit is not deemed to be at an end, even if the seller has refused to receive them back.

(5) When goods are delivered to a ship chartered by the buyer it is a question depending on the circumstances of the particular case, whether they are in the possession of the master as a carrier, or as agent to the buyer.

(6) Where the carrier or other bailee or custodier wrongfully refuses to deliver the goods to the buyer, or his agent in that behalf, the transit is deemed to be at an end.

(7) Where part delivery of the goods has been made to the buyer, or his agent in that behalf, the remainder of the goods may be stopped in transitu, unless such part delivery has been made under such circumstances as to show an agreement to give up possession of the whole of the goods.

46. *How stoppage in transitu is effected.*

(1) The unpaid seller may exercise his right of stoppage in transitu either by taking actual possession of the goods, or by giving notice of his claim to the carrier or other bailee [or custodier] in whose possession the goods are. Such notice may be given either to the person in actual possession of the goods or to his principal. In the latter case the notice, to be effectual, must be given at such time and under such circumstances that the principal, by the exercise of reasonable diligence, may communicate it to his servant or agent in time to prevent a delivery to the buyer.

(2) When notice of stoppage in transitu is given by the seller to the carrier, or other bailee [or custodier] in possession of the goods, he must re-deliver the goods to, or according to the directions of, the seller. The expenses of such re-delivery must be borne by the seller.

Re-sale by buyer or seller

47. *Effect of sub-sale or pledge by buyer.* Subject to the pro-visions of this Act, the unpaid seller's right of lien [or retention] or stoppage in transitu is not affected by any sale, or other dis-position of the goods which the buyer may have made, unless the seller has assented thereto.

Provided that where a document of title to goods has been lawfully transferred to any person as buyer or owner of the goods, and that person transfers the document to a person who takes the document in good faith and for valuable consideration, then, if such last-mentioned transfer was by way of sale the unpaid seller's right of lien [or retention] or stoppage in transitu is defeated, and if such last-mentioned transfer was made by way of pledge or other disposition for value, the unpaid seller's right of lien [or retention] or stoppage in transitu can only be exercised subject to the rights of the transferee.

48. *Sale not generally rescinded by lien or stoppage in transitu.*

(1) Subject to the provisions of this section, a contract of sale is not rescinded by the mere exercise by an unpaid seller of his right of lien [or retention] or stoppage in transitu.

(2) Where an unpaid seller who has exercised his right of lien [or retention] or stoppage in transitu re-sells the goods, the buyer acquires a good title thereto as against the original buyer.

(3) Where the goods are of a perishable nature, or where the unpaid seller gives notice to the buyer of his intention to re-sell, and the buyer does not within a reasonable time pay or tender the price, the unpaid seller may re-sell the goods and recover from the original buyer damages for any loss occasioned by his breach of contract.

(4) Where the seller expressly reserves the right of resale in case the buyer should make default, and on the buyer making default, re-sells the goods, the original contract of sale is thereby rescinded, but without prejudice to any claim the seller may have for damages.

PART V

ACTIONS FOR BREACH OF THE CONTRACT

Remedies of the seller

49. *Action of price.*

(1) Where, under a contract of sale, the property in the goods has passed to the buyer, and the buyer wrongfully neglects or refuses to pay for the goods according to the terms of the contract,

the seller may maintain an action against him for the price of the goods.

(2) Where, under a contract of sale, the price is payable on a day certain irrespective of delivery, and the buyer wrongfully neglects or refuses to pay such price, the seller may maintain an action for the price, although the property in the goods has not passed, and the goods have not been appropriated to the contract.

(3) Nothing in this section shall prejudice the right of the seller in Scotland to recover interest on the price from the date of tender of the goods, or from the date on which the price was payable, as the case may be.

50. *Damages for non-acceptance.*

(1) Where the buyer wrongfully neglects or refuses to accept and pay for the goods, the seller may maintain an action against him for damages for non-acceptance.

(2) The measure of damages is the estimated loss directly and naturally resulting, in the ordinary course of events, from the buyer's breach of contract.

(3) Where there is an available market for the goods in question the measure of damages is *primâ facie* to be ascertained by the difference between the contract price and the market or current price at the time or times when the goods ought to have been accepted or, if no time was fixed for acceptance, then at the time of the refusal to accept.

Remedies of the buyer

51. *Damages for non-delivery.*

(1) Where the seller wrongfully neglects or refuses to deliver the goods to the buyer, the buyer may maintain an action against the seller for damages for non-delivery.

(2) The measure of damages is the estimated loss directly and naturally resulting, in the ordinary course of events, from the seller's breach of contract.

(3) Where there is an available market for the goods in question the measure of damages is *primâ facie* to be ascertained by the difference between the contract price and the market or current price of the goods at the time or times when they ought to have been delivered, or, if no time was fixed, then at the time of the refusal to deliver.

52. *Specific performance.* In any action for breach of contract to deliver specific or ascertained goods the court may, if it thinks fit, on the application of the plaintiff, by its judgment [or decree] direct that the contract shall be performed specifically, without

F

giving the defendant the option of retaining the goods on payment of damages. The judgment [or decree] may be unconditional, or upon such terms and conditions as to damages, payment of the price, and otherwise, as to the court may seem just, and the application by the plaintiff may be made at any time before judgment [or decree].

The provisions of this section shall be deemed to be supplementary to, and not in derogation of, the right of specific implement in Scotland.

53. *Remedy for breach of warranty.*

(1) Where there is a breach of warranty by the seller, or where the buyer elects, or is compelled, to treat any breach of a condition on the part of the seller as a breach of warranty, the buyer is not by reason only of such breach of warranty entitled to reject the goods; but he may

- (*a*) set up against the seller the breach of warranty in diminution or extinction of the price; or
- (*b*) maintain an action against the seller for damages for the breach of warranty.

(2) The measure of damages for breach of warranty is the estimated loss directly and naturally resulting, in the ordinary course of events, from the breach of warranty.

(3) In the case of breach of warranty of quality such loss is *primâ facie* the difference between the value of the goods at the time of delivery to the buyer and the value they would have had if they had answered to the warranty.

(4) The fact that the buyer has set up the breach of warranty in diminution or extinction of the price does not prevent him from maintaining an action for the same breach of warranty if he has suffered further damage.

(5) Nothing in this section shall prejudice or affect the buyer's right of rejection in Scotland as declared by this Act.

54. *Interest and special damages.* Nothing in this Act shall affect the right of the buyer or the seller to recover interest or special damages in any case where by law interest or special damages may be recoverable, or to recover money paid where the consideration for the payment of it has failed.

Part VI

SUPPLEMENTARY

55. *Exclusion of implied terms and conditions.* Where any right, duty, or liability would arise under a contract of sale by implication of law, it may be negatived or varied by express

agreement or by the course of dealing between the parties, or by usage, if the usage be such as to bind both parties to the contract.

56. *Reasonable time a question of fact.* Where, by this Act, any reference is made to a reasonable time the question what is a reasonable time is a question of fact.

57. *Rights, &c., enforceable by action.* Where any right, duty, or liability is declared by this Act, it may, unless otherwise by this Act provided, be enforced by action.

58. *Auction sales.* In the case of a sale by auction:
(1) Where goods are put up for sale by auction in lots, each lot is *primâ facie* deemed to be the subject of a separate contract of sale:
(2) A sale by auction is complete when the auctioneer announces its completion by the fall of the hammer, or in other customary manner. Until such announcement is made any bidder may retract his bid:
(3) Where a sale by auction is not notified to be subject to a right to bid on behalf of the seller, it shall not be lawful for the seller to bid himself or to employ any person to bid at such sale, or for the auctioneer knowingly to take any bid from the seller or any such person: Any sale contravening this rule may be treated as faudulent by the buyer:
(4) A sale by auction may be notified to be subject to a reserve or upset price, and a right to bid may also be reserved expressly by or on behalf of the seller.
Where a right to bid is expressly reserved, but not otherwise, the seller, or any one person on his behalf, may bid at the auction.

59. *Payment into court in Scotland when breach of warranty alleged.* In Scotland where a buyer has elected to accept goods which he might have rejected, and to treat a breach of contract as only giving rise to a claim for damages, he may, in an action by the seller for the price, be required, in the discretion of the court before which the action depends, to consign or pay into court the price of the goods, or part thereof, or to give other reasonable security for the due payment thereof.

60. *Repealed.*

61. *Savings.* (1) The rules in bankruptcy relating to contract of sale shall continue to apply thereto, notwithstanding anything in this Act contained.
(2) The rules of the common law, including the law merchant, save in so far as they are inconsistent with the express provisions

of this Act, and in particular the rules relating to the law of principal and agent and the effect of fraud, misrepresentation, duress [or coercion], mistake, or other invalidating cause, shall continue to apply to contracts for the sale of goods.

(3) Nothing in this Act or in any repeal effected thereby shall affect the enactments relating to bills of sale, or any enactment relating to the sale of goods which is not expressly repealed by this Act.

(4) The provisions of this Act relating to contracts of sale do not apply to any transaction in the form of a contract of sale which is intended to operate by way of mortgage, pledge, charge, or other security.

(5) Nothing in this Act shall prejudice or affect the landlord's right of hypothec or sequestration for rent in Scotland.

62. *Interpretations of terms.*

(1) In this Act, unless the context or subject matter otherwise requires:

Action includes counterclaim and set off, and in Scotland condescendence and claim and compensation:

Bailee in Scotland includes custodier:

Buyer means a person who buys or agrees to buy goods:

Contract of sale includes an agreement to sell as well as a sale:

Defendant includes in Scotland defender, respondent, and claimant in a multiplepoinding:

Delivery means voluntary transfer of possession from one person to another:

Document of title to goods has the same meaning as it has in the Factors Acts:

Factors Acts mean the *Factors Act*, 1889, the *Factors (Scotland) Act*, 1890, and any enactment amending or substituted for the same:

Fault means wrongful act or default:

Future Goods means goods to be manufactured or acquired by the seller after the making of the contract of sale:

Goods include all chattels personal other than things in action and money, and in Scotland all corporeal moveables except money. The term includes emblements, industrial growing crops, and things attached to or forming part of the land which are agreed to be severed before sale or under the contract of sale:

Lien in Scotland includes right of retention:

Plaintiff includes pursuer, complainer, claimant in a multiplepoinding and defendant or defender counterclaiming:

Property means the general property in goods, and not merely a special property:

Quality of goods includes their state or condition:

Sale includes a bargain and sale as well as a sale and delivery:

Seller means a person who sells or agrees to sell goods:

Specific goods means goods identified and agreed upon at the time a contract of sale is made:

Warranty as regards England and Ireland means an agreement with reference to goods which are the subject of a contract of sale, but collateral to the main purpose of such contract, the breach if which gives rise to a claim for damages, but not to a right to reject the goods and treat the contract as repudiated.

As regards Scotland, a breach of warranty shall be deemed to be a failure to perform a material part of the contract.

(2) A thing is deemed to be done "in good faith" within the meaning of this Act when it is in fact done honestly, whether it be done negligently or not.

(3) A person is deemed to be insolvent within the meaning of this Act who either has ceased to pay his debts in the ordinary course of business, or cannot pay his debts as they become due, whether he has committed an act of bankruptcy or not, and whether he has become a notour bankrupt or not.

(4) Goods are in a "deliverable state" within the meaning of this Act when they are in such a state that the buyer would under the contract be bound to take delivery of them.

63. *Repealed.*

64. *Short title.* This Act may be cited as the *Sale of Goods Act,* 1893.

LAW COMMISSION'S DRAFT CLAUSES

The Law Commission's first Report on the Amendments to the Sale of Goods Act contained an appendix in which the proposed draft clauses were set out as follows:

1. *Implied undertakings as to title, etc.* For section 12 of the principal Act (implied conditions as to title, and implied warranties as to quiet possession and freedom from encumbrances) there shall be substituted the following section:—

"12.—(1) In every contract of sale, other than one to which subsection (2) of this section implies, there is—

(a) An implied condition on the part of the seller that in the case of a sale, he has the right to sell the goods, and in the case of an agreement to sell, he will have the right to sell the goods at the time when the property is to pass; and

(b) An implied warranty that the goods shall be free from any charge or encumbrance not disclosed or known to the buyer before the contract is made and that the buyer shall enjoy quiet possession of the goods except so far as it may be disturbed by the owner of any charge or encumbrance so disclosed or known.

(2) In a contract of sale in the case of which there appears from the contract or is to be inferred from the circumstances of the contract an intention that the seller should not transfer the property in the goods, but only such title as he or a third person may have, there is—

(a) An implied warranty that all charges or encumbrances known to the seller and not known to the buyer have been disclosed to the buyer before the contract is made; and

(b) An implied warranty that neither—

(i) the seller; nor

(ii) in a case where the parties to the contract intend that the seller should transfer only such title as a third person may have, that person; nor

(iii) anyone claiming through or under the seller or that third person otherwise than under a charge or encumbrance disclosed or known to the buyer before the contract is made;

will disturb the buyer's quiet possession of the goods."

2. *Sale by description.*   Section 13 of the principal Act (sale by description) shall be renumbered as subsection (1) of that section, and at the end there shall be inserted the following subsection:

"(2) A sale of goods shall not be prevented from being a sale by description by reason only that, being exposed for sale, they are selected by the buyer."

3. *Implied undertakings as to quality or fitness.*   For section 14 of the principal Act (implied undertakings as to quality or fitness) there shall be substituted the following section:

"14.   (1) Except as provided by this section and section 15 of this Act and subject to the provisions of any other enactment, there is no implied condition or warranty as to the quality or fitness for any particular purpose of goods supplied under a contract of sale.

(2) Where the seller sells goods in the course of a business, there is an implied condition that the goods are of merchantable quality, except that there is no such condition—

(*a*) As regards defects specifically drawn to the buyer's attention before the contract is made; or

(*b*) If the buyer examines the goods before the contract is made, as regards defects which that examination ought to reveal.

(3) Where the seller sells goods in the course of a business and the buyer, expressly or by implication, makes known to the seller any particular purpose for which the goods are bought, there is an implied condition that the goods are reasonably fit for that purpose, whether or not that is a purpose for which such goods are commonly bought, except where the circumstances show that the buyer does not rely, or that it is unreasonable for him to rely, on the seller's skill or judgment.

(4) An implied condition or warranty as to quality or fitness for a particular purpose may be annexed to a contract of sale by usage.

(5) The foregoing provisions of this section apply to a sale by a person who in the course of a business is acting as agent for another as they apply to a sale by a principal in the course of a business, except where that other is not selling in the course of a business and the agent takes reasonable steps to bring that fact to the notice of the buyer before the contract is made."

4. *Exemption clauses.*   Section 55 of the principal Act (exclusion of implied terms and conditions) shall be renumbered as subsection (1) of that section and at the end there shall be inserted the following subsections:

"(2) An express condition or warranty does not negative a

condition or warranty implied by this Act unless inconsistent therewith.

(3) Notwithstanding anything in subsection (1) of this section, any term—

(a) Which is contained in or applies to a contract of sale and which purports to exclude or restrict, or has the effect of excluding or restricting, the operation of all or any of the provisions of section 12 of this Act or any liability of the seller for breach of a condition or warranty implied by any such provision; or

(b) Which is contained in or applies to a contract for a consumer sale and which purports to exclude or restrict, or has the effect of excluding or restricting, the operation of all or any of the provisions of sections 13 to 15 of this Act or any liability of the seller for breach of a condition or warranty implied by any such provision;

shall be void."

Alternative A

"(4) In this section "consumer sale" means a sale of goods (other than a sale by auction) by a seller in the course of a business where the goods—

(a) Are of a type ordinarily bought for private use or consumption; and

(b) Are sold to a person who does not buy or hold himself out as buying them in the course of a business for one of the purposes mentioned in subsection (5) below.

(5) The said purposes are—

(a) Disposing of the goods by way of sale, hire or hire purchase in the course of the buyer's business;

(b) Consuming or processing them in the course of that business;

(c) Using them for providing a service which it is an object of that business to provide.

(6) In the case of a consumer sale where the goods are sold to a person who buys or holds himself out as buying them in the course of a business but for a purpose other than one mentioned in subsection (5) above, the court may treat the sale for the purposes of this section as not being a consumer sale if satisfied that, having regard to the size and terms of the transaction, and all other relevant circumstances, it is reasonable to do so.

(7) The onus of proving that a sale falls to be treated for the purposes of this section as not being a consumer sale shall lie on the party so contending.

(8) This section is subject to the provisions of section 61(6) of this Act."

Alternative B

"(4) Any term which is contained in or applies to a contract of sale of goods other than a consumer sale and which purports to exclude or restrict, or has the effect of excluding or restricting, the operation of all or any of the provisions of sections 13 to 15 of this Act or any liability of the seller for breach of a condition or warranty implied by any such provision shall not be enforceable to the extent that it is shown that it would not be fair or reasonable in the circumstances of the case to allow reliance on the term.

(5) In this section "consumer sale" means a sale of goods (other than a sale by auction) by a seller in the course of a business where the goods—

(a) Are of a type ordinarily bought for private use or consumption; and

(b) Are sold to a person who does not buy or hold himself out as buying them in the course of a business.

(6) The onus of proving that a sale falls to be treated for the purposes of this section as not being a consumer sale shall lie on the party so contending.

(7) This section is subject to the provisions of section 61(6) of this Act."

5. *Conflict of laws.*

(1) After section 55 of the principal Act there shall be inserted the following section:

"55A. Where the proper law of a contract for the sale of goods would, apart from a term that it should be the law of some other country or a term to the like effect, be the law of England and Wales or Scotland, or where any such contract contains a term which purports to substitute, or has the effect of substituting, provisions of the law of some other country for all or any of the provisions of sections 12 to 15 and 55 of this Act, those sections shall, notwithstanding that term but subject to section 61(6) of this Act, apply to the contract."

(2) In section 1(4) of the Uniform Laws on International Sales Act, 1967 (which provides that no provision of the law of any part of the United Kingdom shall be regarded as a mandatory provision for the purposes of the Uniform Law on the International Sale of Goods so as to override the choice of the parties) for the words from "no provision" to the end of the subsection there shall be substituted the words "no provision of the law of England and Wales, Scotland or Northern Ireland, except sections 12 to 15, 55 and 55A of the Sale of Goods Act, 1893, shall be regarded as a mandatory provision within the meaning of that Article."

6. *International sales.* In section 61 of the principal Act (savings) there shall be inserted after subsection (5) thereof the following subsection—

"(6) Nothing in sections 55 or 55A of this Act shall prevent the parties to a contract for the international sale of goods from negativing or varying any right, duty or liability which would otherwise arise by implication of law under sections 12 to 15 of this Act."

7. *Interpretation.*

(1) In section 62(1) of the principal Act (definitions) at the appropriate points in alphabetical order there shall be inserted the following definitions:

"business" includes a profession and the activities of any government department, local authority or statutory undertaker:

"contract for the international sale of goods" means a contract of sale of goods made by parties whose places of business (or, if they have none, habitual residences) are in the territories of different States and—

(a) the contract involves the sale of goods which are at the time of the conclusion of the contract in the course of carriage or will be carried from the territory of one State to the territory of another; or

(b) The acts constituting the offer and acceptance have been effected in the territories of different States; or

(c) Delivery of the goods is to be made in the territory of a State other than that within whose territory the acts constituting the offer and the acceptance have been effected.

For the purposes of this definition Northern Ireland, the Channel Islands and the Isle of Man shall be treated as different States from Great Britain."

(2) After section 62(1) of the principal Act there shall be inserted the following subsection:

"(1A) Goods of any kind are of merchantable quality within the meaning of this Act if they are as fit for the purpose or purposes for which goods of that kind are commonly bought as it is reasonable to expect having regard to their price, any description applied to them and all the other circumstances; and any reference in this Act to unmerchantable goods shall be construed accordingly."

8. *Short title, citation, construction, commencement, saving and extent.*

(1) This Act may be cited as the Sale of Goods Act, 1969.

(2) This Act and the principal Act may be cited as the Sale of Goods Acts, 1893 and 1969.

(3) In this Act "the principal Act" means the Sale of Goods Act, 1893.

(4) In ascertaining the meaning of any enactment as amended by this Act regard may be had to a report of the Law Commission and the Scottish Law Commission recommending that that enactment be amended.

(5) This Act shall come into operation at the expiration of a period of one month beginning with the date on which it is passed.

(6) This Act does not apply to contracts of sale made before its commencement, except that section 55(3) [and (4) of Alternative B] of the principal Act as amended by this Act applies to terms agreed on before the commencement of this Act, if applied to contracts made after its commencement.

(7) This Act does not extend to Northern Ireland.

HIRE-PURCHASE ACT, 1965

PART I

AGREEMENTS TO WHICH PARTS II, III AND IV OF ACT APPLY

1. *Meaning of "hire-purchase agreement," "credit-sale agreement" and "conditional sale agreement."*

(1) In this Act (subject to the following provisions of this Part of this Act)—

"hire-purchase agreement" means an agreement for the bailment of goods under which the bailee may buy the goods, or under which the property in the goods will or may pass to the bailee;

"credit-sale agreement" means an agreement for the sale of goods under which the purchase price is payable by five or more instalments, not being a conditional sale agreement;

"conditional sale agreement" means an agreement for the sale of goods under which the purchase price or part of it is payable by instalments, and the property in the goods is to remain in the seller (notwithstanding that the buyer is to be in possession of the goods) until such conditions as to the payment of instalments or otherwise as may be specified in the agreement are fulfilled.

(2) Where by virtue of two or more agreements, none of which by itself constitutes a hire-purchase agreement as defined by the preceding subsection, there is a bailment of goods and either the bailee may buy the goods, of the property therein will or may pass to the bailee, the agreements shall be treated for the purposes of this Act as a single agreement made at the time when the last of the agreements was made.

2. *Limits of value for purposes of Parts II, III and IV.*

(1) Subject to the following provisions of this Part of this Act, references in Parts II, III and IV of this Act to hire-purchase agreements and to conditional sale agreements, and references in Part II of this Act to credit-sale agreements, shall be construed in accordance with the following provisions of this section.

(2) References in Parts II, III and IV of this Act to a hire-purchase agreement or a conditional sale agreement shall be construed respectively as references to a hire-purchase agreement

(as defined by the preceding section) or a conditional sale agreement (as so defined) under which the hire-purchase price or total purchase price, as the case may be, does not exceed £2,000.

(3) In Part II of this Act, except in any provision to which the next following subsection applies, any reference to a credit-sale agreement shall be construed as a reference to a credit-sale agreement (as defined by the preceding section) under which the total purchase price—

(a) Exceeds £30, but

(b) Does not exceed £2,000.

(4) In any provision of Part II of this Act to which this subsection is expressed to apply, any reference to a credit-sale agreement shall be construed as a reference to a credit-sale agreement (as defined by the preceding section) under which the total purchase price does not exceed £2,000.

PART II

GENERAL PROVISIONS

Requirements in connection with making agreements

5. *Enforcement conditional on compliance with specified requirements.*

(1) Where goods are let under a hire-purchase agreement, or are sold, or agreed to be sold, under a credit-sale agreement or a conditional sale agreement, then (subject to the exercise of any power of the court under section 10 of this Act) the owner or seller shall not be entitled to enforce the agreement unless:

(a) The agreement is signed by the hirer or buyer, and by or on behalf of all other parties to the agreement, and

(b) The requirements of sections 6 and 7 of this Act, and the requirements of section 8 or (as the case may be) section 9 of this Act, are complied with.

(2) Where by virtue of the preceding subsection the owner or seller is not entitled to enforce an agreement:

(a) He shall not be entitled to enforce any contract of guarantee relating to that agreement;

(b) No security given by the hirer or buyer in respect of money payable under the agreement, or given by a guarantor in respect of money payable under a contract of guarantee relating to the agreement, shall be enforceable against the hirer or buyer, or against the guarantor, as the case may be, by the holder of such a security; and

(c) If it is a hire-purchase agreement or a conditional sale agreement, the owner or seller shall not be entitled to enforce any right to recover the goods from the hirer or buyer.

6. *Requirements as to cash price.*

(1) The requirements of this section, in relation to an agreement, are that, before the agreement is made:

(a) The cash price of the goods has been stated in writing to the hirer or buyer by the owner or seller, otherwise than in the agreement, or

(b) If the hirer or buyer has inspected the goods or like goods, then, at the time of his inspection, tickets or labels were attached to or displayed with the goods clearly stating the cash price, either of the goods as a whole or of all the different articles or sets of articles comprised therein, or

(c) The hirer or buyer has selected the goods by reference to a catalogue, price list or advertisement which clearly stated the cash price, either of the goods as a whole or of all the different articles or sets of articles comprised therein.

(2) In this Part of this Act "cash price", in relation to any goods, means the price at which the goods may be purchased by the hirer or buyer for cash.

7. *Requirements as to contents and form of agreements.*

(1) The requirements of this section, in relation to an agreement, are that:

(a) The agreement contains a statement of the hire-purchase price or total purchase price, as the case may be, and of the cash price of the goods to which the agreement relates, and of the amount of each instalment by which the hire-purchase price or total purchase price is to be paid, and of the date, or the mode of determining the date, on which each instalment is payable;

(b) The agreement contains a list of the goods to which the agreement relates sufficient to identify them;

(c) The agreement, at the time when it is signed by the hirer or buyer, complies with the requirements of any regulations made under subsection (2) of this section;

(d) The agreement complies with the requirements of any regulations made under section 32 of this Act; and

(e) If it is a hire-purchase agreement or a conditional sale agreement, it contains a notice, which is at least as prominent as the rest of the contents of the agreement, in the terms set out in Schedule 1 or (as the case may be) Schedule 2 to this Act.

(2) The Board of Trade may by regulations provide that, in

any document which, on being signed as mentioned in section 5(1)(a) of this Act, constitutes a hire-purchase agreement, a credit-sale agreement or a conditional sale agreement, the signature of the hirer or buyer shall be inserted in a space marked in such manner, and accompanied in the document by such words, as may be specified in the regulations; and the regulations may include provision as to the location of those words in relation to the space in which the signature is inserted, and may prescribe such other requirements (whether as to type, size, colour or disposition of lettering or otherwise) as the Board may consider appropriate for securing that the words come to the attention of the hirer or buyer at the time when he is about to sign the document.

8. *Requirements as to copies where hirer or buyer signs at appropriate trade premises.*

(1) The requirements of this section, in relation to an agreement which is signed by the hirer or buyer at appropriate trade premises, are that copies are delivered or sent to the hirer or buyer in accordance with the following provisions of this section.

(2) If either:

(a) The agreement is signed by or on behalf of all other parties immediately after it is signed by the hirer or buyer, and a copy of the agreement is there and then delivered to him, or

(b) The agreement having been signed by or on behalf of all other parties before it is signed by the hirer or buyer, a copy of the agreement is delivered to him immediately after he signs the agreement,

and (in either case) the copy so delivered complies with the requirements of any regulations made under section 32 of this Act, the delivery of that copy shall be taken to have fulfilled the requirements of this section in relation to that agreement.

(3) If, in a case not falling within paragraph (a) or paragraph (b) of the last preceding subsection:

(a) Either:

(i) The relevant document was presented, and not sent, to the hirer or buyer for his signature, and immediately after he signed it there was delivered to him a copy of that document in the form in which it then was, or

(ii) The relevant document was sent to the hirer for his signature, and at the time when it was sent there was also sent to him a copy of that document in the form in which it then was, and

(b) In either case, a copy of the agreement is delivered or sent to the hirer or buyer within seven days of the making of the agreement, then, if each copy delivered or sent to the hirer or buyer as mentioned in paragraph (a) or paragraph (b) of this subsection complies with the requirements of any regulations made under section 32 of this Act, the delivery or sending of those copies shall be taken to have fulfilled the requirements of this section in relation to that agreement.

(4) In this and the next following section "the relevant document" means the document which, on being signed by the hirer or buyer and by or on behalf of all other parties to the agreement, became the hire-purchase agreement, credit-sale agreement or conditional sale agreement, as the case may be.

9. *Requirements as to copies where hirer or buyer signs elsewhere than at appropriate trade premises.*

(1) The requirements of this section, in relation to an agreement which is signed by the hirer or buyer at a place other than appropriate trade premises, are that copies are delivered or sent to the hirer or buyer in accordance with the following provisions of this section.

(2) A copy of the relevant document (in this Part of this Act referred to as "the first statutory copy") must be delivered or sent to the hirer or buyer as follows, that is to say:

(a) If the relevant document is presented, and not sent, to the hirer or buyer for his signature, a copy of that document, in the form in which it then is, must be delivered to him immediately after he signs it;

(b) If the relevant document is sent to the hirer or buyer for his signature, a copy of that document, in the form in which it then is, must be sent to him at the time when that document is sent.

(3) Within seven days of the making of the agreement, a copy of the agreement (in this Part of this Act referred to as "the second statutory copy") must be sent by post to the hirer or buyer.

(4) The first statutory copy and the second statutory copy must each contain such a statement of the rights of the hirer or buyer under section 11 of this Act, and of matters relating to or consequential upon the exercise of those rights, as may be prescribed by regulations made by the Board of Trade; and that statement must be so contained in such position, and must comply with such other requirements (whether as to type, size, colour or disposition of lettering or otherwise) as may be so prescribed.

(5) Any statement which, in accordance with regulations made under the last preceding subsection, is contained either in the first statutory copy or in the second statutory copy must specify the name of a person to whom, and an address to which, notice of cancellation may be sent; and (without prejudice to any other

respect in which, in accordance with section 57(3) of this Act, the regulations may make different provision as between the first statutory copy and the second statutory copy, or as between copies delivered and copies sent) different names and addresses may be so specified in the first statutory copy and the second statutory copy of the same document.

(6) The first statutory copy and the second statutory copy must each comply with the requirements of any regulations made under section 32 of this Act.

10. *Power of court to dispense with requirements of sections 6 to 9.*

(1) Subject to the following provisions of this section, if in any action the court is satisfied that a failure to comply with any of the requirements specified in sections 6 to 9 of this Act has not prejudiced the hirer or buyer, and that it would be just and equitable to dispense with the requirement, the court may, subject to any conditions that it thinks fit to impose, dispense with that requirement for the purposes of the action.

(2) The power conferred by the preceding subsection shall not be exercisable in relation to the requirement specified in section 9(3) of this Act except where the second statutory copy has been sent to the hirer or buyer but not within the period of seven days of the making of the agreement.

(3) The power conferred by subsection (1) of this section shall not be exercisable in relation to the requirement imposed by section 9(4) of this Act.

(4) For the avoidance of doubt it is hereby declared that in subsection (1) of this section the reference to the requirements specified in sections 6 to 9 of this Act includes the requirements of any regulations made under section 32 of this Act, in so far as any such requirements relate to hire-purchase agreements, credit-sale agreements and conditional sale agreements, or to copies delivered or sent as mentioned in section 8 or section 9 of this Act.

Right of cancellation

11. *Notice of cancellation.*

(1) The provisions of this section shall have effect where a person (in this section referred to as "the prospective hirer or buyer") signs a document (in this section referred to as "the relevant document") which:

(a) Constitutes a hire-purchase agreement, a credit-sale agreement or a conditional sale agreement, or

(b) Would constitute such an agreement if executed by or on behalf of another person as owner or seller of the goods to which it relates, and (in either case) the relevant document is signed by the prospective hirer or buyer at a place other than appropriate trade premises.

(2) At any time after he has signed the relevant document and before the end of the period of four days beginning with the day on which he receives the second statutory copy, the prospective hirer or buyer may serve a notice under this section (in this Act referred to as a "notice of cancellation"):

(a) On the owner or seller, or
(b) On any person who (whether by virtue of section 12(3) of this Act or otherwise) is the agent of the owner or seller for the purpose of receiving such a notice.

(3) A notice of cancellation served as mentioned in the last preceding subsection shall have effect if, however expressed, it indicates the intention of the prospective hirer or buyer to withdraw from the transaction to which the relevant document relates.

(4) Where the prospective hirer or buyer serves a notice of cancellation, then:

(a) If, at the time when that notice is served, the relevant document constitutes a hire-purchase agreement, a credit-sale agreement or a conditional sale agreement, the service of the notice shall operate so as to rescind that agreement;
(b) In any other case, the service of the notice shall operate as a withdrawal of any offer to enter into such an agreement which is contained in, or implied by, the relevant document, and as notice to the owner or seller that any such offer is withdrawn.

(5) In this section "owner or seller," in relation to the relevant document, means the person who, at the time when the document is signed by the prospective hirer or buyer, is specified in the document as the person who is to let the goods on hire to him or to sell the goods to him, as the case may be:

Provided that, if no person is so specified at that time, any person by whom, or on whose behalf, the document is executed at any subsequent time, and who is then specified in the document as the person letting or selling the goods, shall for the purposes of this section be deemed to be, and at all material times to have been, the owner or seller in relation to that document.

(6) In sections 12 to 15 of this Act "the prospective hirer or buyer," "the relevant document" and "owner or seller" have the same meanings as in this section.

12. *Service of notice of cancellation*.

(1) For the purposes of section 11 of this Act a notice of cancellation:

(a) Shall be deemed to be served on the owner or seller if it is sent by post addressed to a person specified in a statement contained either in the first statutory copy or in the second statutory copy of the relevant document as being a person to whom such a notice may be sent, and is addressed to that person at an address so specified, and

(b) Where the preceding paragraph applies, shall be deemed to be served on the owner or seller at the time when it is posted.

(2) The preceding subsection shall have effect without prejudice to the service of a notice of cancellation (whether by post or otherwise) in any way in which the notice could be served apart from that subsection, whether the notice is served on the owner or seller or on a person who (whether by virtue of the next following subsection or otherwise) is the agent of the owner or seller for the purpose of receiving such a notice.

(3) Any person who conducted any antecedent negotiations, but is not the owner or seller, shall be deemed to be the agent of the owner or seller for the purpose of receiving any notice of cancellation served by the prospective hirer or buyer.

(4) A notice of cancellation which is sent by post to a person at his proper address, otherwise than in accordance with subsection (1) of this section, shall be deemed to be served on him at the time when it is posted.

(5) So much of section 26 of the Interpretation Act, 1889, as relates to the time when service is deemed to have been effected shall not apply to a notice of cancellation.

13. *Re-delivery and interim care, of goods comprised in notice of cancellation.*

(1) The provisions of this section shall have effect where a notice of cancellation is served, and at any time, whether before or after the service of that notice, any of the goods to which the relevant document relates are in the possession of the prospective hirer or buyer, having come into his possession in consequence, or in anticipation, of his signing that document.

(2) The prospective hirer or buyer shall not be under any obligation (whether arising by contract or otherwise) to deliver the goods except at his own premises and in pursuance of a request in writing signed by or on behalf of the person entitled to possession of the goods and served on the prospective hirer or buyer either before, or at the time when, the goods are collected from his premises, and any such obligation shall be subject to any lien, or other right to retain the goods, which he may have under section 14(2) or section 15(3) of this Act.

(3) If the prospective hirer or buyer:

(a) Delivers the goods (whether at his own premises or else-where) to an authorised person, or to a person designated for the purpose by an authorised person, or

(b) Sends the goods at his own expense to an authorised person,

he shall be taken to have done so with the consent of that author-ised person and (if that person is not for the time being entitled to possession of the goods) with the consent of the person who is so entitled, and shall be discharged from any obligation (whether arising by contract or otherwise) to retain the goods or to deliver them to any person so entitled.

(4) Subject to the following provisions of this section, the prospective hirer or buyer shall be under an obligation to take reasonable care of the goods until the end of the period of twenty-one days beginning with the date of service of the notice of cancellation.

(5) Where the prospective hirer or buyer delivers the goods as mentioned in paragraph (a) of subsection (3) of this section, his obligation to take care of the goods shall thereupon cease; and if he sends the goods to an authorised person as mentioned in paragraph (b) of that subsection, he shall be under an obligation to take reasonable care to see that they are received by that person and are not damaged in transit to him, but in other res-pects his obligation to take care of the goods shall cease on his sending the goods to that person.

(6) Where, at any time during the period of twenty-one days mentioned in subsection (4) of this section, the prospective hirer or buyer receives such a request as is mentioned in sub-section (2) of this section, and unreasonably refuses or unreason-ably fails to comply with it, his obligation to take reasonable care of the goods shall continue until he delivers or sends the goods as mentioned in paragraph (a) or paragraph (b) of subsection (3) of this section.

(7) Any obligation under subsections (4) to (6) of this section shall be owed to the person for the time being entitled to possession of the goods, and any breach of that obligation shall be actionable, at the suit of that person, as a breach of statutory duty.

(8) Except as provided by subsections (4) to (7) of this section, the prospective hirer or buyer shall not be under any obligation (whether arising by contract or otherwise) to take care of the goods by reason of their having come into his possession as men-tioned in subsection (1) of this section.

(9) In this section "authorised person" means a person falling within any one or more of the following descriptions, that is to say:

(a) The person who conducted any antecedent negotiations in pursuance of which the prospective hirer or buyer signed the relevant document;

(*b*) The person for the time being entitled to possession of the goods;

(*c*) The owner or seller;

(*d*) Any person who is specified, as mentioned in section 12(1)(*a*) of this Act, as a person to whom a notice of cancellation may be sent,

and any reference to the premises of the prospective hirer or buyer is a reference to the premises which in the relevant document are specified as his address.

14. *Further consequences of notice of cancellation.*

(1) Where a notice of cancellation operates so as to rescind a hire-purchase agreement, a credit-sale agreement or a conditional sale agreement:

(*a*) That agreement, and any contract of guarantee relating thereto, shall be deemed never to have had effect, and

(*b*) Any security given by the prospective hirer or buyer in respect of money payable under the agreement, or given by a guarantor in respect of money payable under such a contract of guarantee, shall be deemed never to have been enforceable.

(2) On the service of a notice of cancellation, any sum which:

(*a*) Has been paid by the prospective hirer or buyer in respect of the goods to which the relevant document relates, whether it has been paid before the signature of the document or in pursuance of any provision contained in that document, and

(*b*) Is comprised (or would, if the document constituted a hire-purchase agreement, a credit-sale agreement or a conditional sale agreement, be comprised) in the hire-purchase price or total purchase price or (if it is not or would not be so comprised) has in pursuance of any antecedent negotiations been paid to, or for the benefit of, the owner or seller, or has in pursuance of any such negotiations been paid to, or for the benefit of, any person (other than the owner or seller) who conducted those negotiations,

shall be recoverable by the prospective hirer or buyer from the person to whom it has been paid; and, if the prospective hirer or buyer is in possession of those goods, he shall have a lien on them for any sum which he is entitled to recover by virtue of this subsection.

(3) Any obligation to pay any sum which, if it had been paid before the service of a notice of cancellation, would have been recoverable by the prospective hirer or buyer under the last preceding subsection, shall be extinguished on the service of such a notice.

(4) Any sum recoverable under subsection (2) of this section shall be recoverable as a simple contract debt in any court of competent jurisdiction.

15. *Effect of notice of cancellation where goods given in part-exchange.*

(1) The provisions of this section shall have effect where a notice of cancellation is served, and, in pursuance of any antecedent negotiations conducted by him, a person (in this section referred to as "the dealer") has agreed to take goods in part-exchange and those goods have been delivered to the dealer.

(2) Unless, before the end of the period of ten days beginning with the date of service of the notice of cancellation, the goods in question are delivered to the prospective hirer or buyer, and are then in a condition which is substantially as good as when they were delivered to the dealer, the prospective hirer or buyer shall be entitled to recover from the dealer a sum equal to the part-exchange allowance.

(3) During the period of ten days referred to in the last preceding subsection the prospective hirer or buyer, if he is in possession of the goods to which the relevant document relates, shall be entitled to retain possession of them until either:

    (*a*) The goods agreed to be taken in part-exchange are delivered to him in such a condition as is mentioned in that subsection, or

    (*b*) A sum equal to the part-exchange allowance is paid to him;

and if, immediately before the end of that period, he continues by virtue of this subsection to be entitled to retain possession of the goods to which the relevant document relates, he shall have a lien on those goods for any sum which he is entitled to recover by virtue of the last preceding subsection.

(4) Any sum recoverable under subsection (2) of this section shall be recoverable as a simple contract debt in any court of competent jurisdiction.

(5) Where the prospective hirer or buyer recovers from the dealer a sum equal to the part-exchange allowance, then, if the title of the prospective hirer or buyer to the goods agreed to be taken in part-exchange has not vested in the dealer, that title shall so vest on the recovery of that sum.

(6) For the purposes of this section:

    (*a*) The dealer shall be taken to have agreed to take goods in part-exchange if, in pursuance of the antecedent negotiations, he has either purchased or agreed to purchase those goods or has accepted or agreed to accept them as part of the consideration for the transaction to which the relevant document relates, and (*b*) The part-exchange allowance shall be taken to be the sum which, in the antecedent negotiations, was agreed to be allowed in respect of the goods referred to in the preceding paragraph, or, if no such sum was agreed, the part-exchange allowance shall be taken to be such sum as in all the circumstances it would have been reasonable to allow in respect of those goods if no notice of cancellation had been served.

Representations, conditions and warranties

16. *Dealer to be agent of owner or seller in respect of certain representations.*

(1) Where a person (in this section referred to as "the owner or seller") lets goods under a hire-purchase agreement, or sells or agrees to sell goods under a credit-sale agreement or a conditional sale agreement, any representations with respect to the goods to which the agreement relates which were made, either orally or in writing, to the hirer or buyer by a person other than the owner or seller in the course of any antecedent negotiations conducted by that other person shall be deemed to have been made by him as agent of the owner or seller.

(2) Nothing in this section shall exonerate any person from any liability (whether criminal or civil) to which he would be subject apart from this section.

(3) Section 2(4) of this Act applies to this section.

(4) In this section "representations" includes any statement or undertaking, whether constituting a condition or a warranty or not, and references to making representations shall be construed accordingly.

17. *Implied conditions and warranties.*

(1) In every hire-purchase agreement and in every conditional sale agreement there shall be implied:

(*a*) A condition on the part of the owner or seller that he will have a right to sell the goods at the time when the property is to pass;

(*b*) A warranty that the hirer or buyer shall have and enjoy quiet possession of the goods;

(*c*) A warranty that the goods shall be free from any charge or encumbrance in favour of any third party at the time when the property is to pass.

(2) Subject to the next following subsection, and to section 18 of this Act, in every hire-purchase agreement and in every conditional sale agreement there shall be implied a condition that the goods will be of merchantable quality.

(3) Where the hirer or buyer has examined the goods or a sample of them, the condition referred to in subsection (2) of this section shall not be implied by virtue of that subsection in respect of defects which the examination ought to have revealed.

(4) Where the hirer under a hire-purchase agreement, or the buyer under a conditional sale agreement, whether expressly or by implication:

(a) Has made known to the owner or seller, or to a servant or agent of the owner or seller, the particular purpose for which the goods are required, or

(b) In the course of any antecedent negotiations has made that purpose known to any other person by whom those negotiations were conducted, or to a servant or agent of such a person,

there shall, subject to the provisions of section 18 of this Act, be implied a condition that the goods will be reasonably fit for that purpose.

(5) Nothing in this or the next following section shall prejudice the operation of any other enactment of rule of law whereby any condition or warranty is to be implied in any hire-purchase agreement or conditional sale agreement.

18. *Provisions as to exclusion of implied conditions and warranties.*

(1) Where under a hire-purchase agreement or a conditional sale agreement goods are let or agreed to be sold as second-hand goods, and:

(a) The agreement contains a statement to that effect, and a provision that the condition referred to in section 17(2) of this Act is excluded in relation to those goods, and

(b) It is proved that before the agreement was made the provision in the agreement so excluding that condition was brought to the notice of the hirer or buyer and its effect made clear to him,

that condition shall not be implied in the agreement in relation to those goods.

(2) Where under a hire-purchase agreement or a conditional sale agreement goods are let or agreed to be sold as being subject to defects specified in the agreement (whether referred to in the agreement as defects or by any other description to the like effect), and:

(a) The agreement contains a provision that the condition referred to in section 17(2) of this Act is excluded in relation to those goods in respect of those defects and

(b) It is proved that before the agreement was made those defects, and the provision in the agreement so excluding that condition, were brought to the notice of the hirer or buyer and the effect of that provision was made clear to him,

that condition shall not be implied in the agreement in respect of those defects.

(3) The condition and warranties specified in subsection (1) of section 17 of this Act, and, except as provided by subsection (3) of that section and by subsections (1) and (2) of this section, the condition specified in subsection (2) of that section, shall be implied notwithstanding any agreement to the contrary.

(4) The owner or seller shall not be entitled to rely on any provision in a hire-purchase agreement or conditional sale agreement excluding or modifying the condition referred to in section 17(4) of this Act unless he proves that before the agreement was made that provision was brought to the notice of the hirer or buyer and its effect was made clear to him.

19. *Further implied conditions in special cases.*

(1) Where goods are let under a hire-purchase agreement, or are agreed to be sold under a conditional sale agreement, and the goods are so let or agreed to be sold by reference to a sample, there shall be implied in the agreement:

(a) A condition that the bulk will correspond with the sample in quality, and

(b) A condition that the hirer or buyer will have a reasonable opportunity of comparing the bulk with the sample.

(2) Where goods are let under a hire-purchase agreement, or are agreed to be sold under a conditional sale agreement, and are so let or agreed to be sold by description, there shall be implied in the agreement a condition that the goods will correspond with the description; and if the goods are let or agreed to be sold under the agreement by reference to a sample, as well as by description, it shall not be sufficient that the bulk of the goods corresponds with the sample if the goods do not also correspond with the description.

20. *Special provisions as to conditional sale agreements.*

(1) Section 11(1)(c) of the Sale of Goods Act, 1893 (whereby in certain circumstances a breach of a condition in a contract of sale is to be treated only as a breach of warranty) shall not apply to conditional sale agreements.

(2) A breach of a condition (whether express or implied) to be fulfilled by the seller under a conditional sale agreement shall be treated as a breach of warranty, and not as grounds for rejecting the goods and treating the agreement as repudiated, if (but only if) it would have fallen to be so treated had the condition been

contained or implied in a corresponding hire-purchase agreement as a condition to be fulfilled by the owner.

(3) A conditional sale agreement shall be treated as not being a contract of sale for the purposes of sections 12 to 15 of the Sale of Goods Act, 1893 (which imply certain conditions and warranties in contracts of sale).

(4) In this section "corresponding hire-purchase agreement" means a hire-purchase agreement relating to the same goods as the conditional sale agreement and made between the same parties and at the same time and in the same circumstances and, as nearly as may be, in the same terms as the conditional sale agreement.

Duties to supply information and documents

21. *Owner or seller to supply information and copy to hirer or buyer.*

(1) At any time before the final payment has geen made under a hire-purchase agreement, a credit-sale agreement or a conditional sale agreement, any person entitled to enforce the agreement against the hirer or buyer shall, within four days after he has received a request in writing from the hirer or buyer, and the hirer or buyer has tendered to him the sum of 2s. 6d. for expenses, supply to the hirer or buyer a copy of the agreement, together with a statement signed by that person or his agent showing:

   (*a*) The amount paid by or on behalf of the hirer or buyer;

   (*b*) The amount which has become due under the agreement but remains unpaid, and the date on which each unpaid instalment became due, and the amount of each such instalment; and

   (*c*) The amount which is to become payable under the agreement, and the date, or the mode of determining the date, on which each future instalment is to become payable, and the amount of each such instalment.

(2) In the event of a failure without reasonable cause to comply with the preceding subsection, then, while the default continues:

   (*a*) No person shall be entitled to enforce the agreement against the hirer or buyer or to enforce any contract of guarantee relating to the agreement, and, in the case of a hire-purchase agreement or a conditional sale agreement, the owner or seller shall not be entitled to enforce any right to recover the goods from the hirer or buyer, and

   (*b*) No security by the hirer or buyer in respect of money payable under the agreement, or given by a guarantor in respect of money payable under a contract of guarantee

relating to the agreement, shall be enforceable against the
hirer or buyer or the guarantor by any holder thereof,

and, if the default continues for a period of one month, the
person in default shall be liable on summary conviction to a fine
not exceeding £25.

(3) If a copy supplied to a hirer or buyer in pursuance of a
request made by him under this section does not comply with
such requirements of any regulations made under section 32 of
this Act as relate thereto, the last preceding subsection shall apply
as if that copy had not been supplied to him.

(4) In relation to a credit-sale agreement under which the
total purchase price does not exceed £30, subsection (1) of this
section shall apply with the substitution, for the words "a copy
of the agreement," of the words "a copy of any note or memorandum of the agreement."

(5) Section 2(4) of this Act applies to this section.

22. *Requirements relating to contracts of guarantee.*

(1) A contract of guarantee relating to a hire-purchase agreement, a credit-sale agreement or a conditional sale agreement,
and any security given by a guarantor in respect of money payable
under such a contract, shall (subject to the following provisions
of this section) not be enforceable unless, within seven days of
the making of the contract of guarantee or the making of the
hire-purchase agreement, credit-sale agreement or conditional sale
agreement, whichever is the later, there is delivered or sent to the
guarantor:

(a) A copy of the hire-purchase agreement, credit-sale agreement or conditional sale agreement, and

(b) A copy of a note or memorandum of the contract of guarantee, being a note or memorandum signed by the guarantor
or by a person authorised by him to sign it on his behalf.

(2) Subject to the next following subsection, such a contract
of guarantee, and any such security, shall also not be enforceable
unless:

(a) Each copy delivered or sent as mentioned in the preceding
subsection, and

(b) The note or memorandum of the contract of guarantee,

complies with the requirements of any regulations made under
section 32 of this Act, in so far as any such requirements relate
thereto.

(3) If in any action the court is satisfied that a failure to comply
with any requirement imposed by subsection (1) of this section,
or with any such requirement as is mentioned in the last preceding
subsection, has not prejudiced the guarantor, and that it would

be just and equitable to dispense with that requirement, the court may, subject to any conditions that it thinks fit to impose, dispense with that requirement for the purposes of the action.

23. *Further documents to be supplied to guarantor.*

(1) Where a contract of guarantee relating to a hire-purchase agreement, a credit-sale agreement or a conditional sale agreement is for the time being in force, and the final payment under that agreement has not been made, any person entitled to enforce the contract of guarantee against the guarantor, shall, within four days after he has received a request in writing from the guarantor, and the guarantor has tendered to him the sum of 2s. 6d. for expenses, supply to the guarantor the documents specified in the next following subsection.

(2) The documents referred to in the preceding subsection are:

(a) A copy of the hire-purchase agreement, credit-sale agreement or conditional sale agreement, or, in the case of a credit-sale agreement under which the total purchase price does not exceed £30, a copy of any note or memorandum of the agreement; and

(b) A copy of a note or memorandum of the contract of guarantee; and

(c) A statement signed by, or by the agent of, the person to whom the request in writing referred to in the preceding subsection is made, showing the matters specified in paragraphs (a) to (c) of section 21(1) of this Act.

(3) In the event of a failure without reasonable cause to comply with subsection (1) of this section, then, while the default continues:

(a) No person shall be entitled to enforce the contract of guarantee against the guarantor, and

(b) No security given by the guarantor in respect of money payable under that contract shall be enforceable against the guarantor by any holder of that security,

and, if the default continues for a period of one month, the person in default shall be liable on summary conviction to a fine not exceeding £25.

(4) If a copy supplied to a guarantor in pursuance of a request made by him under this section does not comply with such requirements of any regulations made under section 32 of this Act as relate thereto, the last preceding subsection shall apply as if that copy had not been supplied to him.

(5) Section 2(4) of this Act applies to this section.

24. *Hirer or buyer to give information to owner or seller.*

(1) Where by virtue of a hire-purchase agreement or a condi-

tional sale agreement a hirer or buyer is under a duty to keep the goods comprised in the agreement in his possession or control, the hirer or buyer shall, on receipt of a request in writing from the owner or seller, inform the owner or seller where the goods are at the time when the information is given, or, if it is sent by post, at the time of posting.

(2) If a hirer or buyer fails without reasonable cause to give that information within fourteen days of the receipt of the notice, he shall be liable on summary conviction to a fine not exceeding £25.

Defaults in payment

25. *Notice of default.*

(1) The provisions of this section shall have effect where goods are let under a hire-purchase agreement, or are agreed to be sold under a conditional sale agreement, and that agreement, or any other agreement, contains a provision (however expressed, and whether limited to defaults in payment or not) whereby, apart from this section, on the occurrence of, or at a time to be ascertained by reference to, a default in the payment of one or more instalments or other sums payable by the hirer or buyer, such of the consequences mentioned in the next following subsection as are specified in that provision (in this section referred to as "the specified consequences") would follow.

(2) The consequences referred to in the preceding subsection are that the hire-purchase agreement or conditional sale agreement, or (in the case of a hire-purchase agreement) the bailment of the goods, shall terminate, or shall be terminable, or that the owner or seller shall have a right to recover possession of the goods.

(3) If default is made in the payment of one or more sums to which that provision (in this subsection referred to as "the relevant provision") applies, the specified consequences shall not follow by reason of that default unless the owner or seller serves on the hirer or buyer, by post or otherwise, a notice (in this Act referred to as a "notice of default") stating the amount which has become due, but remains unpaid, in respect of sums to which the relevant provision applies, and requiring the amount so stated to be paid within such period (not being less than seven days beginning with the date of service of the notice) as may be specified in the notice.

(4) Where a notice of default is served, the specified consequences shall not follow before the end of the period specified in the notice by reason of any default to which the notice relates; and, if before the end of that priod the amount specified in the notice is paid or tendered by or on behalf of the hirer or buyer or

any guarantor, the specified consequences shall not follow thereafter by reason of any such default.

(5) In a case where the specified consequences are that the hire-purchase agreement or conditional sale agreement, or (in the case of a hire-purchase agreement) the bailment of the goods, may be terminated by notice given by the owner or seller, a notice of default may include a notice terminating the hire-purchase agreement or conditional sale agreement, or the bailment, as the case may be, at or after the end of the period specified therein in accordance with subsection (3) of this section, subject to a condition that the termination is not to take effect if before the end of that period the amount specified in the notice of default is paid or tendered as mentioned in the last preceding subsection.

Right of hirer or buyer to terminate agreement

27. *Right to terminate agreement.*

(1) At any time before the final payment under a hire-purchase agreement or conditional sale agreement falls due, the hirer or buyer shall (subject to the next following subsection) be entitled to terminate the agreement by giving notice of termination in writing to any person entitled or authorised to receive the sums payable under the agreement.

(2) In the case of a conditional sale agreement, where the property in the goods, having become vested in the buyer, is transferred to a person who does not become the buyer under the agreement, the buyer shall not thereafter be entitled to terminate the agreement under this section.

(3) Subject to the last preceding subsection, where a buyer under a conditional sale agreement terminates the agreement under this section after the property in the goods has become vested in him, the property in the goods shall thereupon vest in the person (in this subsection referred to as "the previous owner") in whom it was vested immediately before it became vested in the buyer:

Provided that if the previous owner has died, or any other event has occurred whereby that property, if vested in him immediately before that event, would thereupon have vested in some other person, the property shall be treated as having devolved as if it had been vested in the previous owner immediately before his death or immediately before that event, as the case may be.

(4) Nothing in this section shall prejudice any right of a hirer or buyer to terminate a hire-purchase agreement or conditional sale agreement otherwise than by virtue of this section.

28. *Liability of hirer or buyer giving notice of termination.*

(1) Where the hirer under a hire-purchase agreement, or the buyer under a conditional sale agreement, terminates the agreement by virtue of the last preceding section, then, subject to the following provisions of this section, and without prejudice to any liability which has accrued before the termination, he shall be liable:

(a) In the case of a hire-purchase agreement, to pay the amount (if any) by which one-half of the hire-purchase price exceeds the total of the sums paid and the sums due in respect of the hire-purchase price immediately before the termination, or

(b) In the case of a conditional sale agreement, to pay the amount (if any) by which one-half of the total purchase price exceeds the total of the sums paid and the sums due in respect of the total purchase price immediately before the termination,

or if (in either case) the agreement specifies a lesser amount, he shall be liable to pay the amount so specified.

(2) If in any action the court is satisfied that a sum less than the amount specified in paragraph (a) or paragraph (b) of the preceding subsection (as the case may be) would be equal to the loss sustained by the owner or seller in consequence of the termination of the agreement by the hirer or buyer, the court may make an order for the payment of that sum in lieu of that amount.

(3) Where a hire-purchase agreement or conditional sale agreement has been terminated under the last preceding section, the hirer or buyer, if he has failed to take reasonable care of the goods, shall be liable to pay damages for the failure.

(4) Where a hirer or buyer, having terminated a hire-purchase agreement or conditional sale agreement under the last preceding section, wrongfully retains possession of the goods, then, in any action brought by the owner or seller to recover possession of the goods from the hirer or buyer, the court, unless it is satisfied that having regard to the circumstances it would not be just and equitable to do so, shall order the goods to be delivered to the owner or seller without giving the hirer or buyer an option to pay the value of the goods.

(5) The preceding provisions of this section shall have effect subject to the provisions of section 55 of this Act.

Avoidance of certain provisions and contracts

29. *General provisions.*

(1) Any provision to which this subsection applies shall be void.

(2) The preceding subsection applies to any provision in any agreement (whether a hire-purchase agreement, credit-sale agreement or conditional sale agreement or not):

(a) Whereby an owner or seller, or any person acting on his behalf, is authorised to enter upon any premises for the purpose of taking possession of goods which have been let under a hire-purchase agreement or agreed to be sold under a conditional sale agreement, or is relieved from liability for any such entry, or

(b) Whereby the right conferred by section 27 of this Act to terminate a hire-purchase agreement or a conditional sale agreement is excluded or restricted, or whereby any liability, in addition to the liability imposed by section 28 of this Act, is imposed on a hirer or buyer by reason of the termination of a hire-purchase agreement or conditional sale agreement under the said section 27, or

(c) Whereby a hirer or buyer, after the termination in any manner whatsoever of a hire-purchase agreement or conditional sale agreement or (in the case of a hire-purchase agreement) of the bailment, is (apart from any liability which has accrued before the termination) subject to a liability to pay an amount which exceeds whichever is the lesser of the two following amounts, that is to say:

  (i) The amount mentioned in paragraph (a) or (as the case may be) in paragraph (b) of section 28(1) of this Act, and

  (ii) An amount equal to the loss sustained by the owner or seller in consequence of the termination of the agreement or bailment, or

(d) Whereby any person acting on behalf of an owner or seller in connection with the formation or conclusion of a hire-purchase agreement, credit-sale agreement or conditional sale agreement is treated as, or deemed to be, the agent of the hirer or buyer, or

(e) Whereby an owner or seller is relieved from liability for the acts or defaults of any person acting on his behalf in connection with the formation or conclusion of a hire-purchase agreement, credit-sale agreement or conditional sale agreement.

(3) There shall also be void any provision in any agreement (whether a hire-purchase agreement, credit-sale agreement or conditional sale agreement or not):

(a) Excluding or restricting the operation of any enactment contained in sections 11 to 15 of this Act or the exercise of any right conferred by such an enactment or imposing any liability in consequence of the exercise of such a right, other than or in addition to any liability imposed by such an enactment, or

(b) Excluding or restricting the operation of any enactment contained in section 16 or section 31 of this Act, or

(c) Excluding or modifying any condition implied by virtue of section 19 of this Act.

(4) Any contract, whether oral or in writing, which apart from this subsection would have effect as a contract to enter into a hire-purchase agreement, a credit-sale agreement or a conditional sale agreement (as distinct from a contract constituting such an agreement) shall be void.

(5) Section 2(4) of this Act applies to subsections (2) and (3) of this section.

Supplementary provisions

31. *Agency for purpose of receiving notices.*

(1) Where a person has made an offer to enter into a hire-purchase agreement, a credit-sale agreement or a conditional sale agreement, in a case not falling within section 11(1) of this Act, and wishes to withdraw that offer before it is accepted, any person who conducted any antecedent negotiations shall be deemed to be the agent of any other person concerned for the purpose of receiving notice that the offer is withdrawn.

(2) Where the hirer or buyer under a hire-purchase agreement, a credit-sale agreement or a conditional sale agreement claims to have a right to rescind the agreement, any person who conducted any antecedent negotiations shall be deemed to be the agent of the owner or seller for the purpose of receiving any notice rescinding the agreement which is served by the hirer or buyer.

(3) In subsection (1) of this section "other person concerned", in relation to an offer, means any person who would be in a position to accept the offer if it were not withdrawn; and in the last preceding subsection "rescind" does not include:

(a) The service of a notice of cancellation, or

(b) The termination of an agreement under section 27 of this Act, or by the exercise of a right or power in that behalf expressly conferred by the agreement.

(4) The preceding provisions of this section shall have effect without prejudice to the operation of section 12(3) of this Act.

(5) Section 2(4) of this Act applies to this section.

32. *Legibility of documents.*

(1) The Board of Trade may make regulations prescribing such requirements (whether as to type, size, colour or disposition

G

of lettering, quality or colour of paper, or otherwise) as the Board may consider appropriate for securing that documents to which this section applies are easily legible.

(2) Subject to the next following subsection, the documents to which this section applies are documents of any of the following descriptions, that is to say:

(a) Any hire-purchase agreement, credit-sale agreement or conditional sale agreement;

(b) Any such copy as is mentioned in subsection (2) or subsection (3) of section 8 or in subsection (2) or subsection (3) of section 9 of this Act;

(c) Any copy supplied to a hirer or buyer in pursuance of a request made by him under section 21 of this Act;

(d) Any note or memorandum of a contract of guarantee relating to a hire-purchase agreement, credit-sale agreement or conditional sale agreement, and any such copy as is mentioned in paragraph (a) or paragraph (b) of section 22(1) of this Act;

(e) Any such copy as is mentioned in paragraph (a) or paragraph (b) of subsection (2) of section 23 of this Act which is supplied to a guarantor in pursuance of a request made by him under subsection (1) of that section.

(3) Without prejudice to the operation of section 57(3) of this Act in relation to any regulations made under this section, any such regulations:

(a) May specify which parts of the contents of a document to which the regulations apply are permitted to consist of handwriting or a reproduction of handwriting, and may prescribe different requirements in relation to so much of the contents of such a document as is permitted to consist, and consists, of handwriting or a reproduction of handwriting and in relation to the remainder of the contents of such a document; and

(b) May except from any of the requirements of the regulations any marginal notes or other subsidiary parts of a document.

(4) In relation to so much of any document falling within paragraph (a) or paragraph (b) of subsection (2) of this section as consists of:

(a) Words or other matters prescribed by regulations made under section 7(2) of this Act, or

(b) A statement required to be contained therein as prescribed by regulations made under section 9(4) of this Act,

any regulations made under this section shall have effect subject to the provisions of the regulations referred to in paragraph (a) or paragraph (b) of this subsection, as the case may be.

PART III

Protected goods

33. *Meaning of "protected goods."*

(1) For the purposes of this Part of this Act goods are "protected goods" if for the time being the following conditions are fulfilled, that is to say:

(a) That the goods have been let under a hire-purchase agreement, or agreed to be sold under a conditional sale agreement;

(b) That one-third of the hire-purchase price or total purchase price has been paid (whether in pursuance of a judgment or otherwise) or tendered by or on behalf of the hirer or buyer or a guarantor; and

(c) That the hirer or buyer has not terminated the hire-purchase agreement or conditional sale agreement, or (in the case of a hire-purchase agreement) the bailment, by virtue of any right vested in him.

(2) In this Part of this Act "the agreement," in relation to any protected goods, means the hire-purchase agreement or conditional sale agreement in respect of which those conditions are fulfilled.

34. *Restriction on right to recover possession of protected goods.*

(1) The owner (where the agreement is a hire-purchase agreement) or the seller (where it is a conditional sale agreement) shall not enforce any right to recover possession of protected goods from the hirer or buyer otherwise than by action.

(2) If the owner or seller recovers possession of protected goods in contravention of the preceding subsection, the agreement, if not previously terminated, shall terminate, and:

(a) The hirer or buyer shall be released from all liability under the agreement, and shall be entitled to recover from the owner or seller, in an action for money had and received, all sums paid by the hirer or buyer under the agreement or under any security given by him in respect thereof, and

(b) Any guarantor shall be tntitled to recover from the owner or seller, in an action for money had and received, all sums paid by him under the contract of guarantee or under any security given by him in respect thereof.

Action by owner for possession

35. *Action by owner to recover possession of protected goods from hirer.*

(1) This section applies to any action brought by the owner to enforce a right to recover possession of protected goods from the hirer, where the owner has not previously, in contravention of section 34(1) of this Act, recovered possession of part of the goods let under the agreement.

(2) Subject to such exceptions as may be provided for by county court rules, all the parties to the agreement, and any guarantor, shall be made parties to the action.

(3) Pending the hearing of the action, the court shall, in addition to any other powers, have power, on the application of the owner, to make such orders as the court thinks just for the purpose of protecting the goods from damage or depreciation, including orders restricting or prohibiting the use of the goods or giving directions as to their custody.

(4) Subject to the following provisions of this Part of this Act, on the hearing of the action the court may, without prejudice to any other power:

(a) Make an order for the specific delivery of all the goods to the owner, or

(b) Make an order for the specific delivery of all the goods to the owner and postpone the operation of the order on condition that the hirer or any guarantor pays the unpaid balance of the hire-purchase price at such times and in such amounts as the court, having regard to the means of the hirer and of any guarantor, thinks just, and subject to the fulfilment by the hirer or a guarantor of such other conditions as the court thinks just, or

(c) Make an order for the specific delivery of a part of the goods to the owner and for the transfer to the hirer of the owner's title to the remainder of the goods.

(5) In this Part of this Act any reference to an order for the specific delivery of goods to the owner is a reference to an order for the delivery of those goods to the owner without giving the hirer an option to pay their value.

(6) In the following provisions of this Part of this Act "postponed" means postponed in pursuance of subsection (4)(b) of this section, and any reference to postponement shall be construed accordingly.

36. *Circumstances in which postponed order may be made.*

(1) The operation of an order for the specific delivery of goods to the owner shall not be postponed unless the hirer satisfies the court

that the goods are in his possession or control at the time when the
order is made.

(2) If in an action to which the last preceding section
applies an offer as to conditions for the postponement of the
operation of an order is made by the hirer, and accepted by the
owner, in accordance with rules of court, the court (subject to the
next following subsection) may thereupon make the order, and
postpone its operation, in accordance with the offer without
hearing evidence as to any of the matters mentioned in subsection
(4)(*b*) of the last preceding section and in subsection (1) of this
section.

(3) Where a guarantor is a party to the action, an order shall
not be made in pursuance of the last preceding subsection before
the date fixed for the hearing of the action.

37. *Restriction on orders transferring owner's title.*

(1) The court shall not exercise any power under this Part of
this Act to make an order for the transfer to the hirer of the
owner's title to part of the goods to which the agreement relates
unless the court is satisfied that the amount which the hirer has
paid in respect of the hire-purchase price exceeds the price of
that part of the goods by at least one-third of the unpaid balance
of the hire-purchase price.

(2) In this section "price", in relation to any part of the goods
to which the agreement relates, mean such part of the hire-
purchase price as is assigned to that part of the goods by the
agreement, or, if no such assignment is so made, it means such
part of the hire-purchase price as the court may determine.

38. *Effect of postponed order.*

(1) While the operation of an order for the specific delivery of
goods to the owner is postponed, the hirer shall, subject to the
following provisions of this section, be deemed to be a bailee of the
goods under and on the terms of the agreement.

(2) No further sum shall be or become payable by the hirer or
a guarantor on account of the unpaid balance of the hire-purchase
price, except in accordance with the terms of the order.

(3) The court may make such further modification of the terms
of the agreement, and of any contract of guarantee relating
thereto, as the court considers necessary having regard to the
variation of the terms of payment.

(4) If, while the operation of the order is postponed, the hirer
or a guarantor fails to comply with any condition of the postponement, or with any term of the agreement as varied by the
court, or wrongfully disposes of the goods, the owner shall not
take any civil proceedings against the hirer or guarantor other-

wise than by making an application to the court by which the order was made:

Provided that, in the case of a breach of a condition relating to the payment of the unpaid balance of the hire-purchase price, it shall not be necessary for the owner to apply to the court for leave to execute the order unless the court has so directed.

(5) When the unpaid balance of the hire-purchase price has been paid in accordance with the terms of the order, the owner's title to the goods shall vest in the hirer.

Money claims by owner

41. *Restriction on separate action.* After the owner has begun an action to which section 35 of this Act applies, he shall not take any step to enforce payment of any sum due under the agreement, or under any contract of guarantee relating to the agreement, except by claiming the sum in that action.

Action for possession, and money claims, by seller under conditional sale agreement

45. *Application of ss. 35 to 44 to conditional sale agreements.*

(1) The provisions of sections 35 to 44 of this Act shall have effect in relation to protected goods where the agreement is a conditional sale agreement, subject to the modifications specified in the following provisions of this section.

(2) Subject to the next following subsection, those provisions shall apply as if:

(*a*) Any reference to the hirer were a reference to the buyer;

(*b*) Any reference to the owner were a reference to the seller;

(*c*) Any reference to the hire-purchase price were a reference to the total purchase price; and

(*d*) Any reference to a hire-purchase agreement, or to goods let under the agreement, were a reference to a conditional sale agreement, or to goods agreed to be sold under the agreement, as the case may be.

(3) For section 38(1) of this Act there shall be substituted the following subsection:

"(1) While the operation of an order for the specific delivery of goods to the seller is postponed, the buyer shall, subject to the following provisions of this section, be deemed to be in possession of the goods under and on the terms of the agreement, other than any term providing for the property in the goods to vest in the buyer at any time before the payment of the whole of the total purchase price."

Supplementary provisions

47. *Successive agreements.*

(1) The provisions of this section shall have effect where:

(*a*) Goods have been let under a hire-purchase agreement, and, at any time after one-third of the hire-purchase price has been paid or tendered, the owner makes a further hire-purchase agreement with the hirer, or, as seller, makes a conditional sale agreement with the hirer as buyer, or

(*b*) Goods have been agreed to be sold under a conditional sale agreement, and, at any time after one-third of the total purchase price has been paid or tendered, the seller makes a further conditional sale agreement with the buyer, or, as owner, makes a hire-purchase agreement with the buyer as hirer,

and (in either case) the subsequent agreement relates to the whole or any part of those goods, with or without other goods.

(2) In any case falling within the preceding subsection, section 33 of this Act shall have effect in relation to the subsequent agreement as if paragraph (*b*) of subsection (1) of that section were omitted.

PART IV

PROVISIONS RELATED TO PARTS II AND III

51. *Appropriation of payments.*

(1) Where a hirer or buyer is liable to make payments in respect of:

(*a*) Two or more hire-purchase agreements, or

(*b*) Two or more conditional sale agreements, or

(*c*) One or more hire-purchase agreements and one or more conditional sale agreements,

and he is liable to make those payments to the same owner or seller, he shall be entitled, on making any payment in respect of the agreements which is not sufficient to discharge the total amount then due under all the agreements, to appropriate the sum so paid by him in either of the ways mentioned in the next following subsection.

(2) The hirer or buyer may appropriate the sum in question:

(*a*) In or towards the satisfaction of the sum due under any one of the agreements, or

(*b*) In or towards the satisfaction of the sums due under any two or more of the agreements in such proportions as he thinks fit.

(3) If the hirer or buyer fails to make any such appropriation, the payment shall by virtue of this subsection be appropriated towards the satisfaction of the sums due under the several agreements respectively in the proportions which those sums bear to one another.

(4) The preceding provisions of this section shall have effect notwithstanding any agreement to the contrary.

54. *Exclusion of conditional sale agreements from certain enactments relating to sale of goods.* For the purposes of section 9 of the Factors Act, 1889 and of section 25(2) of the Sale of Goods Act, 1893 (under which, notwithstanding that the property in the goods has not been transferred to him, a person who has bought or agreed to buy goods and is in possession of them can confer a good title to the goods) the buyer under a conditional sale agreement shall be deemed not to be a person who has bought or agreed to buy goods.

PART V

SUPPLEMENTARY PROVISIONS

57. *Regulations.*

(1) Any power of the Board of Trade to make regulations under this Act shall be exercisable by statutory instrument.

(2) Anything required or authorised by or under this Act to be done by, to or before the Board of Trade may be done by, to or before the President of the Board, any Minister of State with duties concerning the affairs of the Board, any secretary, under-secretary or assistant secretary of the Board or any person authorised in that behalf by the President.

(3) Where a power to make regulations is exercisable by virtue of this Act, regulations made in the exercise of that power may make different provision in relation to different classes of cases.

(4) Any power (exercisable in accordance with section 61(2) of this Act) to make regulations under this Act before the date of the commencement of this Act shall include power, by any regulations so made, to revoke any regulations made under any of the enactments which, as from that date, are repealed by this Act.

58. *Interpretation.*

(1) In this Act, except in so far as the context otherwise requires, the following expressions have the meaning hereby assigned to them respectively, that is to say:

    "action," "buyer" (except in relation to a conditional sale agreement), "delivery," "goods," "property," "sale," "seller" (except in relation to a conditional sale agreement) and "warranty" have the meanings assigned to them respectively by the Sale of Goods Act, 1893;

"appropriate trade premises," in relation to a document means premises at which either the owner or seller (as defined by section 11(5) of this Act) normally carries on a business, or goods of the description to which the document relates, or goods of a similar description, are normally offered or exposed for sale in the course of a business carried on at those premises;

"buyer," in relation to a conditional sale agreement, means the person who agrees to purchase goods under the agreement and includes a person to whom the rights or liabilities of that person under the agreement have passed by assignment or by operation of law;

"conditional sale agreement," "credit-sale agreement" and "hire-purchase agreement" have the meanings assigned to them by Part I of this Act;

"contract of guarantee," in relation to a hire-purchase agreement, credit-sale agreement or conditional sale agreement, means a contract, made at the request (express or implied) of the hirer or buyer, either to guarantee the performance of the hirer's or buyer's obligations under the hire-purchase agreement, credit-sale agreement or conditional sale agreement, or to indemnify the owner or seller against any loss which he may incur in respect of that agreement, and "guarantor" shall be construed accordingly;

"hire-purchase price" (subject to subsection (2) of this section) means the total sum payable by the hirer under a hire-purchase agreement in order to complete the purchase of goods to which the agreement relates, exclusive of any sum payable as a penalty or as compensation or damages for a breach of the agreement;

"hirer" means the person who takes or has taken goods from an owner under a hire-purchase agreement and includes a person to whom the hirer's rights or liabilities under the agreement have passed by assignment or by operation of law;

"notice of cancellation" has the meaning assigned to it by section 11(2) of this Act;

"owner" means the person who lets or has let goods to a hirer under a hire-purchase agreement and includes a person to whom the owner's property in the goods or any of the owner's rights or liabilities under the agreement has passed by assignment or by operation of law;

"seller," in relation to a conditional sale agreement, means the person who agrees to sell goods under the agreement and includes a person (other than the buyer) to whom that person's property in the goods or any of that person's rights or liabilities under the agreement has passed by assignment or by operation of law;

"total purchase price" (subject to subsection (2) of this section) means the total sum payable by the buyer under a credit-sale agreement or a conditional sale agreement, exclusive of any sum payable as a penalty or as compensation or damages for a breach of the agreement.

(2) For the purposes of this Act, any sum payable by the hirer under a hire-purchase agreement, or by the buyer under a conditional sale agreement, by way of a deposit or other initial payment, or credited or to be credited to him under the agreement on account of any such deposit or payment, whether that sum is to be or has been paid to the owner or seller or to any other person or is to be or has been discharged by a payment of money or by the transfer or delivery of goods or by any other means, shall form part of the hire-purchase price or total purchase price, as the case may be.

(3) In this Act "antecedent negotiations," in relation to a hire-purchase agreement, credit-sale agreement or conditional sale agreement, means any negotiations or arrangements with the hirer or buyer whereby he was induced to make the agreement or which otherwise promoted the transaction to which the agreement relates; and any reference in this Act to the person by whom any antecedent negotiations were conducted is a reference to the person by whom the negotiations or arrangements in question were conducted or made in the course of a business carried on by him.

(4) The last preceding subsection:

(a) Shall have effect in relation to a document to which section 11 of this Act applies, but which does not constitute a hire-purchase agreement; a credit-sale agreement or a conditional sale agreement, as if references to the agreement and to making the agreement were references respectively to the document and to signing the document and any reference to the hirer or buyer were a reference to the prospective hirer or buyer (within the meaning of that section), and

(b) For the purposes of section 31(1) of this Act, shall have effect in relation to any offer to enter into a hire-purchase agreement, credit-sale agreement or conditional sale agreement as if any reference to the agreement were a reference to the offer and any reference to the hirer or buyer were a reference to the person making the offer.

(5) For the purposes of this Act any negotiations conducted,

or arrangements or representations made, by a servant or agent, if conducted or made by him in the course of his employment or agency, shall be treated as conducted or made by his employer or principal; and anything received by a servant or agent, if received by him in the course of his employment or agency, shall be treated as received by his employer or principal.

In this subsection "representations" has the same meaning as in section 16 of this Act, and references to making representations shall be construed accordingly.

(6) Without prejudice to the operation of section 1(2) of this Act, any reference in this Act to a document which constitutes a hire-purchase agreement, credit-sale agreement or conditional sale agreement shall be construed as including a reference to a document which together with one or more other documents constitutes such an agreement, and any reference to a document which, if executed by or on behalf of another person, would constitute such an agreement shall be construed accordingly.

(7) Except in so far as the context otherwise requires, any reference in this Act to an enactment shall be construed as a reference to that enactment as amended or extended by or under any other enactment, including this Act.

SCHEDULE 1

NOTICE TO BE INCLUDED IN HIRE-PURCHASE AGREEMENT
NOTICE

Right of Hirer to terminate Agreement

1. The hirer may put an end to this agreement by giving notice of termination in writing to any person who is entitled to collect or receive the hire-rent.

2. He must then pay any instalments which are in arrear at the time when he gives notice. If, when he has paid those instalments, the total amount which he has paid under the agreement is less than (*here insert the minimum amount which the hirer is required to pay in accordance with the provisions of sections 28(1) and 55 of this Act*) he must also pay enough to make up that sum, unless the court determines that a smaller sum would be equal to the owner's loss.

3. If the goods have been damaged owing to the hirer having failed to take reasonable care of them, the owner may sue him for the amount of the damage unless that amount can be agreed between the hirer and the owner.

4. The hirer should see whether this agreement contains provisions allowing him to put an end to the agreement on terms

more favourable to him than those just mentioned. If it does, he may put an end to the agreement on those terms.

Restriction of Owner's right to recover Goods

5. *[After (*here insert an amount calculated in accordance with the provisions of sections 33 and 55 of this Act*) has been paid, then,] unless the hirer has himself put an end to the agreement, the owner of the goods cannot take them back from the hirer without the hirer's consent unless the owner obtains an order of the court.

6. If the owner applies to the court for such an order, the court may, if the court thinks it just to do so, allow the hirer to keep either:

(a) The whole of the goods, on condition that the hirer pays the balance of the price in the manner ordered by the court; or

(b) A fair proportion of the goods having regard to what the hirer has already paid.

SCHEDULE 2

NOTICE TO BE INCLUDED IN CONDITIONAL SALE AGREEMENT NOTICE

Right of Buyer to terminate Agreement

1. The buyer may put an end to this agreement by giving notice of termination in writing to any person who is entitled to collect or receive the instalments of the purchase price.

2. He must then pay any instalments which are in arrear at the time when he gives notice. If, when he has paid those instalments, the total amount which he has paid under the agreement is less than (*here insert the minimum amount which the buyer is required to pay in accordance with the provisions of sections 28(1) and 55 of this Act*) he must also pay enough to make up that sum, unless the court determines that a smaller sum would be equal to the seller's loss.

3. If the goods have been damaged owing to the buyer having failed to take reasonable care of them, the seller may sue him for the amount of the damage unless that amount can be agreed between the buyer and the seller.

* If the agreement is a subsequent agreement to which section 47 of this Act applies, the words in square brackets should be omitted.

4. The buyer should see whether this agreement contains provisions allowing him to put an end to the agreement on terms more favourable to him than those just mentioned. If it does, he may put an end to the agreement on those terms.

Restriction of Seller's right to recover Goods

5. *[After (*here insert an amount calculated in accordance with the provisions of sections 33 and 55 of this Act*) has been paid, then,] unless the buyer has himself put an end to the agreement, the seller of the goods cannot take them back from the buyer without the buyer's consent unless the seller obtains an order of the court.

6. If the seller applies to the court for such an order, the court may, if the court thinks it just to do so, allow the buyer to keep either:

- (*a*) The whole of the goods, on condition that the buyer pays the balance of the price in the manner ordered by the court; or
- (*b*) A fair proportion of the goods having regard to what the buyer has already paid.

* If the agreement is a subsequent agreement to which section **47** of this Act applies, the words in square brackets should be omitted.

HIRE-PURCHASE REGULATIONS
1965 No. 1646

The Hire-Purchase (Documents) (Legibility and Statutory Statements) Regulations 1965

The Board of Trade, in pursuance of the powers conferred upon them by sections 7(2), 9(4), 32 and 57(4) of the Hire-Purchase Act, 1965, and by sections 7(2), 9(4), 32 and 53(4) of the Hire-Purchase (Scotland) Act, 1965, hereby making the following Regulations:

PART I

LEGIBILITY OF DOCUMENTS

1. Every document to which this Part of these Regulations apply shall comply with the following provisions of the said Part.
2.

(1) The paper of the document shall be white and, except as otherwise provided in these Regulations, the lettering of the document shall be black or dark grey.

(2) The lettering, apart from any signature, shall be clear.

3.

(1) The following parts of the contents of the document may consist of handwriting or a reproduction of handwriting, that is to say:

(a) Particulars relating to any person named in the document;
(b) Particulars of the goods;
(c) The financial particulars of any transaction, including the date on which, or the period for which, any payment is to be made;
(d) Any signature or copy thereof;
(e) Any date;
(f) Any amount (whether in figures or words) inserted in the notice mentioned in section 7(1)(e) of the Act or in a copy of that notice;
(g) In the case of a document referred to in Regulation 6(1)(b) or a copy of such a document, the words "all the" or the

190

number referred to in Regulation 6(2) included within the
space outlined for the signature of the buyer.

(2) Except as provided in paragraph (1) of this Regulation the
contents of the document shall not consist of handwriting or a
reproduction thereof.

(3) Any signature may be in any colour, and the colour of the
lettering in any other part of the contents of the document which
by virtue of this Regulation may consist of, and which does
consist of, handwriting may be blue.

4.

(1) The lettering in the document shall be roman or upright
sanserif.

(2) The height of the smallest letter in the document shall be
not less than .056 of an inch, and the width of any column in the
document shall not exceed $4\frac{1}{2}$ inches:

Provided that the limit on the width of the column shall not
'apply to any part of the document if the height of the smallest
letter in that part of the document is not less than .067 of an inch.

(3) Subject to the provision of Regulation 7(7) hereof the lettering in the document shall not be in capital letters except that
capital letters may be used:

(a) For the initial letters of words; or

(b) In headings.

(4) The provisions of this Regulation shall not apply to:

(a) Any part of the contents of the document which by virtue
of Regulation 3 may consist of, and which does consist of,
handwriting or a reproduction thereof;

(5) The provisions of paragraph (3) of this Regulation shal
not apply to any part of the contents of the document which by
virtue of Regulation 3 may consist of handwriting or a reproduction of handwriting.

5. This Part of these Regulations shall apply to documents of
the following descriptions, that is to say:

(a) Any hire-purchase agreement, any credit-sale agreement
under which the total purchase price exceeds £30 or any
conditional sale agreement;

(b) Any such copy as is mentioned in subsection (2) or subsection (3) of section 8 or in subsection (2) or subsection (3)
of section 9 of the Act;

(c) Any copy supplied to the hirer or buyer in pursuance of a
request made by him under section 21 of the Act;

(d) Any note or memorandum of a contract of guarantee relating to a hire-purchase agreement, a credit-sale agreement

under which the total purchase price exceeds £30 or a conditional sale agreement and any such copy as is mentioned in paragraph (a) or paragraph (b) of section 22(1) of the Act;

(e) Any such copy as is mentioned in paragraph (a) or paragraph (b) of subsection (2) of section 23 of the Act which is supplied to the guarantor in pursuance of a request made by him under subsection (1) of that section.

PART II

STATUTORY STATEMENTS—SPACE FOR SIGNATURE

6.

(1) The following provisions of this Regulation shall apply to every document which, on being signed as mentioned in section 5(1)(a) of the Act:

(a) Constitutes a hire-purchase agreement, or

(b) Constitutes a conditional sale agreement, or

(c) Constitutes a credit-sale agreement under which the total purchase price exceeds £30.

(2) The signature of the hirer or buyer, as the case may be, shall be inserted in a space in the document outlined in the manner indicated in Part I of the Schedule hereto and accompanied by the words specified in that Part which are appropriate to that document and set out in the form therein indicated and, in the case of a document referred to in paragraph (1)(b) of this Regulation, those words shall include immediately before the word "instalments" the words "all the" or the number of the instalments which must be paid before the goods will become the property of the buyer:

Provided that nothing in this paragraph shall require there to be any particular number of words to a line.

(3) The width of the outlined area shall be not less than 3¾ inches, and its height shall be not less than 1¾ inches in the case of a credit-sale agreement and not less than 2 inches in the case of any other agreement; and the thickness of the outlining shall be not less than .025 of an inch.

(4) The colour of the lettering within the outlined area and of the outlining of that area shall be red and the height of the smallest letter within the outlined area shall be not less than .067 of an inch.

(5) Paragraph (4) of this Regulation shall not apply to any words which by virtue of Regulation 3(1)(g) may be, and which are, in handwriting or a reproduction of handwriting, but the lettering of those words may be red.

(6) The distance vertically between any of the words which are to appear in the outlined area above the place for signature and:

    (*a*) In the case of a hire-purchase agreement or a conditional sale agreement, any of the words which are to appear below that place, or

    (*b*) In the case of a credit-sale agreement, the lower horizontal line of the outlined area

shall be not less than 1 inch.

(7) Nothing in this Regulation shall prohibit the inclusion within the outlined area of any postage stamp which does not obscure any of the words required by this Regulation to be included within the outlined area.

PART III

STATUTORY STATEMENTS—RIGHT OF CANCELLATION

7.

(1) In a case to which section 9 of the Act applies the first statutory copy and the second statutory copy in relation to the relevant document shall contain the statements specified, respectively, in sections 1 and 2 of Part II of the Schedule hereto set out in, and outlined in, the manner therein indicated; and the following provisions of this Regulation shall apply in the case of each copy:

Provided that nothing in this paragraph shall require there to be any particular number of words to a line.

(2) The statement shall appear on the page which contains particulars of the goods to which the relevant document relates.

(3) The width of the outlined area shall be not less than 6 inches and its height shall be not less than $2\frac{1}{4}$ inches in the first statutory copy and not less than $2\frac{1}{2}$ inches in the second statutory copy; and the thickness of the outlining shall be not less than .025 of an inch.

(4) The colour of the lettering and the outlining of the area shall be red.

(5) The height of the smallest letter within the outlined area shall be not less than .067 of an inch.

(6) Where the lettering of the name and address required to be included within the outlined area consists of handwriting or a reproduction of handwriting that lettering may be, but shall not be required by virtue of paragraph (4) of this Regulation to be, in red, and paragraph (5) of this Regulation shall not apply to that lettering.

(7) The words "NOTICE TO CUSTOMER: RIGHT OF CANCELLATION" shall be in capital letters.

H

Part IV

GENERAL

8.

(1) In these Regulations the words "letter" and "lettering" include figures.

(2) In the application of these Regulations to England Wales:

(a) References to a hire-purchase agreement, a conditional sale agreement and a credit-sale agreement shall be construed as references respectively to a hire-purchase agreement, a conditional sale agreement and a credit-sale agreement to which Part II of the Hire-Purchase Act, 1965 for the time being applies;

(b) Any reference to the Act shall be construed as a reference to the Hire-Purchase Act, 1965.

(3) In the application of these Regulations to Scotland:

(a) References to a hire-purchase agreement, a conditional sale agreement and a credit-sale agreement shall be construed as references respectively to a hire-purchase agreement, a conditional sale agreement and a credit-sale agreement to which Part II of the Hire-Purchase (Scotland) Act, 1965 for the time being applies;

(b) Any reference to the Act shall be construed as a reference to the Hire-Purchase (Scotland) Act, 1965;

(c) In Regulation 5(d) the words "note or memorandum of a" shall be omitted.

(4) The Hire-Purchase (Documents) (Legibility and Statutory Statements) Regulations, 1964(a) and the Hire-Purchase (Documents) (Legibility and Statutory Statements) (Amendment) Regulations, 1965(b) are hereby revoked.

(5) The Interpretation Act, 1889(c) shall apply to the interpretation of these Regulations as it applies to the interpretation of an Act of Parliament and as if these Regulations and the Regulations hereby revoked were Acts of Parliament.

(6) These Regulations may be cited as the Hire-Purchase (Documents) (Legibility and Statutory Statements) Regulations, 1965, and shall come into operation on 1st October 1965.

SCHEDULE

PART I

Specified words to be included in outlined space for signature

1. Where the document contains the terms of a hire-purchase agreement:

This document contains the terms of a hire-purchase agreement. Sign it only if you want to be legally bound by them.

Signature
of hirer

The goods will not become your property until you have made all the payments. You must not sell them before then.

---

2. Where the document contains the terms of a conditional sale agreement:

This document contains the terms of a conditional sale agreement. Sign it only if you want to be legally bound by them.

Signature
of buyer

The goods will not become your property until you have paid................instalments. You must not sell them before then.

---

3. Where the document contains the terms of a credit-sale agreement:

> This document contains the terms of a credit-sale agreement. Sign it only if you want to be legally bound by them.
>
>
> Signature
> of buyer

PART II

STATUTORY STATEMENTS—RIGHT OF CANCELLATION

Section 1

Statement to be included in the first statutory copy

NOTICE TO CUSTOMER : RIGHT OF CANCELLATION

You have for a short time a legal right to cancel this agreement. You can do this by writing, saying that you are cancelling the agreement, to...

If you do cancel this agreement, any money you have already paid must be returned to you. If you have given any property in part-exchange, the property—or its value—must also be returned to you. If you have got the goods, you need take no action to return them but can wait for them to be collected. You need not hand them over unless you have received a written request to do so and have had your money and property back. If you wish, however, you may yourself take or send the goods to the person named above.

Section 2

Statement to be included in the second statutory copy

NOTICE TO CUSTOMER : RIGHT OF CANCELLATION

You have for a short time a legal right to cancel this agreement. You can do this by writing, saying that you are cancelling the agreement, to..................

You must post your letter before the end of the third day after the day on which you receive this copy of the agreement.

If you do cancel this agreement, any money you have already paid must be returned to you. If you have given any property in part-exchange, the property—or its value—must also be returned to you. If you have got the goods, you need take no action to return them but can wait for them to be collected. You need not hand them over unless you have received a written request to do so and have had your money and property back. If you wish, however, you may yourself take or send the goods to the person named above.

EXAMINATION TECHNIQUE

1. Two types of question. The student working for a law paper in an accountancy, company secretarial or other professional examination must prepare himself to answer two types of question. First, there is the kind of question which demands an exposition or discussion of a particular topic or principle. Second, there is the *problem* demanding the application of legal principles to a given situation. These two kinds of question should be considered separately.

2. Text-book questions. This kind of question is designed to test the student's knowledge and understanding of the subject. Sometimes, these questions are little more than a test of memory, but often the examiner will be looking for a grasp of the subject Here are some points for guidance.

- (a) *Read the question very carefully.* This advice seems obvious enough, but many students fail to do this. It may help to underline the part of the question that tells you what you have to do.
- (b) *Make an outline plan of your answer.* At this stage you should know exactly what the examiner wants from you. If the question is widely drawn, you will need a widely drawn plan. If the question is narrowly drawn, you will need a narrowly drawn plan. It is important to be sure that the aim and scope of your plan exactly satisfy the question. Your outline plan will probably consist of four or five key sentences arranged in logical sequence. Statutes and cases to be cited should be indicated in your plan.
- (c) *Write an answer based on the plan.* Stick to the plan and try to set out the answer in an attractive way. There is no harm in letting your plan "show through" the answer in the form of sub-headings if you so wish. In law examinations, it is usually best to write in a simple and direct style. You should aim at clarity and precision. If you are at all unsure of your English style, use short sentences.

3. Some worked examples.

Q: *Explain in detail the duty of the seller to deliver the right quantity of goods.*

A: It is the seller's contractual duty to deliver to the buyer the quantity of goods he agreed to sell under the contract.

Where a contract of sale stipulates the quantity of goods to be sold, the stipulation as to quantity is part of the description of the goods. It follows, therefore, that *s.* 13 of the *Sale of Goods Act,* 1893, applies, giving rise to an implied condition that the quantity delivered corresponds with the quantity contracted for. Moreover, where there is a term in the contract to the effect that the goods shall be packed in containers each containing a specified quantity of goods, it is the duty of the seller to conform to this requirement. Should the seller deliver the correct total quantity of goods, but in containers holding different quantities from those agreed on, there is a breach of the implied condition as to correspondence with description, and the buyer may reject the goods: *re Moore & Landauer* (1921).

Where the seller delivers to the buyer a quantity of goods less than he contracted to sell, the buyer may reject them, but if the buyer accepts the goods so delivered he must pay for them at the contract rate: *s.* 30 (1).

Where the seller delivers to the buyer a quantity of goods larger than he contracted to sell, the buyer may accept the goods included in the contract and reject the rest, or he may reject the whole. If the buyer accepts the whole of the goods so delivered, he must pay for them at the contract rate: *s.* 30 (2).

By *s.* 30 (3), where the seller delivers to the buyer goods of the contract description mixed with goods of a different description, not included in the contract, the buyer may accept the goods which are in accordance with the contract and reject the rest, or he may reject the whole. In *Dawood* v. *Heath* (1961) the buyer elected to accept only those goods which were of the contract description. In this case there was a contract for the sale of 50 tons of steel sheets, the consignment to comprise an equal number of sheets each of the following lengths: 6, 7, 8, 9 and 10 feet. The seller delivered 50 tons of sheets of length 6 feet and it was held that the buyer was entitled to accept one-fifth and reject four-fifths of the consignment. That is to say, the buyers were entitled to reject the part of the consignment which should have consisted of 7, 8, 9 and 10 foot lengths.

The rules as to delivery of the right quantity are strictly applied by the court. The seller who delivers a quantity different from that contracted for will be in breach of contract unless the discrepancy is minute, for *de minimis non curat lex* ("the law does not concern itself with trifles"): *Shipton Anderson* v. *Weil* (1912). Thus where there is a contract for the sale of a large bulk of goods, it is usual for the seller to stipulate a margin within which to operate.

Q. *What conditions are implied in a contract of sale of goods by sample?*

A: In a contract of sale of goods by sample the following conditions are implied under the provisions of the *Sale of Goods Act*, 1893:

(*a*) There is an implied condition that the bulk shall correspond with the sample in quality: *s.* 15, *S.G.A.* Where the bulk does not correspond with the sample, there is a breach of this implied condition even though a simple process would restore the goods to the quality of the sample: *Ruben* v. *Faire Bros.* (1948).

(*b*) There is an implied condition that the buyer shall have a reasonable opportunity of comparing the bulk with the sample: *s.* 15, *S.G.A.*

(*c*) There is an implied condition that the goods shall be free from any defect rendering them unmerchantable which would not be apparent on reasonable examination of the sample: *s.* 15, *S.G.A.* But a "reasonable examination" is not the most exhaustive examination possible. The standard of knowledge of the buyer must be taken into account when deciding what is reasonable: *Godley* v. *Perry* (1959).

(*d*) Where there is a contract for the sale of goods by sample as well as by description, it is not sufficient that the bulk of the goods corresponds with the sample if the goods do not also correspond with the description: there is an implied condition that the goods shall correspond with the description: *s.* 13, *S.G.A.*

Any of the implied conditions considered above may be negatived by a valid exemption clause to that effect: *s.* 55, *S.G.A.*

Q: *When is there an implied term in a sale of goods contract that the goods are fit for any particular purpose?*

A: Section 14 of the *Sale of Goods Act*, 1893, provides that there is no implied warranty or condition as to the fitness for any particular purpose of the goods supplied under a contract of sale; except that where the buyer, expressly or by implication, makes known to the seller the particular purpose for which the goods are required, so as to show that he relies on the seller's skill and judgment, and where the goods are of a description which it is in the course of the seller's business to supply (whether he be the manufacturer or not), there is an implied condition that the goods shall be reasonably fit for such purpose.

Where the goods have a self-evident purpose, *e.g.* a hot water bottle, as in *Priest* v. *Last* (1903), or a pair of underpants, as in *Grant* v. *Australian Knitting Mills* (1936), the seller will be deemed to know the purpose for which the goods are required. In these circumstances, the implied condition as to fitness for purpose arises even though the buyer does not expressly state that purpose, reliance on the seller's skill and judgment being assumed in such cases.

Where the goods have no self-evident purpose, the question whether the buyer relied on the seller's skill and judgment will depend on the circumstances of the case. In *Hill* v. *Ashington Piggeries* (1969), the sellers manufactured a mink food to the formula of the buyers, the sellers having made it clear that they knew nothing about the nutritional requirements of mink. When some of the food contained a chemical which was toxic to mink but harmless to other animals, it was held that there had been no reliance on the seller's skill and judgment with respect to ingredients which might be toxic to mink alone. But in *Kendall* v. *Lillico* (1968), where the seller knew that the ground nuts he sold were to be used ultimately for cattle and poultry food, it was held that the buyer had relied on the seller's skill and judgment, and that the seller was liable for breach of the implied condition of fitness for purpose when it was found that the nuts were toxic for poultry.

In the case of a private sale there is no implied condition as to fitness for purpose, for the Act stipulates that the goods must be of a description which it is in the course of the seller's business to supply.

The implied condition as to fitness arises in connection with goods *supplied* under a contract of sale. It therefore follows that there may be an implied condition as to fitness for purpose in connection with a box, carton or bottle which contains the goods covered by the sale, but which is returnable to the seller: *Geddling* v. *Marsh* (1920).

Where there is a contract for the sale of a specified article under its patent or other trade name, there is no implied condition as to its fitness for any particular purpose: *s. 14, S.G.A.* But where there is a sale of an article under its patent or trade name and the buyer expressly stipulates the purpose for which he requires the article, there may be an implied condition as to fitness for that purpose: *Baldry* v. *Marshall* (1925).

The implied condition as to fitness for purpose may be negatived by a valid exemption clause in the contract of sale: *s. 55, S.G.A.* Also, the condition is not implied where the goods are not fit for the buyer's purpose because of some abnormal circumstances not known to the seller: *Griffiths* v. *Peter Conway* (1939).

Q: *When does the property in the goods pass from seller to buyer under a contract of sale?*

A: No property in goods can pass from seller to buyer unless and until the goods are ascertained: *s. 16, Sale of Goods Act,*

1893. Goods are ascertained when they are identified in accordance with the agreement after the time when the contract of sale was made: *re Wait* (1926).

Where there is a contract for the sale of specific or ascertained goods, the general rule is that property passes when it is intended by the parties that it shall pass: *s.* 17, *S.G.A.* For the purpose of ascertaining the intention of the parties, regard shall be had to the terms of the contract, express and implied, and the circumstances of the case.

Section 18 of the *S.G.A.* provides a set of rules for discovering the intention of the parties. But these rules are used only where a different intention does not appear. The rules are as follows:

Rule 1: Where there is an unconditional contract for the sale of specific goods, in a deliverable state, the property in the goods passes to the buyer when the contract is made, and it is immaterial whether the time of payment or the time of delivery, or both, be postponed.

Rule 2: Where there is a contract for the sale of specific goods and the seller is bound to do something to the goods for the purpose of putting them into a deliverable state, the property does not pass until such thing be done, and the buyer has notice thereof. (Goods are in a deliverable state when they are in such a state that the buyer would under the contract be bound to take delivery of them: *s.* 62, *S.G.A.*)

Rule 3: Where there is a contract for the sale of specific goods in a deliverable state, but the seller is bound to weigh, measure, test or do some other act or thing with reference to the goods for the purpose of ascertaining the price, the property does not pass until such act or thing be done, and the buyer has notice thereof.

Rule 4: When the goods are delivered to the buyer on approval or "on sale or return" or other similar terms, the property therein passes to the buyer:

(*a*) When he signifies his approval or acceptance to the seller or does any other act adopting the transaction.

(*b*) If he does not signify his approval or acceptance to the seller but retains the goods without giving notice of rejection, then, if a time has been fixed for the return of the goods, on the expiration of such time, and, if no time has been fixed, on the expiration of a reasonable time. What is a reasonable time is a question of fact.

Rule 5: (*i*) Where there is a contract for the sale of unascertained or future goods by description, and goods of that description and in a deliverable state are unconditionally appropriated to the contract, either by the seller with the assent of the buyer, or by the buyer with the assent of the seller, the property in the goods thereupon passes to the buyer. Such assent may be express or implied, and may be given either before or after the appropriation is made.

(*ii*) Where, in pursuance of the contract, the seller delivers the goods to the buyer or to a carrier or other bailee (whether named by the buyer or not) for the purpose of transmission to the buyer, and does not reserve a right of disposal, he is deemed to have unconditionally appropriated the goods to the contract.

Q: *In what circumstances does a sale take place in market overt? What special rule applies to market overt?*

A: A sale in a shop in the City of London is deemed to be a sale in market overt when the following conditions are satisfied:

(*a*) The sale must take place in business hours on a business day.

(*b*) The entire transaction must take place in the part of the shop which is open to the public. If, for example, the sale takes place in a private back room of the shop premises, the sale cannot be in market overt.

(*c*) The goods must be of the class usually sold in that shop.

(*d*) The shopkeeper must be the seller and not the buyer.

Outside the City of London, market overt obtains only in markets where the usage has been established.

Where goods are sold in market overt, the buyer acquires a good title to the goods, provided he buys them in good faith and without notice of any defect or want of title on the part of the seller: *s.* 22, *S.G.A.* A thing is deemed to be done in good faith when it is in fact done honestly, whether it be done negligently or not: *s.* 62, *S.G.A.*

The Law Reform Committee Report on Transfer of Title, 1966, contains a recommendation for the modification of *s.* 22 on the ground that the rule is capricious in its application. The majority of the Committee recommended that *s.* 22 be replaced by a provision that a person who buys goods by retail at trade premises or by public auction acquires a good title provided he buys in good faith. By "trade premises," the Committee meant premises open to the public at which goods of the same or a similar description to those sold are normally offered for sale by retail in the course of a business carried on at those premises. This definition would not include a street market.

Q: *When is a seller of goods deemed to be an "unpaid seller"? In what circumstances may an unpaid seller exercise a statutory right of lien?*

A: The seller of goods is deemed to be an "unpaid seller" within the meaning of the *Sale of Goods Act,* 1893, when the whole of the price has not been paid or tendered, or when a negotiable instrument has been received as conditional payment and has been dishonoured: *s.* 39, *S.G.A.*

The unpaid seller of goods who is in possession of them is entitled to retain possession until payment or tender of the price in the following circumstances:

(a) Where the goods have been sold without any stipulation as to credit; or

(b) Where the goods have been sold on credit, but the terms of credit have expired; or

(c) Where the buyer becomes insolvent: *s.* 41, *S.G.A.*

The unpaid seller's lien is subject to the provisions of the *Sale of Goods Act,* 1893; thus the lien will be defeated by the right of a person to whom the buyer transferred documents of title relating to the goods, provided they were received in good faith and for value: *ss.* 47 and 25, *S.G.A. Ant. Jurgens Margarinefabrieken* v. *Dreyfus* (1914). Moreover, the unpaid seller's right of lien arises by implication of law and may, therefore, be negatived or varied by agreement between the parties: *s.* 55, *S.G.A.*

The unpaid seller loses his right of lien on the goods in the following circumstances:

(a) When he delivers the goods to a carrier or other bailee for the purpose of transmission to the buyer without reserving the right of disposal of the goods; or

(b) When the buyer or his agent lawfully obtains possession of the goods; or

(c) By waiver of the right: *s.* 43, *S.G.A.*

(d) When the price is paid or tendered: *s.* 41, *S.G.A.*

4. Problems. Examination questions which take the form of problems are designed to discover whether the student is able to recognise and apply the relevant legal principles to a given situation.

(a) *Read the problem very carefully.* The problem will include a number of facts. Consider each fact stated and then study the instructions. You may be told, for example, to advise one of the parties, or to comment on the legal position. Whatever the instruction, you should carry it out exactly.

(b) *Decide what legal principles are applicable.*

(c) *Make an outline plan of your answer.* Your plan should include an indication of the principles to be applied. Where there are several principles, the sequence should be such as to bring out the relationship between them: for example, where your problem requires the application of an exception to a general rule, state first the general rule and follow it with the exception. Where two conflicting rules seem to apply, state both rules. Jot down the names of cases or section numbers of statutes to be cited as authorities for the rules stated. If you cannot remember the section numbers, just cite the statute. Complete your plan by making a brief note of the result obtained when the relevant principles are applied to the facts of the problem. Do not worry if you do not reach a definite solution.

(d) *Write your answer based on the plan.* Aim at a concise statement of the rules applicable, giving an authority for each rule stated. You should be able to remember the most important section numbers of the *Sale of Goods Act*, but where you cannot remember the section number you should, nevertheless, give the Act as your authority for the rule. Where you need to cite a case as an authority for a rule, the name of the case is often sufficient. If you wish to mention the facts of a decided case, confine yourself to those which are relevant to the point under discussion. Do not launch out into a long rigmarole including irrelevant details of the case. Merely identify and isolate those facts which are of legal significance. Many examiners deliberately omit a fact from a problem. Where this happens, you should supply the alternative facts yourself, stating clearly in your answer that you are doing so. This usually leads to an answer which branches out into two limbs, one for each of the alternatives which you have supplied for yourself.

5. Worked examples.

Q: *Sydney, a market gardener, has had dealings with Malcolm and Rodney as follows:*

(a) *Sydney agreed to sell to Malcolm, a wholesale greengrocer, a consignment of tomatoes at a price of £100. Sydney attempted to deliver this consignment at the stipulated time, but by then the market price of tomatoes had fallen to £85, and Malcolm refused to accept delivery, having bought more cheaply elsewhere. Sydney then returned the tomatoes to his storehouse, where they remained until they perished.*

(b) *Sydney agreed to buy from Rodney, a motor dealer, a new "Trademaster" lorry for use in his business. The list price of the "Trademaster" was £1,500. A week before the date of delivery of the vehicle, Sydney realised that he could not afford it, so he wrote to Rodney explaining that he would not be able to accept delivery as agreed. Rodney's profit on the transaction would have been £200.*

Sydney now wishes to know his legal position in connection with these two contracts. Advise him.

A: Section 50 of the *Sale of Goods Act*, 1893, provides that:

(*a*) Where the buyer wrongfully neglects or refuses to accept and pay for the goods, the seller may maintain an action against him for damages for non-acceptance.

(*b*) The measure of damages is the estimated loss directly and naturally resulting, in the ordinary course of events, from the buyer's breach of contract.

(*c*) Where there is an available market for the goods in question the measure of damages is *primâ facie* to be ascertained by the difference between the contract price and the market or current price at the time when the goods ought to have been accepted, or, if no time was fixed for acceptance, then at the time of the refusal to accept.

Applying *s.* 50 to Sydney's transactions:

(*a*) *Sydney* v. *Malcolm:* When Malcolm refused to accept delivery of the consignment of tomatoes at the stipulated time, there was a clear breach of contract, giving Sydney the right to maintain an action against him for damages for non-acceptance according to *s.* 50 (1), *S.G.A.*

As to the question of the measure of damages, it is submitted that it is almost certain that the court would consider this a suitable case for the application of the *primâ facie* rule in *s.* 50 (3). Thus, the damages likely to be awarded against Malcolm will be the difference between £100 and £85, *i.e.* £15. Sydney should be further advised that he was at fault in failing to mitigate his loss after Malcolm's refusal to accept the goods. He should have sold them elsewhere.

(*b*) *Rodney* v. *Sydney:* When Sydney refused to accept delivery of the "Trademaster" lorry, he was in breach of his contract with Rodney, giving Rodney the right to sue for damages for non-acceptance: *s.* 50 (1), *S.G.A.*

In this case, the list price of the vehicle is fixed and, therefore, the *primâ facie* rule in *s.* 50 (3), *S.G.A.*, is not properly applicable. The damages likely to be awarded against Sydney will depend on whether or not there was a demand for "Trademaster" lorries in the locality at the time of the breach. If there was such a demand for this type of vehicle so that Rodney had no difficulty in finding another buyer for the model ordered by Sydney, then only nominal damages will be awarded against him: *Charter* v. *Sullivan* (1957). If, on the other hand, there was little or no demand for "Trademasters," the measure of damages will be the amount of profit lost by Rodney on the failure of the transaction, *i.e.* £200. Sydney should be advised accordingly.

Q: *Freddy agrees to buy a wireless set from Martin, a dealer in radio and electrical goods. Before the agreement was completed, Freddy explained to Martin that he wanted the set for use with his record player. It was agreed that the price should be paid by twelve monthly instalments of £1 10s. and that property should not pass until payment of the final instalment. There was also an exemption clause in the agreement—which was in writing—to the effect that no implied conditions or warranties should arise, whether at common law or under any statute. The wireless set was not, in fact, adaptable to use with a record player. Freddy now wishes to know whether he is entitled to return the set to Martin and to recover the instalment already paid. The set has just been delivered,—advise Freddy.*

A: Section 17 (4) of the *Hire-Purchase Act*, 1965, provides that in the case of a conditional sale agreement as defined in that Act, where the buyer has made known to the seller the particular purpose for which the goods are required there shall be an implied condition that the goods shall be reasonably fit to that purpose. By *s.* 18 (4), the seller may not rely on clause purporting to exclude liability under *s.* (17) 4 unless he proves that the clause was brought to the notice of the buyer and its effect made clear to him before the agreement was concluded.

The agreement between Freddy and Martin is a conditional sale agreement as defined in the *H.-P.A.*, 1965. Assuming that the contract in writing contains a statement of the cash price and the total purchase price and the statutory notice of the buyers' rights, and is signed by both parties, the contract generally is enforceable by Martin. But the exemption clause, in so far as it purports to exclude implied terms arising from any statute, will not take effect so as to exclude the implied condition as to fitness for purpose under the *Hire-Purchase Act.*

Since Freddy made known to Martin the particular purpose for which he required the wireless set, *i.e.* to use with his record player, there is an implied condition that the wireless set was fit for that purpose. The exemption clause does not exclude this implied condition unless Martin is able to prove that the clause was brought to Freddy's notice before the contract was made and that its effect was made clear to him. If Martin is unable to prove these matters, Freddy will be entitled to return the set to Martin and to recover any money paid.

Q: *Giles, a farmer, agreed to sell his entire wheat crop to Timothy, a grain merchant. It was agreed that the price should be fixed after the harvest by the valuation of Matthew. When Matthew was on his way to Giles' farm to make a valuation of the crop, he was killed in a road accident. Giles has now delivered to Timothy a third of the crop, which Timothy has taken into his warehouse. Timothy has just informed Giles that he intends not to accept delivery of the remaining two-thirds of the crop. Advise Giles.*

A: The *Sale of Goods Act, s.* 62, provides that "goods" includes emblements. Therefore, where emblements (*i.e.* annual crops produced by agricultural labour) are agreed to be sold, the contract is a contract of sale of goods, even though the crop is still growing at the time the contract is made.

The *S.G.A.* further provides that where there is an agreement to sell goods on the terms that the price is to be fixed by the valuation of a third party, and such third party cannot or does not make such valuation, the agreement is thereby avoided; provided that if the goods or any part thereof have been delivered to and appropriated by the buyer he must pay a reasonable price therefore: *s.* 9 (1).

The contract between Giles and Timothy is, therefore, a contract of sale of goods and governed by the *Sale of Goods Act,* 1893. Owing to the death of Matthew before he could make a valuation of the crop, the agreement to sell the wheat is avoided, except that Timothy is bound to pay a reasonable price for the part of the crop which has been delivered to him and which he has appropriated by storing in his warehouse. Timothy is under no obligation to accept delivery of the remaining two-thirds of Giles' crop.

Giles should be advised accordingly.

6. Mixed questions. In some examinations, it is usual to find questions in two parts, the first of which requires the exposition of a rule of law, while the second part requires the student to attempt a problem. Usually, the rules needed for the solution of the problem are included in the first part of the question, and should not therefore be restated fully when answering the second part. It is good practice to show clearly in your answer the point at which you complete the first part and begin the second part. Here is an example of this kind of question, together with a suggested answer.

Q: (a) *What are the statutory rules as to the sale of goods by public auction?*

(b) *Henry, an auctioneer, agreed to sell John's oak table, the sale to be subject to a reserve price of £20. Subsequently, Henry inadvertently knocked it down to Peter for £15. Discuss Peter's rights.*

A: (a) The main statutory rules as to sale of goods by auction are to be found in s. 58 of the *Sale of Goods Act*, 1893, and s. 1 of the *Auctions (Bidding Agreements) Act*, 1927.

Section 58 of the *S.G.A.* provides as follows:

(i) Where goods are put up for sale by auction in lots, each lot is *primâ facie* deemed to be the subject of a separate contract of sale.

(ii) A sale by auction is complete when the auctioneer announces its completion by the fall of the hammer, or in other customary manner. Until such announcement is made any bidder may retract his bid:

(iii) Where a sale by auction is not notified to be subject to a right to bid on behalf of the seller, it shall not be lawful for the seller to bid himself or to employ any person to bid at such sale, or for the auctioneer knowingly to take any bid from the seller or any such person: any sale contravening this rule may be treated as fraudulent by the buyer:

(iv) A sale by auction may be notified to be subject to a reserve or upset price, and a right to bid may also be reserved expressly by or on behalf of the seller. Where a right to bid is expressly reserved, but not otherwise, the seller, or any one person on his behalf, may bid at the auction.

Section 1 of the *Auctions (Bidding Agreements) Act*, 1927, provides that if any dealer agrees to give, or gives, or offers any gift or consideration to any other person as an inducement or reward for abstaining, or for having abstained, from bidding at a sale by auction, he shall be guilty of a criminal offence. The selection further provides that any person who agrees to accept any such gift or consideration shall also be guilty of a criminal offence. For the purposes of this section, "dealer" means a person who in the normal course of his business attends sales by auction for the purpose of purchasing goods with a view to reselling them.

(b) *Problem:*

Where a sale by auction is notified under s. 58, *S.G.A.* to be subject to a reserve price, every bid is "a conditional offer subject to its being up to the reserve price": *per* Sir Richard Henn Collins, M.R., in *McManus* v. *Fortescue* (1907). Thus, where the bidders have been notified that there is a reserve price and the auctioneer inadvertently knocks down to a bidder for a price less than the reserve price, there is no contract of sale.

Peter's rights will, therefore, depend upon whether the bidders at the sale were notified that there was a reserve price on the table.

If Henry did not give due notification that the sale was subject to a reserve price, there is a valid contract between Peter and John for the sale of the table for £15. If delivery is refused, Peter may bring an action for damages for breach of contract.

If, on the other hand, Henry gave due notification that the sale was subject to a reserve price, there is no contract for the sale of the table to Peter, whose bid was below the reserve price and of no legal effect: *McManus* v. *Fortescue* (1907).

7. Sitting the examination. Here are some hints which may help you to make the most of your knowledge when the day of the examination arrives.

(a) *Read the paper through several times.* Put a mark against the questions which you know you can answer well. Do not start to answer them at this stage.

(b) *Make outline plans* for all the answers to be attempted. Few students can write good answers without some sort of planning. In a three-hour examination, it is worth spending 20–30 minutes in studying the questions and making the plans. (During this first half hour or so in the examination room, you should not be put off by other candidates around you who may be writing their answers furiously from the moment they sit down. Their answers are probably not very good.) When you have finished the plans, divide the remaining time *equally* between the questions to be attempted, so that you know exactly how long you have for each answer.

(c) *Write your answers.* Begin with the questions which you can answer well. Stick to your time schedule or you will be rushed at the end. If you do not finish an answer within the time planned, *leave it.* Go on to the next question. Go back to the unfinished question at the end if you have managed to leave time.

(d) *Read your work.* Try to leave five or ten minutes at the end of the examination for reading and checking for small errors of spelling, punctuation, etc.

SPECIMEN EXAMINATION QUESTIONS

1. Distinguish between a condition and a warranty in connexion with a contract of sale of goods; and mention (a) the conditions, and (b) the warranties which are implied in every contract of sale of goods.

M, a retailer of milk, supplied C with milk which contained typhoid germs, and C's daughter was infected thereby and died.

Discuss the legal position. *C.I.S.: December* 1962.

2. (a) Carefully describe the rights of an unpaid seller under a contract of sale of goods.

(b) B bought from S 100 bales of cotton ex *Hercules,* which was at the time on her way to London. When the ship arrived in London, B handed a cheque for the price of the cotton to S's London agent and received delivery orders on the warehouse where the cotton was stored. B endorsed the delivery orders to T and received payment from him. The cheque which B had issued was dishonoured and S, through his London agent, refuses now to allow T to remove the cotton from the warehouse. Advise the parties. *C.I.S.: December* 1963.

3. (a) When, if at all, may a seller who is not the owner of the goods pass a good title to the buyer?

(b) M has obtained a wireless set from P on hire purchase terms. After having paid all the instalments but one, M sells the set to Q, who buys it in good faith. P now claims the set from Q. State the reasons whether P is likely to succeed. *C.I.S.: December* 1964.

4. Upon what principles will damages for breach of a contract for the sale of goods be assessed? When will a court order the specific delivery of goods which are the subject of such a contract? *C.C.S.: June* 1964.

5. What are the duties of the buyer and seller respectively in c.i.f. contracts of sale? *C.C.S.:* June 1964.

6. (a) What rules govern the effect of the destruction of goods which have been the subject of a contract of sale?

(b) What is an acceptance of goods which have been sold and what is its significance? *C.C.S.: December* 1964.

7. (a) Dan agrees to buy 5,000 tons of iron from Ed. Ed sends him 10,000 tons. Dan takes 4,000 tons and sends back 6,000 tons. What is the legal position?

(b) Fred sells Gus 100 bags of rice, the particular bags being unascertained. When will the property in the goods pass? Why may it be important to know the answer to this question? *C.C.S.: June* 1961.

8. Explain with illustrations what is meant by "in course of transit" in connexion with the seller's right to stop the goods in transitu. *C.C.S.: December* 1962.

9. In what circumstances is a buyer deemed to have accepted the goods he has bought? Why may it be important to know whether he has accepted the goods? *C.C.S.: June* 1963.

10. Explain the term "stoppage in transitu." What are the vendor's remedies when he exercises this right and the buyer nevertheless received the goods? *A.C.C.A.: December* 1964.

11. With particular reference to the *Sale of Goods Act,* 1893, write an explanatory note upon *each* of the following points:

(a) Delivery of the wrong quantity.
(b) Instalment delivery.
(c) Sale by description.
(d) Sale by sample. *A.C.C.A.: June* 1962

12. Give two examples in which the title to goods may be effectively transferred to a bona fide purchaser by a seller who has no title or only a defective title to the goods sold. State the necessary conditions for each example you quote. *A.C.C.A.: June* 1962.

13. A deposited with a silversmith in the City of London some valuable jewellery whilst he went on holiday. B on visiting the shop purchased part of the jewellery. Did B get good title? State your reasons. *A.C.C.A.: June* 1962.

14. In regard to the sale of goods, what warranties and conditions are implied when the buyer (a) makes known the purpose for which the goods are required; (b) buys by description from a seller of goods of that description?

A was injured owing to an explosion caused by explosive

material hidden in a patent smokeless fuel; on what grounds can he recover for his injuries, if at all?   *A.C.C.A.: December* 1964.

15. In connexion with the sale of goods state (*a*) what rights, in addition to those of lien and stoppage in transit, the unpaid seller has against the goods on breach of a contract; (*b*) whether the seller can sue the buyer for the price if the property in the goods has not passed; (*c*) in an action for the price, whether interest may be awarded on the debt.   *A.C.C.A.: December* 1962.

16. (*a*) State in general terms what is meant by "a right of stoppage in transitu."

(*b*) How is stoppage in transitu effected?   *C.A.: May* 1964.

17. (*a*) What are the provisions of the *Sale of Goods Act*, 1893, as to when a buyer is deemed to have accepted the goods delivered to him?

(*b*) Are these provisions in any way limited if a buyer has not had a reasonable opportunity to examine the goods after they have been delivered to him.   *C.A.: May* 1962.

18. (*a*) What are the conditions implied in a contract for the sale of goods by sample?

(*b*) A contract for sale by sample provided that payment was to be made on arrival, against shipping documents. The buyer accordingly paid for the goods before he had an opportunity of examining them. On examination he found that the bulk did not correspond with the sample. Could he reject the goods, and, if so, on what grounds?   *C.A.: November* 1963.

19. Under the terms of a contract for the sale of goods the buyer was under an obligation to pay for the goods on a certain day. The day has now passed and the buyer has not made the payment.

    (*a*) In what circumstances can the seller:
       (*i*) exercise his statutory right to resell the goods and
       (*ii*) recover from the buyer any loss on the transaction?
    (*b*) Would it make any difference if the seller had a right under the contract to resell in the event of the buyer not paying on the appointed date?   *C.A.: May* 1964

20. Brown inspects a load of 3 tons of potatoes at Allen's warehouse and agrees to buy them for £30, Allen to wash them and pack them in 1 cwt sacks for collection by Brown. Allen's workmen complete the washing and bagging on the same day

and the sacks are set aside for collection by Brown. During the night the warehouse and its contents are destroyed by fire.

Can Allen make Brown pay the agreed price for the potatoes? *C.A.: November 1964.*

21. (*a*) In relation to a sale of goods, what is meant by a warranty?

(*b*) What is the test as to whether a statement made by a seller during the making of the contract for sale amounts to a warranty or a mere expression of opinion? *C.A.: November 1964.*

22. State in detail the various reasons why it is important to know when the property in goods agreed to be sold passes. *C.A.: May 1963.*

23. (*a*) When goods are sold by description but not by sample, are there any, and if so what, implied conditions as to the goods and their fitness for any particular purpose?

(*b*) How is an implied condition affected by an express condition? *C.A.: May 1963*

24. A seller who is not the owner of goods cannot pass a good title to a purchaser. State six exceptions to this rule. *C.A.: May 1963.*

25. What, if any, rights has Williams in the following cases:

(*a*) Williams buys from Brown an "Imperial Automatic Sewing Machine." When delivered the machine will not work.

(*b*) Williams buys from Clark a ton of cattle cake made by X & Co. The cattle cake, which has been carelessly manufactured, contains prussic acid, and Williams's cattle are poisoned.

(*c*) Williams, without previously inspecting it, buys a house from Edwards which proves to be uninhabitable. *C.A.: May 1962.*

26. A buyer is normally entitled to reject goods on breach of a condition; state the circumstances when a buyer cannot do this.

If a contract contains a clause prohibiting the rejection of goods, what is the position? *A.C.C.A.: June 1965.*

27. Distinguish between contracts for the sale of goods, sales of goods, credit sales, conditional sales and hire-purchase agreements. What are the principal rules applying to conditional sales? *C.C.S.: June 1965.*

28. What is the essential feature of a c.i.f. contract? In such a contract what are (a) the seller's duties; (b) the buyer's right of rejection? *C.C.S.: June* 1965.

29. (a) State the rules determining when the property in goods sold passes from the seller to the buyer.

(b) B, a wholesale bookseller, sold to L 100 copies of X's text-took on company law, the particular copies not being ascertained. B in due course personally delivered 40 copies of the book to L and informed L that the remaining 60 copies were in his (B's) warehouse and would be dispatched as soon as B's van driver had returned from sick leave. A fortnight later B's warehouse is totally destroyed by fire and the books are lost. Consider whether L will have to pay for the 60 books lost in the fire. *C.I.S.: December* 1969.

30. (a) In what circumstances has an unpaid seller of goods

(i) a right of lien;
(ii) a right of stoppage in transit;
(iii) a right of resale?

(b) When are these rights lost? *C.I.S.: June* 1969.

31. In connexion with the Hire Purchase Act, 1965 discuss the hirer's right

(i) to cancel the agreement;
(ii) to terminate the agreement. *C.I.S.: June* 1969.

32. (a) State the main conditions which are implied by statute in a contract for the sale of goods.

(b) M agreed to sell to P a quantity of honey which was described as "English honey, warranted only equal to sample." The honey actually delivered by M was equal to sample but was imported honey. Discuss whether P is entitled to refuse to accept the honey. *C.I.S.: December* 1968.

33. (a) What conditions as to quality of goods sold are implied in contracts for the sale of goods?

(b) A bought an electric blanket (made by Hotseat Ltd.) from B, who keeps an electrical goods shop. A gave the blanket to C as a Christmas present and the first time C used the blanket it caught fire and C was injured. C wishes to sue B or the manufacturers. What is the legal position? *A.C.C.A.: June* 1969.

34. In what circumstances may a seller who is not the owner of goods sold, pass an effective title to the buyer? *A.C.C.A.: December* 1969.

35. (*a*) How does a contract for the sale of goods differ from a contract for work and materials?

(*b*) A contracted to build a racing car for B, to B's specifications. When delivered the car proved to be roadworthy but was unsuitable for racing. B now wishes to return the car and recover his money. Explain the legal position. *A.C.C.A.: June* 1967.

36. Explain how the parties to a contract of sale of goods are affected where in a sale of specific goods the subject matter of the contract has perished. If instead of "perishing" the goods have deteriorated only, are the parties similarly affected? *A.C.C.A.: June* 1966.

37. In contracts for the sale of goods, what conditions are implied by statute as to (*a*) quality of the goods, and (*b*) their fitness for any particular purpose? *A.C.C.A.: December* 1966.

38. Where a contract for the sale of goods does not expressly cover the passing of the property in goods, what statutory rules are applied to ascertain the intentions of the parties? *A.C.C.A.: December* 1967.

39. What exceptions are there to the rule that a seller of goods cannot pass a better title to the goods than he possesses himself? *A.C.C.A. June* 1968.

40. What terms are implied by statute in hire-purchase contracts? *A.C.C.A.: December* 1968.

41. Explain briefly the rights of an unpaid seller against the goods sold. *A.C.C.A.: December* 1968.

42. Smith, a cattle dealer, sold to Jones, a dairyman, a cow for £50. Smith knew Jones wanted the cow for dairy purposes. Jones took away the cow but did not pay for it. Although Smith did not know it the cow at the time of sale was suffering from tuberculosis. Smith refuses to take back the animal and threatens to sue for the £50. What are the respective rights of Smith and Jones? *C.A.: November* 1968.

43. A wine merchant contracts to sell to a customer five dozen bottles of a particular brand of champagne. At the time of the contract the wine merchant's whole stock of wine had been destroyed by fire, but he was not aware of this fact.

What is the effect (if any) on the legal rights of the parties? *C.A.: November* 1968.

44. Whilst shopping in the High Street Mrs. James sees in the window of an electrical shop a Wundawash washing machine which she inspects and decides to buy on hire purchase. She explains to the salesman that her husband has expressly forbidden her to sign any hire purchase agreements without his prior consent and the salesman accordingly gives her the hire-purchase agreement to take home and show to her husband. That evening Mr. James carefully reads the document and agrees that his wife may have the machine. She accordingly signs the hire purchase agreement in the presence of a witness, and Mr. James also signs as guarantor. The following day she returns to the shop, hands over the completed hire purchase agreement, and pays the deposit on the machine. Four days later Mrs. James reads in the newspaper that Wundawash are bringing out a new washing machine which will make the one she has just bought obsolete. She immediately goes round to the shop to try to cancel her order, but the salesman refuses to permit her to do so.

Can Mrs. James cancel the agreement and if so is the dealer entitled to retain her deposit? *C.A.: November* 1968.

45. (a) In a contract for the sale of goods what are the buyer's remedies for misrepresentation?

(b) Can these remedies be excluded by agreement between the buyer and the seller? *C.A.: November* 1969.

46. (a) Immediately before going on holiday Jones goes to his local garage and sees a car which he decides to buy and he pays for it by cheque. He explains that he wants it delivered on his return from holiday in two weeks' time, and the garage agrees to deliver it to his house in time for his return. Two days later the car is accidentally damaged whilst on the garage's premises through no fault of anyone. Who is responsible for the cost of the repairs?

(b) Would your answer be different, and if so why, if the garage failed to deliver the car in time for Jones's return, and the accidental damage took place $2\frac{1}{2}$ weeks after the date of purchase whilst the car was still in the possession of the garage? *C.A.: November* 1969.

47. State shortly the obligations under the Hire Purchase Act, 1965 of the owner of goods let on hire-purchase with regard to the merchantable quality of the goods. *C.A.: November* 1969.

48. (a) If goods are delivered to a buyer on approval, when does the property pass?

(b) By a false representation made by Jones that he could sell

their goods to actresses, jewellers were induced to hand him brace-
lets and watches on approval.   As soon as Jones received these
articles he handed them to women who, on his instructions, pawned
them.   The pawnbrokers acted in good faith.

Can the jewellers recover the articles from the pawnbrokers?
C.A.: May 1970.

49. (*a*) When is a seller of goods deemed to be an "unpaid
seller"?

(*b*) How are the rights of the "unpaid seller" affected by:

(*i*) a part delivery of the goods;

(*ii*) a sub-sale of the goods by the purchaser?

C.A.: May 1970.

50. On 1st January 1969 Smith agreed to purchase a boat from
Brown for £600 and paid him £200 as a deposit.   Smith did not
take delivery and delayed making payment of the balance of the
purchase money.   On 14th April Brown wrote to Smith that unless
the money was paid by 30th April 1969 the boat would be re-sold
and the deposit would be forfeited.   Smith did not pay on the
given date, but a fortnight later he saw Brown and offered him the
balance of £400, but Brown told him the boat had been sold on
7th May for £700.

On these facts, what are the respective rights and liabilities of
Smith and Brown, and in particular is Smith entitled to claim from
Brown the return of his deposit and who is entitled to the profit
on resale?   State the principles of law involved.   *C.A.: May* 1970.

51. (*a*) In what circumstances, if at all, will the manufacturer
of potentially dangerous goods be liable in damages to the ultimate
user of the goods?

(*b*) E enters the shop of a chemist and asks for some tooth
paste which will help to soothe his sore gums.   The chemist
recommends brand X, and E buys a tube.   If, after using the
toothpaste, E sustains a serious inflammation of the gums will he
be able to claim damages from (*i*) the chemist, (*ii*) the maker of
the tooth-paste or (*iii*) at all?   Give reasons for your answer and
indicate whether it would be different if E had asked for brand X
by name, having seen it advertised on television?   *C.I.S.: June*
1967.

52. (*a*) What remedies has the buyer of goods against the seller
where the latter has been guilty of a breach of contract?

(*b*) Some months before the investiture of the Prince of Wales,
W, a Welsh shopkeeper, orders from M, a manufacturer, a large
quantity of commemorative drinking mugs for delivery one week

before the investiture. In fact, the mugs are delivered to him one week after the investiture. State with reasons whether W will be legally entitled

    (*i*) to refuse to accept delivery of the mugs, and
    (*ii*) to claim damages from M.   *C.I.S.: June* 1970.

53. (*a*) In what circumstances will a person who buys goods from someone who is not their owner acquire a good title to them?

(*b*) X's bicycle has been stolen from outside his house. In due course X traces the bicycle to Y who had bought it in good faith from a third party. Will X be able to recover his bicycle from Y, and, if so, will he have to compensate Y, for the price that he had paid for it? *C.I.S.: June* 1968.

54. (*a*) What is meant by a c.i.f. contract?

(*b*) What are the duties of the seller under such a contract?

(*c*) What are the duties of the buyer under this contract?
                                       C.I.S.: December 1967.

INDEX

221